Community Mental Health

A PRACTICAL GUIDE

Loren R. Mosher

Lorenzo Burti

W.W. NORTON & COMPANY · *NEW YORK · LONDON*

A NORTON PROFESSIONAL BOOK

This has been abriged from the original hardcover edition that was published in 1989

Library of Congress Cataloging-in-Publication Data

Mosher, Loren R.
   Community mental health : a practical guide / Loren R. Mosher and
Lorenzo Burti. — Rev. ed., abridged.
      p.   cm.
   Includes bibliographical references and index.
   ISBN 0-393-70165-4
   1. Community mental health services.   I. Burti, Lorenzo.
II. Title.
RA790.M615   1994
362.2′2 — dc20   93-28408   CIP

W.W. Norton & Company, Inc., 500 Fifth Avenue, New York, New York 10110
W.W. Norton & Company, Ltd., 10 Coptic Street, London WC1A 1PU

3 4 5 6 7 8 9 0

Foreword

PERSONALLY, I HATE FOREWORDS. I hardly ever read them (or only after having read the book), and I have never written one—until now. I hate forewords because in them somebody tells you how you should read and understand a book that somebody else, who certainly is more competent, has written. This is not fair. Let the author speak for himself! Listen to the author!

However, after having read Mosher and Burti's *Community Mental Health*, I accept the honor of writing a foreword for it with pleasure and grace. Because this is a wonderful book! It is exceptional, I think, in several ways. First of all, it clearly and understandably says so many things, grounded on elementary commonsense and humanity, which all of us who as psychiatrists or other professionals within the social field "know" or "feel" in some way, but without clear consciousness, so that we cannot fully use this knowledge in our everyday work with psychiatric patients. This book tells us, in great detail, how to translate our intuitions into clear, conscious, and operational understanding, and how to translate this new understanding into concrete day-to-day activities, into organizational structures, into precise therapeutic goals and approaches, and into adequate methods of evaluation.

Therefore, in my view, Mosher and Burti's work is not just a book on "community psychiatry" (or on "social psychiatry," as it is called elsewhere), but on "psychiatry tout court": It explains the context in which every kind of psychiatric intervention occurs, and it shows on this basis how this context should be utilized and structured to best meet the needs of our patients.

This book is also most welcome, because it presents a desperately needed complement — or rather counterpart — to the currently predominating technical, biological, and drug-oriented psychiatry. After a certainly too unilateral predomination of psychodynamic and sociodynamic concepts during the previous decades, contemporary psychiatry in the United States and elsewhere is, in fact, in danger of falling victim to another reductionistic "paradigm of understanding," namely the biological and medical one. Even though modern advances in understanding the biophysiological bases of brain functioning are certainly very impressive and promising, and even if it may be true, as Wilhelm Griesinger (mid–19th century German organic psychiatrist) said more than a century ago, that many illnesses or problems are essentially brain illnesses and brain problems, these brains and their disturbances still belong to a complete human being and take place within a global psychological, social, physical, and organizational context! The suffering individual, even when suffering from a "purely organic" disease, such as, for instance, Alzheimer's disease or brain injury, still needs to be perceived, understood, respected, and treated within this global situation. If not, he will be reduced to a mere disturbed brain function, to an anonymous "biological mechanism." In other words, his "psyche" — that is, the very thing the psychiatrist has to care for — will be neglected and destroyed.

This book tells us how to avoid such a danger by putting psychiatric patients and psychiatric problems into context. It is, therefore, a "*psycho-ecological book*" — and as such it is, I believe, a book of the psychiatry of the future.

Another fascinating aspect of this book is the fact that it represents an extraordinarily complete overview, as well as a synthesis, of the best and most interesting American and Italian experiences of the last 20 years in community psychiatry. In other words, this book is heavily grounded on experience. On the one hand, we have the personal experiences of the two authors, who for many years have worked within some of the most creative and successful projects of modern American and Italian community psychiatry. On the other hand, the book is firmly grounded on specific research; in fact, it probably represents the most complete and illuminating overview of the current body of Anglo-Saxon research and knowledge in relevant psychosocial issues available anywhere. And again, it not only provides a synthesis of the most important findings, but also translates and integrates these findings into down-to-earth measures and practical interventions.

Finally, the book is provocative: It challenges many deeply rooted beliefs and dogmas. Therefore, it will certainly provoke controversial discussions; many readers will (as I do) disagree with certain points or propositions, finding at times that the authors are too radical, that they go too far, or that they are in danger themselves of becoming reductionistic and unilateral on certain issues. Thus, this book certainly also has its limitations. After all, like any other treatise it reflects nothing but one aspect — even if it is a particularly interesting one — of the "current state of error" in our knowledge and understanding of psychiatric complexities and possible ways of dealing with them!

However, in my opinion this by no means prevents a very positive global evaluation of the contribution of the two authors: I hope and believe that Mosher and Burti's book will soon become a kind of "bible of the social worker," as Gerald Caplan's book on *Principles of Preventive Psychiatry*** became more than 20 years ago. And I hope, too, that with its focus on practical issues and global psychosocial context, *Community Mental Health* will become an important element of perhaps the most important common task facing today's psychiatrists of all possible orientations: the task of constructing a truly realistic, multiconditional, biological-psychological-social model of the "psyche" and its disturbances, which will enable us to more adequately understand and treat our patients as real human beings!

Luc Ciompi, M.D.
Professor of Psychiatry and Medical Director,
Sociopsychiatric University Clinic,
Faculty of Medicine,
University of Berne, Switzerland

*Basic Books, 1964.

Contents

SECTION III: A MODEL FOR EFFECTIVE COMMUNITY
MENTAL HEALTH

SECTION IV: INGREDIENTS OF SUCCESS

APPENDIX

Preface

THIS VOLUME IS AN UPDATED, reorganized, condensed version of our 1989 book, *Community Mental Health: Principles and Practice.* It has been specifically rewritten to address the needs of students in all the mental health related disciplines and for those currently working in any capacity in community-based programs.

We have trimmed the original text to leave, and highlight, the most basic principles and practices that flow from them.

CHAPTER 1

What You Can Expect from This Book

THIS BOOK IS ABOUT THE HOW, not just the what, of community mental health. It is a practical, clinical book for community mental health practitioners, workers, clinicians, users, and families.

It is our intention to present an approach to community mental health that will bring together research and experience that have been shown to be both practical and effective. We believe that much more is known about effective community-based treatment than is currently acknowledged or implemented widely (see, for example Beiser, Shore, Peters, & Tatum, 1985, and Burti, Garzotto, Siciliani, Zimmerman-Tansella, & Tansella, 1986). Community mental health is not very fashionable in the U.S. at the moment. Its reputation in the U.S. suffers from attributions of having overpromised and not delivered, of being unscientific, of being dominated by nonphysicians, of being a major accomplice in the "failure" of deinstitutionalization, and most of all, of being ineffective in dealing with the most severely disturbed patients, except insofar as it fosters medication compliance.

These attributions, when seen contextually, become increasingly untenable. A movement that was funded in a way that achieved only one-third of its original aims (750 community mental health centers versus 2000 proposed) can hardly be held responsible for its "failure." Clearly, research into its effectiveness has not been highly regarded or funded. Hence, the question of whether it is "scientifically sound" remains, for a number of

1

observers, largely unanswered. It is indeed currently dominated by nonphysicians who have come to power by default when psychiatrists left it wholesale for more lucrative private office and hospital-based practices (Fenton, Leaf, Moran, & Tischler, 1984; Jerrell & Larsen, 1983; Knesper & Carlson, 1981). The present authors do not believe this nonmedical domination needs to be a problem. However, in practice, it tends to discourage M.D.'s from working in these programs because they don't have the power and control to which they are accustomed. As an accomplice in the "failure" of deinstitutionalization, community mental health's role must be seen in the context of the crucial fact that money did not follow patients out of the hospital.

Our experience, along with access to those of others, has engendered in us a much more positive view. We believe—and will set out "how to" principles to effect this belief—that the vast majority of disturbed and disturbing behavior can be effectively dealt with without the use of places called hospitals. We believe that the *use of the person* interacting with clients is a treatment that can be as powerful as, and have far fewer short- and long-term toxicities than, the drugs (principally neuroleptics) that are so overrelied upon currently. We will set out principles that will help maximize the usefulness of the person as a therapeutic instrument.

We believe that when madness is taken respectfully and seriously it is all too understandable. We will describe principles of interviewing and interaction that will facilitate the process of making madness meaningful. The degree to which an incomprehensibility zeitgeist exists about mad persons is mostly a reflection of the natural human and cultural tendency to wish not to have to deal with our own madness. Our willingness to incarcerate them in hospitals and our unwillingness to have them in our communities are concrete manifestations of this "out of mind, out of sight" attitude. We don't want to understand our own madness.

This zeitgeist is continuously reinforced by psychiatry's current "disease" orientation, which appears to be motivated by economics and its need for medical legitimacy. Thus, psychiatry's current energies are focused on a diagnostic system that lacks construct validity and that decontextualizes the person. The search for biologic causes and treatments related to this diagnostic system is the major focus of current psychiatric research. Psychiatry's power comes from the money it derives from treatment delivered in hospitals where, after all, "diseases" are traditionally treated. About 70% of all mental health expenditures in the U.S. are spent on inpatient care. These are places where, mostly because it is relatively cheap and effective in the short run, drug treatment is predominant. Therapeutic interpersonal interaction is given lip service but not frequently practiced. A pharmaceutical industry-psychiatry cabal has emerged. It is impossible to sustain and transmit a psychosocial treatment philosophy in places where a drug-oriented belief system is preeminent and patients stay only 10 to 15 days. This situation will likely be even more true as cost-containment pressures mount.

We believe that for too long theory has dictated practice rather than the other way around. Dogmatism rather than observation has prevailed. Until the mid '60s the most prevalent dictator was psychoanalytic theory. Today the dictator is reductionistic, antiquated, linear, cause-effect biologic theorizing. Excessive dedication to either results in major blind spots at best, and tunnel vision at worst, in the profession. The practices we espouse are ones that have been shown, pragmatically, to work. We have worked with what now, to us, seems to be a rather sophisticated but unarticulated theory. An aim of this book is to help articulate this theory for effective community mental health interventions.

This book is, in part, a response to our dissatisfaction with prevailing theories and practices. However, we view ourselves as responsible critics in that we offer viable alternatives to what we criticize. For example, psychiatry's current biologic orientation has strongly reinforced the practice of maintaining disturbed and disturbing people indefinitely on neuroleptic drugs. This has, in turn, created a new species, *the tardive dyskinesic*. Effective community treatment is made much more difficult when it is assured that most patients will eventually join this new species. They will, as a result of their psychopharmacologic treatment, be stigmatized by the impossible-to-hide, cosmetic disfigurement of tardive dyskinesia (T.D.).

It is especially painful to us that, in spite of a nearly 5% annual incidence in T.D. (i.e., in four years 20% of neuroleptic-maintained patients will have developed it) (Kane, Woerner, Weinhold, Wagner, Kinon, & Borenstein, 1984), it has become difficult to even raise the question of withdrawal or decreased neuroleptic dosage with psychiatrists presently in the public system. They have no experience with psychotic patients not on neuroleptics. For them not treating psychotics with neuroleptics constitutes malpractice. They fail to understand that more than two-thirds of schizophrenics recovered without drugs before they were available and that long-term outcome is no better today than it was before the introduction of neuroleptics (Bleuler, 1968; Ciompi, 1980; Harding, Brooks, Ashikaga, Strauss, & Breier, 1987a,b; Huber, Gross, Schuttler & Linz, 1980; Niskanen & Achte, 1972). We will describe programs that have successfully treated newly identified psychotic persons with little or no psychotropic medication. We will discuss how currently medicated, long-term clients can be weaned to either very low doses or no medication without substantially increasing the risk of relapse.

We are critical of psychoanalysts who provide important role models, instruction, and supervision to trainees who are treating psychotic individuals. They mostly fail to address in the supervisory process that which is most important to the trainee's patient—how, in the immediate situation, he has been failed by his family, his social network, and the social system. These concerns, as well as the practical, down-to-earth, questions of psychologic and physical survival, are treated as secondary or tertiary manifestations of an evolving psychopathologic process in the individual. Loss of ego boundaries, homosexual panic, overwhelming instinctual drives, symbiotic union, projective identifications, unconscious conflicts, transference distortions, etc., are discussed at length, despite reasonably compelling evidence that the application of these concepts in a psychotherapeutic process several hours a week with a person labeled schizophrenic offers no advantage over supportive reality-oriented psychotherapy (Gunderson, Frank, Katz, Vannicelli, Frosch & Knapp, 1984).

This exercise in therapeutic futility results in the trainee's feeling powerless and exploited. So, he reaches for what he knows he can do if he's a physician—labeling—and for what works—drugs—to restore his potency. Needless to say, if he becomes principally a psychotherapist after graduation he will assiduously avoid these helplessness-engendering disturbed and disturbing clients. This training failure has helped drive psychiatrists out of community psychiatry into hospital and private practice, where the real money and professional gratification are presumed to reside. We will spell out generic psychosocial therapeutic principles that we and others have found effective and that render their purveyors potent.

We are also critical of training programs whose major focus is biologic psychiatry. Although their students are well trained in the use of *DSM-III-R* and drugs, at the same time they learn to focus on the neurotransmitter level, leaving out the individual, his family, the community, and the wider sociocultural context. As a result, it is difficult for them to function in community-based programs. Not infrequently their training has produced in them an attitude that "you can't talk to disease." That is, they have been taught that the major psychiatric disorders (schizophrenia, manic-depression, and major depression) are "brain diseases"; hence it is useless to attempt to understand them by learning about these patient's lives. Ergo, patients with major psychotic disorders are seen only in terms of their medication status and responsiveness. Social factors in the production and course of disorder are given only token attention. As a consequence, they are therapeutically limited and, as is the case with psychoanalytic supervisees and psychotherapy, they feel powerless when medications don't result in an enduring remission. Since at least 40–50% of neuroleptic-maintained schizophrenic patients relapse over a two-year span without strong psychosocial programs, the likelihood of multiple failure experiences is substantial. It is not long before they become disillusioned with these relapsing patients and give them a "chronic mental illness" (i.e., hopeless) label. This is not meant to eschew any possible role for biologic factors in disturbed and disturbing behavior. Rather, it is meant to highlight the fact that at the present time biologic factors are difficult to address therapeutically in individual patients. Unfortunately, training *in* the community for psychiatrists is not very available. We described elsewhere a psychiatric program that does prepare psychiatrists for community-based work (Burti & Mosher, 1986).

As with psychiatrists, many psychologists are overcommitted to a particular theory (most often cognitive behaviorism) that dictates and confines, unnecessarily, what they can see in their clients and do in their work with them. With a few exceptions clinical psychologists have not dedicated themselves to the treatment of psychotic persons. They frequently head agencies that deal with this difficult clientele but don't deal with them directly. They too suffer from having few if any role models for this type of work. The excellent psychotherapeutic skills they've learned during their training are not made available to the most disturbed and disturbing patients. Our generic psychosocial intervention principles are largely derived from research in clinical psychology, in particular on various aspects of psychotherapy (e.g., Bordin, 1979; Frank, 1973; Horowitz & Marmar, 1985; Luborsky, McLellan, Woody, O'Brien & Auerbach, 1985).

We recognize that, because they are not disease-oriented physicians and can't prescribe medications, psychologists tend to be deemed by the medical community as incapable of treating psychotic patients. They may also be prevented from doing so by insurance reimbursement practices and institutional rules. Hence, there are real barriers to their involvement with psychotic patients even if they would like to be.

We are critical of today's social workers. Oversimplified, their current training generally prepares them for one of two tracks—administration or office-based psychotherapy with the worried well. These are legitimate pursuits indeed, but where are the old-fashioned social workers who attended to the needs of whole persons? Mobilizing financial and other resources, environmental manipulation, and community follow-up used to be major foci of social casework. On the assumption that this work is less valuable, it is currently relegated to less talented or less well trained members of the profession. Thus, important potential helpers are kept away from the clientele that could well use their traditional skills. This is, of course, in part a response to social workers' facing the same problems described in the paragraph above for psychologists. This is an especially great loss, as it now appears that what is in fact most *therapeutic* with this clientele is attention to their real life needs. In the context of a positive relationship, discussion of money, work, a place to live and friends is quite helpful. We believe our intervention principles will be highly relevant to the training of a new generation of social workers.

We are critical of nursing because, as a result of its ever growing need to learn new hospital-based procedures and techniques, it has lost much of its time-honored interpersonal caring focus. Nurses are not well represented in community mental health programs. With the exception of public health nurses, they are usually not well prepared to work in the community. Their psychosocial skills have become much less valued and remunerated than their technical ones—as is the case with medicine in general. Again, our psychosocial principles can be profitably utilized by nurses. Unfortunately, they suffer, as do all the mental health professions, from a lack of role models and financial incentives for community mental health nursing.

The training process we have described (Burti & Mosher, 1986) provides the skills needed to address the particular psychologic, interpersonal, and social environmental needs of very disturbed and disturbing persons. It is basically an apprenticeship model with ongoing multidisciplinary supervision from experienced, dedicated role models. Although it refers specifically to the training of psychiatrists, we believe that with modifications to suit local circumstances and added special training for subgroups (e.g., in hypnotherapy for psychotherapy specialists) this type of training program is relevant to all the mental health professions that provide community mental health staff.

Thoughtful readers will by now recognize an emerging paradox: Having said we would present a new and more positive and hopeful view of community mental health, we have begun by calling the relevant professions and the contexts within which they work—especially hospitals (see Chapter 4) on the carpet—a not very positive act. The critique is necessary to provide us with a jumping-off point, as well as background and rationale for why we do things as we do. Although our theoretical stance, insofar as we have one, is an *interpersonal phenomenologic* one, our day-to-day practice has also been strongly influenced by the family therapy movement. We use, on a daily basis, a number of concepts and practices that are associated with this group. An open systems view; contextualization; reframing; use of analogy, metaphor and paradox; always thinking and acting, if possible, in family and social network terms; working with, and in, the social system as it is configured in the community—these are basic tenets that guide our work.

Another basic principle underlying our work is a commitment to semantic simplicity. What we espouse is mostly commonplace and commonsense. We want our language to describe what we do in everyday, jargon-free terms. We do not want to be set apart from the people with whom we deal by our language; rather, we want this volume to be easily understandable to anyone who reads it. We do not have a new theory. We are not attempting to start a new "school" or "institute" or "center" that must define itself through its particular language or therapeutic approach. In fact, nothing in this book is really new. Rather, it is the result of re (again) search (looking). We believe that a great deal of mischief has been created in the lives of unsuspecting madpersons who have been set apart, and then stigmatized, by widespread jargonism — whether biologic, psychoanalytic, behavioristic, or what have you.

For us, a critical attribute of good community mental health workers is their ability to communicate in everyday, colloquially and contextually appropriate street language — that is, to tailor a very clear and relatively simple language to the interpersonal, cultural, ethnic, and religious circumstances in which they find themselves. To help trainees learn this skill we ask them to imagine themselves in a foreign country engaged in a very important conversation with someone who has only rudimentary skill in their language. To be understood they must communicate mostly in the present tense, with simple declarative sentences, using the simplest vocabulary possible. We also encourage them to listen carefully to how this foreigner consistently misuses English language construction and to try to change their own sentence structure to conform to the pattern of misuse and thereby improve their understandability to the other party. Mutual understanding is vitally important to what we do.

Another overarching principle guiding our work is that it is, insofar as possible, client/user/patient-centered. We use this complex slash phrase to indicate that what we espouse should be useful in whatever context the person seeks help; different contexts use different helpee designators. As will be seen in Chapter 3, our principal starting point is, whenever possible: What does the customer want? Lazare and colleagues have written eloquently on this approach (Lazare & Eisenthal, 1979; Lazare, Eisenthal & Frank, 1979). It is from this perspective that we have designed programs. Insofar as possible, program needs take a back seat to client needs. For example, we do not agree with the predetermined lengths of stay so commonly found in community-based transitional residential programs because they are determined by *program* and fiscal, rather than *client*, needs.

Having experience with and knowledge of needs that are at best peripheral to the needs of the help seekers, we acknowledge the validity of such needs. We know that people must be trained for community mental health work and that they must be trained in real life work places. However, this training need must not be met at the expense of the persons for whom the program is designed. In our experience valid needs like training too often become institutionalized. In extreme cases the program comes to exist to meet those needs, rather than the needs of the clients.

A lot of what we have to say is simply common sense. As this fact became clear to us, we began to wonder: Why are we writing such a volume? Shouldn't most of what we have to say be obvious to any thoughtful person? Yes, it should be, but no, it has not been our experience that common sense is highly valued and reinforced in most community programs. It is even less so in large, institution-based programs. Somehow there is a prevailing ethos about dealing with madpersons that demands the suspension of common sense, in favor of complex theories and jargon.

In addition to its client-centered focus, our approach is different from many in its emphasis on what's *right* rather than what's *wrong* with the client. Psychiatry's current obsession with how many Schneiderian symptoms can dance on the head of a schizophrenic is one that our experience has taught us is mostly antitherapeutic in its induction of a we/them separation. Preoccupation with psychopathology has a number of adverse effects: It parades clients' perceived failures in front of them continually. Demoralization, low self-esteem, being down on one's own case are usually the reasons people seek help. Given this, it does not seem very sensible to us to focus the potential helper's attention primarily on these basically negative attributions. The current practice of focusing on symptoms in the individual in order to arrive at a diagnosis is to decontextualize, dehistorify and depower the individual. The person's gestalt is lost. It also results, largely because it takes place in the zoo (office) instead of the jungle (the community), in a thrust toward separating persons from their worlds. This separation, as reinforced by the treatment system, is the source of stigmatization. This separation, when repeatedly experienced, gives a clear message: "We are not ready to attend to your whole person in the world in a serious way." Confirmation of part-human status is an experience reported to us by clients with an alarming frequency.

A psychopathologic focus also has an invidious effect on the diagnoser. The special technical language of diagnosis both separates the labeler from the labeled and provides an *illusion* of understanding. Unfortunately, our present diagnostic system has arbitrarily decided to act *as if* factors that are not directly related to personal psychopathology, such as where the person is seen, race, socioeconomic status, etc., do not influence the assessment of psychopathology. A body of research that demonstrates that a dozen contextual factors influence the diagnostic process, almost always in the direction of greater psychopathology, is unaddressed. Hence, the knowledge we have that could mitigate some of the deleterious aspects of the diagnostic process by forcing it to include the assessment of context are *excluded* from the current diagnostic practice and from training for it. The pain that medical students experience from wrestling with *DSM-III-R* is something to behold. They seem to forever be trying to squeeze a round peg into a minutely defined square hole — with predictable confusion. Although we are critical of the diagnostic process as currently practiced, we recognize that such categorizations may be helpful for recordkeeping, research and communication with other settings. Our perspective is that diagnosis is of limited utility (when trying to help a real patient) and, if overfocused on, a serious impediment to being helpful. Its most pernicious effects are on the relationship between helper and helpee. The distancing that the diagnostic process engenders can preclude the establishment of rapport — the sine qua non of being helpful. Today's psychiatry in particular seems bent on increasing its distance from its customers if the preoccupation it has with diagnosis is any guide — and we believe it is. To label is to pigeonhole and dispense with; unfortunately the labels don't say much about that which is most troubling and important to the person.

We intend to provide readers with a readily understandable set of principles that will enable them to talk with, assess, understand, and develop collaborative goals with disturbed and disturbing individuals. We hope to provide nonconfining recipes to chefs who will use them innovatively rather than prescriptively and let their applicability, not their fashionability, be their test. We acknowledge that a portion of what we propose will not fit well with current conceptions and practices. However, we ask that readers, before rejecting them, first try to understand and put our principles into practice.

Context

CHAPTER 2

The Ups and Downs
of Community Mental Health
in the United States

THE UNITED STATES HAS HAD TWO PERIODS of community psychiatry: the era of "moral treatment" (1740–1840) and 1963 to the present (see Barton & Sanborn, 1977; Beigel & Levinson, 1972; Bellack, 1974; Caplan & Caplan, 1967; Langsley, Berlin & Yarvis, 1981; Zusman & Lamb, 1977). The era of "moral treatment," based on transcendentalist philosophy, and its demise have been ably documented (Bockoven, 1963; Grob, 1973, 1983; Rothman, 1971, 1980). This kind and compassionate form of care, emphasizing mutual responsibility, worked well in the small, relatively homogeneous, New England protestant communities of that era. Unfortunately, massive immigration resulted in rapidly growing urban centers that were unable to apply these principles to the expanding, heterogenous, socially disorganized, communities of post-1840. Interestingly, the situation is much the same today as it was then; good community mental health systems are difficult to implement in rapidly growing megalopolises.

In contrast to Europe, where leprosaria could be converted into asylums (Galzigna & Terzian, 1980), beginning in the 1840s the U.S. built a totally new set of institutions for madpersons. These "new" institutions—ones that plague the U.S. mental health system to this day—began as Dorothea Dix's humanistic response to the misery she encountered in urban almshouses of that era (1840 onward). Madpersons, paupers, prostitutes, criminals and unintelligible foreigners were mixed together in these degrading settings. Today's homeless shelters are a new version of these institutions. However,

13

it was not long before this "reform" had become principally a means of segregating the less attractive (mostly foreign immigrants) and the less competent (mostly the unemployed) from the rest of society. Large numbers of Mediterranean immigrants, exploitative roller-coaster capitalism, and the impact of the philosophy of social Darwinism provided reasons enough to justify disenfranchising and marginalizing so-called madpersons in custodial asylums. After all, they were clearly not the "fittest," hence their survival was of only marginal utility to the society. This attitude led to widespread neglect of public mental hospitals for more than 70 years (1880–1950) (Grob, 1983; Lamb, 1979).

Clifford Beers' *A Mind That Found Itself* (1939), recounting his experiences in Connecticut mental hospitals and his eventual successful self-help approach to his madness led to the development of mental health associations and child guidance clinics that were an early form of community mental health. At about the same time (1909), Adolph Meyer espoused a community-based approach to mental health problems. Unfortunately, neither of these events had any real impact on the state hospital system.

It was not until Deutsch's *Shame of the States* appeared, in 1948, with its exposé of the terrible conditions that existed in these institutions, that a true reform movement began. A number of powerful American Psychiatric Association members convinced the organization that it should spearhead a reform movement to correct the conditions Deutsch had described. The APA was in turn able to obtain the AMA's collaboration in this effort; hence the formation of the Joint Commission (APA and AMA) on Mental Health in 1956. In fact, there were ultimately 36 organizations represented on the Commission.

Interestingly, the Commission's recommendations (1961), were actually quite similar to those made a century earlier by Dr. John Galt (1819–62), the superintendent of Eastern State Hospital in Williamsburg, Virginia. He proposed in 1857 that the patients in his care be let out of the hospital to live and work and be cared for as necessary in a variety of community-based facilities! Galt believed his proposal would be the third revolution in psychiatry—the first being Pinel's unchaining of the insane and the second the development of humane care à la Tuke in England. More than a century later Bellak (1974) would call community mental health psychiatry's third revolution!

Unfortunately, the tides of history washed over Galt's radical proposal before he could implement it. At that time abolition of slavery was of much greater concern than emancipation of the insane. Galt, a confederate loyalist, killed himself following the Union's capture of Williamsburg in the spring of 1862. Although he was only 43, he had been its superintendent for 21 years. To this day Galt's then-radical proposal has received scant attention in the community mental health literature.

The Joint Commission's report is said to have been read cover to cover by President John Kennedy at the urging of his sister Eunice (Jack Ewalt, M.D., personal communication). His enthusiasm for change in the mental health system culminated in a special message to Congress on mental health in February 1963. The legislation authorizing a federally funded system of CMHC's was passed in October 1963 (PL 88-164).

The original bill, in circumventing states in the establishment of this federal program, represented a dramatic violation of traditional federal-state relationships. Basically, since President Pierce's 1854 veto, on constitutional grounds, of legislation that would have provided federal support for care of the indigent insane, the care of the mentally ill had been left the exclusive prerogative of the states. This new federal support for the care of mentally disordered persons, rather than adding to state support, created a parallel and sometimes competitive care system organized by individual locales. In hindsight, this may have been a fatal error for a program with built-in phase-down of federal support. Why should states pick up the tab for a program in whose design and implementation they had had little or no role?

Passage of this legislation resulted in the transformation of the National Institute of Mental Health, one of the traditional research and training-focused institutes of the National Institutes of Health, into an organization with a third functional leg, i.e., service. The CMHC program put the NIMH in the position of directly underwriting payment for a form of "medical" treatment. It was not long, in terms of dollars, before the CMHC tail began to wag the NIMH research and training dog. In 1967, this new functional and fiscal reality led to the NIMH's being formally split off from the parent NIH and given a new administrative status. Many interested parties opposed this move as scientifically and bureaucratically unwise, believing the NIMH would be too exposed politically without the NIH's protective high-science umbrella. However, in times of prodigious growth and prosperity, the more-and-bigger-is-better philosophy is difficult to contain. In retrospect, the critics may have been correct, as the organization has often been politically buffeted. In October 1992 NIMH's research and research training functions were split off from its service elements and returned to the NIH as an institute. This reorganization included the alcohol and drug abuse institutes as well. The three institutes' service elements were combined into a new agency, the Substance Abuse and Mental Health Services Administration (SAMHSA).

The CMHC program made the NIMH an administrator of a federally subsidized treatment system for a subset of the "ill." We presume the implication that this was a liberal venture into socialized medicine was either missed or muted by congressmen and bureaucrats alike as a consequence of the political context of that era. However, given this country's generally ambivalent attitude toward supporting the disenfranchised, it is not surprising that the legislation for this program would be repeatedly modified (see Foley & Sharfstein, 1983, for a complete account). Although Congress kept trying (the legislation was amended *seven* times in 12 years), no one is really sure whether it ever got it right.

The summary objectives of this series of legislative mandates were community mental health centers that would be:

1. Comprehensive; that is, provide inpatient, outpatient, emergency, partial hospitalization and consultation and education services;
2. Accessible and available (24 hours) to all residents of a limited geographical area regardless of ability to pay;
3. Coordinated with other relevant agencies;
4. Able to provide continuity of care; and
5. Emphasizing prevention through consultation and education with agencies and the public.

In a sense, this program obeyed a basic psychological law: the greater the ambivalence about something, the greater the number and types of unrealistic expectations and unsupportable attributions attached to it. The Nixon administration's wish to close out the CMHC program (by giving it to the states) because it was "successful" represents a particularly interesting example of this phenomenon.

The culmination of this program as a social movement was the passage of the Mental Health Systems Act of 1980 — a law based in large part on what had been learned from the CMHC program and its spinoffs. This generally enlightened piece of legislation was repealed in the Omnibus Budget Reconciliation Act of 1981, as part of the Reagan administration's efforts to reduce domestic spending. It was replaced, in reduced dollar amounts, by block grants to the states. This change restored the traditional federal-state relationship the program had violated.

As if it saw the handwriting on the wall for its control of the CMHC program, the NIMH began its Community Support Program (C.S.P.) in 1977. Its origins are best described as personal constructs of a few well placed individuals who then recruited support for them from the field at large (see Mosher, 1986). The Community Support Program did what the CMHC's never had; it moved the programmatic focus of interest from facilities and services in them (i.e., CMHC's) to support networks for individual clients. From the outset it worked directly with state mental health agencies (in contrast to the CMHC program). It is a program whose views promote decentralized, debureaucratized care and force a *systems view* on community mental health. C.S.P. continues to be under the direct control of the NIMH. The 10 elements of a community support system (Turner & Ten Hoor, 1978) (Table 2.1), despite a lack of theoretical cohesiveness and the fact that they mix treatment and nontreatment variables, have come to be widely accepted as the constituents of "good" community programs. The Community Support Program's conceptualizations serve as guidelines for community mental health program development throughout the U.S. CMHC block grant money may be used for their implementation. Because of its attention to political realities, the program has also generated a great deal of state support. Its philosophy has spread, despite the small amounts of federal money it has had to spend, because of frequently convened mega-meetings with representation of all interested parties—from clients to state mental health department heads. Interested readers are referred to *A Network for Caring* (1982) and Stroul (1986, 1987) for more detailed information about C.S.P.

The Community Support Program currently has a new carrot to offer states—money to develop state-wide plans for dealing with the long-term users of the system. The model plan the NIMH (1987) has put together is a good one; what will come of all this remains enigmatic. One major problem with the legislation and the model plan is that both accept as inevitable the notion of large numbers of persons with prolonged mental disorders. For us, a properly organized and operating community system ought to produce fewer and fewer long-term clients by progressively decreasing its use of larger institutions in favor of small, home-like, community-based, normalizing ones.

A status report on the state of community mental health in the U.S. today is difficult. There are some relevant facts: About 750 of the 2000 CMHC's proposed are in operation. About one-quarter of the population of the U.S. has access to one. All 50 states have C.S.P. grants. It appears,

TABLE 2.1
Community Support System Elements

1. Responsible *team*
2. Residential care
3. Emergency care
4. Medical care
5. Halfway house
6. Supervised (supported) apartments
7. Outpatient therapy
8. Vocational training and opportunities
9. Social and recreational opportunities
10. Family and network attention

From Turner & tenHoor, 1978.

overall, that the public mental health system has gotten the C.S.P. message. Psychosocial rehabilitation, supported (supervised) apartment programs, and case management are C.S.P. promulgated notions that have caught on and are growing in popularity and availability. Residential alternatives to hospitalization, neuroleptic-free treatment of psychosis, and the therapeutic importance of psychosocial interventions are notions that have not been as readily accepted. Medical domination, by siphoning off limited resources to support in-hospital care, continues to impede the development of the proper smorgasbord of psychosocially oriented community-based facilities. *We believe that, although the medicalization of madness is clearly an excellent survival strategy for psychiatry, its disease-in-the-person orientation does not optimally serve the interests of users. A family and systems orientation seems a clearly more useful one for community mental health.*

CHAPTER 3

The Context of Public Mental Health

DISTRESS AS PSYCHOPATHOLOGY

PSYCHOPATHOLOGY IS A FORM OF human discomfort and suffering that, ideally, can be alleviated by professional help. But, unfortunately, this process almost always imposes a psychiatric label, a diagnosis. It has been pointed out that it is difficult for a psychiatrist to avoid making a psychiatric diagnosis when the patient has been defined as a psychiatric case by others. A psychiatric diagnosis has been made *before* and independently of the psychiatrist; however, afterwards the psychiatric diagnosis is confirmed just because a psychiatrist is in charge—a self-fulfilling prophecy. When someone seeks treatment on his own, the psychiatrist has more latitude in how he adjudicates the case and whether or not the patient is given a psychiatric label (Goldberg & Huxley, 1980).

In our work we are primarily concerned with needs; we prefer to consider symptoms as communications about unmet needs that may be recognized and met, rather than expressions of hypothetical, underlying, pathological processes, whose classification results in little advantage to the patient. We must understand the message in order to recognize the presenting needs; the psychological mechanisms of symptom formation are of less concern to us.

NEEDS AND REQUESTS

A *need* is the lack of something experienced as essential to the purposes of life. It expresses itself as suffering. If the person is *aware* of the existence of a way to stop the suffering, the need expresses itself as a desire. Therefore, a need may exist objectively, without a clear awareness of it, even if there is suffering. Or the desire may be absent, as in the case of a seriously depressed person. A desire may lead to action; if the subject is unable to obtain what he needs by himself, a desire may be expressed as a *request* (Jervis, 1975).

Providers are not ordinarily asked directly to fill needs; they are confronted with *requests to do something.* Therefore, a request has to be interpreted in order to understand the need behind it.

The first step in the analysis of a request is to question who the real customer is. The term *customer* is currently used to define the real purchaser of the intervention requested. In private practice the patient is generally also the customer: He goes to a professional and asks for help by himself. The patient is a client. In public mental health this rarely happens. Instead, in many cases the patient is brought to the attention of the agency *by others*, often unwillingly; the patient and the customer are not the same person. This topic will be discussed in detail in the interviewing section of Chapter 6.

In order to meet the patient's needs, one has to understand what they are. This is done first by interpreting what the patient presents metaphorically, principally through his symptoms. Traditional clinical psychiatry and especially psychodynamic psychotherapy seem to be most interested in the form of the request (i.e., type of psychopathology), in that the diagnosis is thought to give essential information on the person's mental processes, which are deemed to need a fix. The rationale behind this is that the person's mind *should be changed*; once this is accomplished the person will be able to meet his own needs (the content) by himself.

We are also interested in exploring and understanding the request. However, in sharp contrast to a traditional psychiatric approach, the content of the request, the underlying need, rather than the form, is critical because we believe that *meeting the patient's needs is therapeutic per se.* Doing so empowers the patient, establishes a bond, provides a channel for empathic and meaningful communication, and makes change possible. At times the improvement is prompt and dramatic.

In order to truly *understand the meaning of requests, their context must be considered.* The intervention made in response to a request is also inevitably part of, and denoted by, a context.* For example, antidepressants

---

*The context is not something objective, existing "out there," but depends on how the actors involved in the interaction perceive it. Nor is it stable: it changes over time and can even fluctuate in the course of the interaction.

will likely be accepted more readily by a self-referred depressed person in a private office than by a depressed person brought to the public clinic against his/her will. In many cases, once one knows the context, the patient's seemingly crazy behavior becomes understandable and appropriate and indicates a precise intervention. See, for instance, the example of Piero and Maria in the section on interviewing (Chapter 6).

In general psychotherapists are aware of the importance of the treatment context. For instance, they are careful with regard to the therapeutic setting, ritualizing the encounter in order to provide a definite "psychotherapeutic context." However, less attention is paid to the context surrounding the client and his problem.

When the encounter between client and treater takes place in a public psychiatric service, things are complicated by the fact that the context is ill defined and seldom therapeutic. This is a direct consequence of the characteristics of the participants, i.e., the public psychiatric service, the patient and the treater.

DEFINING THE CONTEXT

Characteristics of Public Health Services

One might believe that a mental health service is a place where psychological disturbances are treated. This is an oversimplification and in many cases not true at all.

In fact, Paul (1978, p. 103) has pointed out that therapeutic effectiveness is *not* the principal goal of the psychiatric system and of its workers: "From top-level administrators, through program directors, to on-line staff, factors other than effective treatment considerations are primary determiners of action." A mental health service, especially a public one, has many attributed characteristics involving multiple goals. Such goals are vaguely stated and often conflict with one another. Besides therapeutic goals there are others related to giving welfare benefits, more or less explicitly stated goals involving social control of disturbing behaviors, consulting goals, legal and administrative ones, etc. There are also internal organizational goals and implicit or even secret ones, regarding career, profit, prestige, or allocation of money and equipment.

In addition to treatment, some common goals and related tasks of mental health agencies are the following:

1. *Control of disturbing behavior.* Mental health services are frequently asked to intervene with a patient, not on his behalf, but on behalf of the community. These are the cases when requests are

made to remove a patient from the street or his apartment because he is perceived as an environmental threat or simply a nuisance to others. Treatment is meant as to "readjust him," which in turn means that he is not a nuisance anymore. Admission to the hospital and heavy medication are the most welcome interventions. This has been defined as forcing conformity as opposed to treatment (see Chapter 4).

These patients might actually be in need of treatment (the most common justification alleged); however, what we wish to stress is that the reason for and the kind of intervention are *not* primarily in the interest of the patient. *This is practically never explicitly admitted*, as therapeutic rationales are always brought forth to justify the intervention.

Custodial care, not treatment, has long been recognized as the principal and "real" function of the mental hospital. Bachrach (1976, p. 19) has pointed out that "mental hospitals must not and cannot be eliminated until alternatives for the functions of asylum and custodial care have been provided."

2. *Dealing with legal medicine and welfare issues*. This has to do with counseling, diagnosing, writing certifications, insurance problems, welfare benefits, etc. In performing these tasks the professional is often rightfully concerned about not reinforcing the patient in his sick role. Sometimes the professional might resent being "used" as a mere bureaucrat, not as a therapist, by the patient or others. Explicitly acknowledging the ever growing bureaucratic components of careers in human services may help prevent disillusionment and frustration.

3. *Filling the gaps of the medical and welfare system*. Let us introduce this concept with an example:

A person is carried to the emergency room at night by the police because he is slightly drunk and acts a little bizarre; he is from out of town and has no money; he was treated by a mental health agency in the past, but presently is working and doing OK. In our system he is likely to be admitted, at least overnight (and we contend he *should be*, if the only alternatives are spending the night in jail or being abandoned), not because of a *specific* psychiatric condition—actually, is it always possible to find, or exclude, a *specific* psychiatric condition?—but because other social services are simply nonexistent. Community services should provide an array of options (see Chapter 9) to meet the different needs; otherwise *improper* use of existing options is the rule.

Characteristics of the Patient

In Italy patients of public services are currently referred to as "users," not as "clients," to stress the difference between a private therapeutic relationship and a public one. While the former is open to free, reciprocal negotiation between the two actors, i.e., provider and patient, the latter is predetermined to a large extent by health and welfare regulations. Therapeutic options for public patients are limited to what the service offers in terms of both programs and professionals. Often the patient cannot choose the therapist.

Welfare provisions greatly add to the secondary gain. The symptom may become a possession and a source of income, hence not to be given up. Being a patient may be a career ending with a retirement on a pension.

Public mental health clients come from the most socially, economically, and educationally disadvantaged strata of society. Because they have little experience with or understanding of office-based psychotherapy, they should not be expected to be good psychotherapy candidates. They are rather like the new immigrant eating his first banana; he ate the peel and threw away the fruit! However, a properly designed program will be very therapeutic for them by decoding their requests so their needs can be met.

Characteristics of the Therapist

The therapist has little more freedom than the patient. He cannot refuse an intervention or select patients and is often required to perform a mainly bureaucratic role for which he had no training. This leads to his being perceived by the patient as an officer rather than a professional. This may be frustrating for a professional, especially if he has psychotherapeutic training.

Unfortunately, mental health professionals have generally been trained for a traditional, purely professional career appropriate only to private practice and resent acting as "health officers" in the community. All this may lead to chronic frustration, burnout, role crisis, etc., and may account for American psychiatrists' disenchantment with CMHC work (Arce & Vergare, 1985; Clark & Vaccaro, 1987). When their skills, delivered with the best of intentions, do not "work" with these patients, professionals are faced with paradoxes: values seem inconsistent, expectations excessive with such difficult patients, and previous training and experience irrelevant for the task (Stern & Minkoff, 1979). The same thing is reported to happen to residents in training in community settings. In order to correct this situation, "good" supervisors should be available, but this is not the case — a final paradox (Minkoff & Stern, 1985). In short, with most "public" cases, the possibility of a free therapeutic contract is seriously hampered by limitations of both the patient and the therapist.

OTHER CONTEXTUAL FACTORS

Consumer/Survivor Organizations

"Ex-psychiatric inmate group" is the label the groups discussed here prefer. However, in order to make this section more inclusive and to simplify the language we will use the terms consumer, survivor, client, user, or patient, usually without the "ex."

The consumer movement in mental health began with the publication, in 1905, of Clifford Beers (1939) autobiographical account of his experiences in mental hospitals of the era. *The Mind That Found Itself*, because of its popular appeal, led over time to the development of the mental health associations and child guidance clinics. These were important background events to the subsequent development of community mental health movement, but did not stimulate widespread grass-roots, consumer-run self-help organizations. Basically, this early movement became professionalized, hence out of the direct control of consumers.

Recent mental health consumerism took hold and grew in the context of the civil rights movement, the legitimized antiauthority Viet Nam protest era, the widespread consumerism of the mid-'70s, and the women's movement. It is driven by shared feelings of outrage, hurt, degradation, and betrayal at the hands of the helping professions, especially psychiatry. The practices of forced hospitalization and medication to which these patients were subjected resulted in a great deal of anger that is being expressed in the movement. Being labeled "mental patient" (as conferred by institutional treatment in particular) led these patients to feel isolated and pariah-like. Promises of help that turned out to be social control led them to feel betrayed and disillusioned with the purveyors of "treatment." Being afflicted with tardive dyskinesia without having given their real informed consent led them to be suspicious of new, technologically advanced treatments. In sum, they have organized to fight for the restoration of their right to be first-class citizens.

The first groups formed in the early 1970s. Their early networking brought them together in 1973 at the first conference on Human Rights and Against Psychiatric Oppression. The ensuing series of conferences (lasting until 1985) brought together ex-patients from around the country. No organization emerged from these annual conferences because the major participants feared recreating the oppressive system they were protesting. In the late 1970s various individual ex-patients were invited (as were family members) to a series of NIMH-sponsored Community Support Program "learning conferences." These parallel series of conferences (Human Rights and CSP) enabled consumers to maintain contact, develop networks, and begin to organize on a local level.

Finally, in 1985, the NIMH awarded a Baltimore consumer group a grant to head a national "consumer conference." A split in the ex-patient movement began at this conference. The basic issue was whether or not the new organization would take a stand against forced treatment. In several subsequent meetings the differences could not be ironed out. By the spring of 1986 two ex-patient groups had been formed: the National Alliance of Mental Patients (NAMP) (Rae Unzicker, Coordinator) and National Mental Health Consumer Association (NMHCA) (headed by Joe Rogers). In 1989 NAMP changed its name to the National Association of Psychiatric Survivors (NAPS).

Basically, NAPS is focused on developing programs totally outside the mental health system, while NMHCA is focused on working for change within the system, including aligning itself with NAMI (National Alliance for the Mentally Ill) goals. Despite this split, as we discussed the development of client-run mutual help groups with a number of persons participating in them, there seemed to emerge a modest consensus around the principles that should govern them. These are not specifically NAPS or NMHCA principles; rather, they are generic to a number of client-run programs:

1. Clients control major governance positions, including all hiring, firing and money management.
2. Participation is totally voluntary. No one will ever be forcibly sent to a hospital; they will not guide an individual's return to the mental health system.
3. Hierarchy is minimal.
4. Staff is responsible to membership and members control the staff.
5. The approach is nonmedical and nonclinical, involving support and caring, and includes consciousness-raising about issues of self-determination, personal responsibility, and autonomy.
6. Education, advocacy and one-to-one help with negotiating the system are high priority activities; that is, accessing entitlements, housing, and providing legal counsel when needed, especially when a person has been committed.
7. Information is provided about such things as psychiatric drugs, civil rights, and options within the psychiatric and other relevant systems.
8. Political action by the organization will be done in various ways, including joining with a variety of coalitions — the poor, the home-

less, Grey Panthers, patient's rights advocates, etc. Other, more traditional forms of pressure (e.g., picketing) will also be used.

These principles are put into practice in drop-in centers staffed by a combination of paid and volunteer persons. The focus is on maximizing self-reliance while utilizing environmental (interpersonal) support as needed. A format that has been evolved is the "mutual speakout." By admitting their common situation, i.e., ex-patients, and criticizing the system in the context of mutual support, consumers find the occasion liberating, organizing, and passion-reviving. The goal is to get more and more distance from the identity as ex-patient so more normalizing activities can be undertaken. One example of this process would be moving from being a staff member or advocate in a self-help center to becoming a community organizer.

The focus of these groups is not so much on bashing psychiatry as it is developing a viable alternative to psychiatry's authority and control. Psychiatric (or other professional) help can be used so long as it is by choice. However, because of their experiences at the hands of psychiatry and the mental health system, ex-patients are very concerned about preservation of their integrity. They worry that cooperation *with* the mental health system will turn into co-optation *by* it.

Some consumer groups see mental health professionals as having a role in helping them form their group and establish their legitimacy. Once this is done they would like the mental health system to:

1. Provide technical information (i.e., regarding drugs, commitment, etc.);
2. Provide material support, such as office space, telephone, and photocopying;
3. Give access to persons who can help them attain goals they have decided upon as a group; and
4. Advocate with, or support their applications to, funding organizations.

At this time (Spring 1993) the more conservative group (NMHCA) currently headed by Fred Fries, Ph.D., seems to be growing. Because it rejects neither the medical model nor involuntary treatment it is more accepting of, and acceptable to, mental health professionals. Overall, the consumer/survivor movement has gained strength since 1988, when this section was initially written. Consumers are running housing programs and cooperative businesses. They are begin trained as case managers and returning to school to obtain professional mental health degrees. A number hold high-level positions within state consumer affairs offices. They sit on most local mental health advisory committees. Perhaps most importantly, they are being accorded greater equality, and the respect that this entails, as stakeholders in the mental health system. However, as compared with the parents and other advocacy groups, they remain poor and relatively politically powerless. This is likely to change in the 1990s.

There are other "consumer" organizations (e.g., the Manic-Depressive Association, Recovery, GROW, etc.); however, we've chosen not to describe them here, hoping this description will be prototypical enough to educate the average reader. Readers interested in more information about the ex-patient movement will find it in Frank (1986) and Miller (1983). Information about client-run programs can be found in Chamberlin (1978), Zinman (1986), Zinman, Harp, and Budd (1987), and from the journals *Phoenix Rising* and *Madness Network News.*

We believe that the continued development of a strong consumer movement should be a high priority of every community mental health program. It is the most direct and clear statement of a program's commitment to the principle of preservation and enhancement of power. The nature of the relationship of client-run programs to the local community mental health system must be allowed to change over time and will vary between locales. What is most critical is that the mental health system *not* attempt to control it or take it over. The system's role should be to provide as much material support and *consultative* expertise as needed to get the program (as defined by users) up and running. After that, the community mental health system should make itself available as needed, with "needed" being defined by the consumers' group. The client-run program can be completely outside the mental health system and serve, for example, a watchdog function for it. Or, it can be at the boundary of the community mental health program by providing a way for clients to make the transition out of the mental health system via the peer support and advocacy offered in a drop-in center.

Parents of Consumers/Survivors

The National Alliance for the Mentally Ill (NAMI) was founded in Madison, Wisconsin in 1979. The national organization brought a number of local organizations of the Alliance for the Mentally Ill under a single umbrella. There are now 1000 affiliates with over 140,000 families involved nationwide. This national organization was presaged by the Schizophrenia Foundation and its local associations, an organization focused on the promulgation of megavitamins as *the* treatment for schizophrenia. A number of local Schizophrenia Association chapters (Schizophrenia Fellowship in Great Britain) changed their names to Alliance and joined NAMI. A number of local Alliance leaders were formerly Schizophrenia Association members.

The history of these local organizations and their various transformations is complex and convoluted and will not be further elaborated here. The essential point is that beginning in the early 1970s groups of parents with disturbed and disturbing children began to coalesce and attempt to make their wishes known. The parents involved were generally white, middle- and upper-middle-class professionals whose mostly male children had received extensive, but usually unsuccessful, psychiatric care. Many of them had spent, in addition to insurance, large sums of their own money for treatment of their disturbed offspring. They shared the common experience of feeling both ripped off and blamed by psychiatry. Many had been, at least implicitly, promised high-priced "cures" that were never delivered. In their interactions with treatment institutions they were frequently attributed responsibility for their offspring's condition. They were angry and highly sensitized to "family bashing," but continued to seek the magic bullet that would cure their offspring once and for all.

In the early '70s parent groups literally leapt on the Hofer-Osmond megavitamin bandwagon as it went by. What happened as a result of this movement was that parents with similar painful and frustrating experiences found each other. They formed support groups, circulated newsletters, had monthly meetings featuring invited professional speakers (megavitamin proponents only in those days), and began legislative lobbying efforts.

As the NIMH was gearing up its Community Support Program (1974–77), consumerism was the order of the day. For example, the 1975 CMHC act amendments were the first to mandate consumer representation (half) on CMHC boards. The meetings convened as part of the Community Support Program's development included these *parents* as consumers. Subsequently the real users (the clients) were also included. These national meetings put local parent groups in touch with each other. We believe this was crucial to the eventual formation of NAMI (see Mosher, 1986). NAMI replaced the previous megavitamin ideology with a new one. It must be emphasized that the positions taken by the national organization on a number of issues are not uniformly supported by local alliance chapters. For example, many local chapters do not favor making involuntary commitment easier (see number 3 below of NAMI's political action platform). Also, local chapters are usually supportive of community mental health programs in their areas.

The basic tenets of the belief system being promulgated by the *National Alliance* are about as follows:

1. Major mental disorders (i.e., schizophrenia, major depression and bipolar illness) are brain diseases.

2. These disorders are genetic in origin.
3. Their genetic underpinning is played out via identifiable biological processes.
4. The family has no role in the production or maintenance of the disorders.
5. The only treatments of relevance are biological in nature.
6. Poor mental health is not the same as mental illness. Social circumstances do not create psychosis.

From this ideology a political action platform has been drawn up by the national organization about as follows:

1. More research into the biologic bases of mental illness is needed. Because psychosocial (i.e., family) factors play no role, no psychosocial research should be supported.
2. As neuroleptic drugs are the only known effective treatment, new and better drugs should be developed and subjected to clinical trials. They will provide subjects for these trials (their offspring).
3. As a biologic illness psychosis should be treated in hospitals. Unfortunately, because of new admission policies, stricter commitment laws, and closing of hospital beds, it is not easy to have someone (their offspring) admitted to a hospital. Hence, it is advocated that mental hospital beds be reopened and commitment made easier. Deinstitutionalization should be stopped via litigation to preserve state hospital budgets. More and improved community-based services are required and should be supported.
4. Since mental illness is somatic/biologic like other illnesses, the National Institute of Mental Health should be renamed the National Institute of Mental Illness and moved back into the NIH fold. Although the name was not changed the NIMH became an NIH institute in October 1992. This move is a concrete example of this organization's political skill and power.
5. Family therapy should be eradicated because it blames families, is really only intended to make families into better caretakers, prevents independence of the offspring, and leaves children no alternatives when parents die. No family therapy research should be supported.
6. Scientists who continue to conduct irrelevant (as defined by NAMI) psychosocially focused research should be educated as to the biologic nature of these disorders and their research carefully scrutinized for flaws, especially any hint of "family bashing." Scientific data that disagree with the ideology will be labeled invalid and disregarded.

7. Training in the relevant mental health disciplines must be carefully scrutinized to be sure students are being taught properly about the biologic basis of mental illness. The organization's curriculum committee will review training program content in psychiatry, psychology, nursing, and social work.

8. Practicing clinicians who continue to advocate psychosocial treatment (especially family therapy) or who question drug treatment for mental illness will be brought to the attention of the relevant licensing bodies as guilty of possible malpractice.

9. Children with neurobiological disorders should not be mixed in with those suffering from abuse, neglect, and family dysfunction.

10. A national health plan should provide mental health coverage parity with other somatic illnesses only for those with severe mental illnesses (as defined in tenet #1 above).

This ambitious program of thought reform has found a number of allies, especially within psychiatry's powerful biologic contingent. Their strong conviction as to the rightness of their cause and to the belief that a true "cure" is just around the corner fuels NAMI parents' fires. For interested readers this summary can be expanded by reading the NAMI newsletter or publications the organization recommends (Hatfield, 1984, 1985; Kanter, 1984; Torrey, 1983; Torrey & Wolfe, 1986; Walsh, 1985).

It is not likely that the family and systems psychosocial approach to community mental health we espouse—even though it never addresses the issue of causation—will be popular with the current NAMI leadership. However, as noted previously, there is a great deal of heterogeneity of point of view within the organization and a number of local affiliates are not in agreement with the national organization's aims. In our experience the local AMI organizations can, and have been, very helpful in advocating in the mental health system and legislatures for good community programs. A number of local chapters have developed quality housing and vocational programs. They, like all parents, want what is best for their individual offspring independent of the organization's firebrand rhetoric. Their functioning as mutual help groups (a more accurate term than self-help) is extremely useful.

What we advocate is quite consistent with these parents' stated wishes: They don't want to be the only care option available to their offspring. The community smorgasbord we describe gives users many options. The programs described should preserve and enhance their offspring's power so they won't need to be excessively dependent on their family. Our position is to try and give clients and their involved families what they want and need and to negotiate around problems that arise in the process. We recommend that support be offered to families of a disturbed offspring independent of whether he/she is living at home. We recommend that their participation be invited in planning processes as one set of players in a complex system. Problems may be encountered around the issue of control. It is our position that no single participant in the system should be in control. However, users' wishes should be addressed first. Community programs should align themselves with parent groups but they should not let them, by themselves, dictate program policies. A proper mix of citizen participation will assure that all relevant points of view are attended to; a balanced position is required for ongoing program functioning.

The Problem of Homelessness

It is a sign of the times that a book on community mental health has a section devoted to something that really is *not* a mental health problem. Mental health workers like ourselves are quite sensitive to the context within which we operate. Attributions of mental health as being responsible for the homelessness problem abound. The mental health field seems to be responding with a combination of guilt and compliance. Psychiatrists are being recruited to volunteer their time in shelters. Psychiatric residents are being trained in them. These dreadful, inhumane institutions have sprung up like topsy. Professionals of every stripe are in attendance in them. All of the activity and rhetoric about the problem seems, to us at least, mostly designed to avoid asking, much less answering, this question: *How can a seemingly civilized, highly affluent society like ours allow somewhere between two and four million of its members to be homeless? What are its root causes and how can we, as a society, address them?* Europeans find this situation inexplicable and unbelievable. Volumes (for example, Lamb, 1984) have been written about it, research on it is proceeding apace, but as a fundamental political and social issue it remains largely unaddressed. The scarcity of decent affordable housing has not yet been thrust into the political limelight as a major domestic issue.

Despite what we're being told, mental illness does not cause homelessness. That many homeless persons are "mentally ill" is not at all surprising. There is probably no more demoralizing experience than the double stress of being without work and having no place to live. A number of those who *do* work (at minimum wage) cannot afford housing in expensive urban areas like New York City, Boston, Washington, Los Angeles, etc. Actually, about 20% (estimates vary greatly) of shelter inhabitants have regular jobs. Most welfare recipients can't afford decent housing in those areas either. Mentally ill or not, these groups are all exposed to the same degrading and dehumanizing conditions in the new urban almshouses — the shelters.

There exists today a belief that most homeless persons are deinstitution-alized mental patients. Let us examine the evidence. Roughly 400,000 patients were deinstitutionalized between 1960 and 1980 (Goldman et al., 1983). About half went home to live with their families. So there is a maximum of 200,000 available to the homeless person pool. Actually, the maximum available is probably less than 100,000 because most persons deinstitutionalized in the 1960–70 decade were geriatric patients placed in nursing homes. Recent studies have found that between 10 and 20% of shelter inhabitants are deinstitutionalized persons (Struening, 1986; Susser & Struening, 1987). Estimates of the numbers of mentally ill in shelter populations vary widely, but 30–40% seems like a fair ballpark figure (Lamb, 1984). The estimates of the number of homeless in 1984 varied between two and four million (Lamb, 1984). Where did they all come from? Clearly, there is no simple answer.

Our analysis of the problem runs like this: Homelessness is basically an economic problem—not enough money to pay for housing. Which groups in our society have the least money? Welfare recipients, the working poor, and the unemployed (obviously overlapping to some extent). Which of these groups increased dramatically in size concomitant with the discovery of the homeless problem in the winter of 1981–82? Between 1980 and 83 unemployment rose from about 7.5% to 10.5%. This represents about three million persons.

In addition to these three million new poor being added to the potentially homeless pool, other factors were at work:

1. The rise in the cost of housing in the 1970–80 decade far out-stripped wage and welfare payment increases for the working poor and welfare recipients.
2. The Reagan and Bush administrations reduced support for development of low income housing and housing subsidy programs. Between FYs 1980 and 1990 the budget of the Department of Housing and Urban Development (HUD), the major source of low-cost housing, was reduced from 35.9 to 14.3 billion dollars.
3. Because of both rapidly rising rents and urban gentrification (there was a 60% decline in the number of single room occupancy hotel rooms in New York City between 1973 and 1980), the cost of available housing moved out of reach for an increasingly large percentage of these groups. The economics of the social context forced them into homelessness.
4. The recession of the late '80s and early '90s has served to perpetuate the problem by preventing the devotion of now scarcer resources

to it. Almost all states and counties are dealing with serious deficits. The disenfranchised are the first to suffer in such situations.

Thus, when the cohort of new poor, i.e., three million new persons collecting unemployment (who became really poor when their unemployment ran out six months or a year later), was added to the preexisting pool, homelessness increased dramatically. It is not surprising that a substantial subset might have *become* mentally ill as a consequence of the confluence of two stressors — unemployment and homelessness.

Based on this analysis, the solution to the problem should be straight forward: Provide either enough money to these people to buy housing on the open market or develop a rent subsidy program in conjunction with buying and rehabilitating housing for which subsidies can be used. With each barrack space in shelters in New York City costing $20,000 and hotel space for families over $300,000 a year, such a program makes good economic — and humanitarian — sense.

Although several pieces of federal legislation (e.g., the "McKinney" Act) have been passed to attempt to deal with the problem, there is no real sense of national urgency about building, rehabilitating, and subsidizing enough housing to assure all Americans access to decent, affordable, permanent housing. These bills usually have an unfortunate feature; they separate programs for mentally ill persons without housing from those for persons without mental illness. They identify and segregate one subset of persons without housing. This not only serves to divert attention from the larger problem (so that it won't be seriously addressed), but also does a grave disservice to these persons.

Housing programs will not, of course, deal with the unfortunate sequelae of homelessness:

1. Demoralization for so long as to render persons so hopeless that they lose all motivation to work — especially at entry level jobs that won't enable them to leave the shelter system.
2. A new form of institutionalism — homeless shelter institutionalism (an interesting oxymoron), stemming from a situation not unlike the one in traditional total institutions, where one group with no other options (the homeless) is required to subjugate itself to another (the shelter providers) in order to obtain the basic necessities of life. Many of the "new" homeless have by now been on the streets for five or more years. Many have become dependent on the shelter system and reluctant to leave it (see Chapter 19).
3. Many of the homeless have serious medical and psychological com-

plications as a result of poor nutrition, exposure, involvement in endemic shelter violence, rape, drug abuse, etc.

Good community mental health programs should have enough affordable housing and intervention available to take in a share of the homeless — those with the most serious psychological difficulties who are *willing* to come in from the cold. Getting the maximum number of homeless into housing and treatment programs will be a test of community program's ability to be flexible and innovative, especially around the use of incentives. That is, the problem now emerging with the homeless is that many of them — some seriously disturbed but many who are not — have embarked on *careers* as homeless persons. They are likely to be unwilling to participate in a process that will reintegrate them into society because they perceive the homeless subculture as more caretaking than the wider society. Innovative approaches to reacculturating these persons and families will need to be developed if this career path is to be interrupted. Developing incentives that will really get their attention is going to be a tall order.

(RE)STRUCTURING THE CONTEXT

Once the context has been recognized, (1) it may just be discussed and defined, or (2) has to undergo a more or less radical restructuring. In the first case, an explicit definition of the context is made by the worker, so that an agreement can be reached with the patient and other interested parties as to "where we are now" and what intervention can be made to suit the patient's needs. Given the vast array of intertwined and often contradictory goals and tasks of a public psychiatric service, this step is essential in order to ascertain if the mental health worker and the client(s) perceive the context in the same way. This also helps the patient to understand what he may expect from the intervention and to define and recognize his own needs.

Defining the context may also be used strategically in the therapeutic process. For example, explicitly defining the context as "custodial" in the case of an involuntary patient clears the air of hypocrisy and provides a honest foundation for the patient-therapist relationship.

In other cases the context needs to be *restructured* because it is strongly antitherapeutic, as happens, for example, in a typical institutional environment where efficiency and discipline prevail over understanding and caring. A radical change of the institution may be the *only real therapeutic* intervention possible in such a case.

These principles characterized deinstitutionalization in Italy, where the primary target of intervention was the institution itself. Not only has there been a gradual discharge of patients into the community, but also the very existence of the "manicomio" has been criticized and resolution made to get rid of it. The term "institutional rehabilitation" was coined to describe this process, implying that change of the whole treatment environment was at stake.

REQUESTS CHANGE ALONG WITH CHANGE IN THE ORGANIZATION

In the process of designing a health service (in our case a psychiatric one) the major difficulty consists in finding concrete answers to the concrete demands coming from the surrounding reality. However, answers, while sticking to reality, should *surpass it as well, in order to transform it.* (Basaglia & Ongaro-Basaglia, 1975; italics added)

It has been suggested that in Italy the ongoing change in the organization of the delivery system is now producing a slow but detectable change in the characteristics of the requests made by patients and significant others. Requests tend to become more differentiated as a function of both the decentralization of services and, especially, the *quality* of interventions provided (De Salvia & Crepet, 1982). When a gamut of alternative interventions is provided, attitudes about mental health are changed both in the public (whose requests change) and in the professionals (with a change of beliefs and clinical practices).

For example, over the past 10 years Liliana, 52, has been in touch with the South Verona Mental Health Service for several episodes of severe depression. She used to go to the emergency room, or be brought by her relatives in critical condition, with the sole request of an admission to the hospital. Now she comes to the Mental Health Center when she feels dispirited and asks either to change medications, or to attend the day program, or to be helped at home with housework she is unable to accomplish. The same shift has been seen with general practitioners: They used to refer patients to the emergency room with a certificate for an admission; now their referrals are much more diversified. When a variety of alternatives is offered, the population is encouraged to present a broader array of *requests*; when only hospitalization is offered, there is a flattening of requests and eventually hospitalization is *the only* request presented when a psychiatric need is perceived. There is some evidence for this. A study (Pancheri, 1986) done in Portogruaro, a city northwest of Venice, showed that 28.2% of patients who had previous multiple hospitalizations asked to be hospitalized when seen in the emergency room. In contrast, no previously untreated patients and only 12.5% of those treated only by their G.P.'s sought hospitalization when seen in the emergency room.

There is also evidence that the existence of mental hospitals tends to induce requests for hospitalization. In research done by the Centro Studi del Ministero della Sanità (Center for Studies of the Department of Health), on a sample of 34 Italian provinces in 1975, the rate of hospitalization was higher in those provinces having a mental hospital than in those without (3.09 vs. 1.59/1,000; Centro Studi Ministero della Sanità, 1977).

WHAT IS "TREATMENT"?

Besides the radical approach described above (restructuring the context in a therapeutic direction), there are other possible options. A common (and certainly much easier) way is one of trying to replicate the private setting within a public institution. We define this as the "flower bed" alternative: A "therapeutic flower bed" is cultivated within the institution/service, whose organization at large, however, is *not* scrutinized. Typically, a therapist locks himself in a room with a patient and tries to make him into a "client," barricading the door against interferences from the institution and the community. This has the advantage of relying on the long experience of private professional practice, especially in the field of dynamic psychotherapy.

One limitation of the "flower bed" approach is that the work done in an hour of therapy is likely to be undone in the other 23 of institutional management. Further, it has the serious disadvantage of being appropriate only for patients who are fit for therapy; given the characteristics of patients referred to public services, the proportion of those meeting the criteria is relatively low. Most public patients are not very motivated for treatment of any kind, even though they might be in an extreme need of it. In the public sector, dealing with unmotivated or even resistant patients is the rule rather than the exception. Therefore, we believe that attitudes regarding motivation and therapeutic contract drawn from private practice are of little relevance in current public practice.

An important corollary of the "flower bed" perspective is that treatment and care are of a different breed, the latter being considered somehow "second class" with respect to treatment and a mere support to it. They are kept also separate, physically and professionally: Treatment takes place in the office, care in the ward; professionals are in charge of treatment, paraprofessionals provide care.

We believe that this distinction is arbitrary, since our patients, in their unique wholeness as individuals, have multiple needs, all important for their well-being. In particular, those patients who are typical of a community service are usually people with multiple needs: The community must provide for all the basic needs that were formerly met by the state hospital.

In addition, there are "new" needs, derived from social evolution, such as being entitled to treatment, not just custody, being entitled to placement in the least restrictive environment, having the right not to be removed from one's own existential and social space, etc.

A community service with global responsibility for a given population has to meet *all* that population's needs directly or indirectly related to mental health. Treatment is not something that is "done" in specific interventions; rather, it is a functional characteristic of the global approach to patients' needs. *The therapeutic intervention does not exist; no intervention is by itself therapeutic or not.* It is the sum of all interventions that has to be "therapeutic," and the service has to be organized in a way to make this possible. Grafting an advanced service, either psychotherapeutic or community-oriented, onto a reactionary institution is nonsensical as it will be swallowed by the pre-existing context.

TOWARDS A MODEL OF TREATMENT IN A COMMUNITY SERVICE

We believe that, in order to provide treatment, a service *has to* offer *prompt, adequate* and *consistent* answers to the needs of the population served:

- *has to:* The service has a responsibility towards the population.
- *prompt* and *adequate:* The service is often the first and the last resort. It cannot postpone interventions, have waiting lists, give evasive and partial answers.
- *consistent:* There must be consistency between values and goals, structure of the service, and therapeutic approach (including techniques).

In brief, treatment means meeting the needs of the population served. However, there is the risk of reinforcing the needs, instead of meeting them, thus making the users chronically dependent upon the service, instead of promoting their independence. This is what happens, for example, when requests are taken literally and without adequate probing, and answers tend to become repetitive—in a word, "institutional." For example, the patient or the family requests multiple hospital admissions and these are granted just to offer respite to the family without an evaluation of the overall scenario or a mid-to-long-term therapeutic strategy and goals. *Putting aside a problem, for no matter how long, acts in the direction of inducing chronicity.* In some cases admission might be inevitable, but a problem-solving *strategy*, at least minimal, must be present as well. *Unfortunately, all too often the limits of the service in providing alternatives to hospitalization become a "clinical" need for admission.*

Being therapeutic depends on *how* one meets needs and with what *goals*. To be therapeutic means to meet needs, but at the same time, ideally, to provide clients with the means and the motivation to work toward satisfying their needs on their own. *The ultimate goal must be to free the patient from the service as he becomes capable of meeting his needs independently.* At the organizational level, the various interventions have to be *integrated* among themselves and *consistently* aim at the therapeutic goal. If the interventions that the service is able to offer are fragmentary and there is no therapeutic continuity, it is unlikely that the patient will become better integrated psychologically, no matter how sophisticated the specific treatments he receives might be.

The previous paragraphs well illustrate how difficult and demanding it is to provide a therapeutic context in a public community setting. However, a public community service has some advantages over the private office or agency. It has more power, because it is both the first filter and the last resort; the patient and the family have to contact the community service, sooner or later, for a number of reasons. Therefore, the therapist has more chances to engage the patient in a therapeutic work and a dropout does not mean end of contacts — the patient will eventually show up again. This may be used strategically. In addition, a community service can rely on a vast array of different possible interventions, some of them very powerful and meaningful for the patient because they directly affect his real existence. We refer to intensive residential care, allocation of welfare benefits, contacts with other social agencies, etc. The task of the worker is to use them in a goal-oriented (therapeutic) way, as defined before.

CHAPTER 4

A Dinosaur to Be:
A Proposal for Limiting Use
of Psychiatric Hospitals

OUR BASIC POSITION IS THAT *hospital*-based care is not necessary for most disturbed and disturbing persons if:

1. In-home family crisis intervention is available;
2. A properly organized intentional social environment (therapeutic community) (see Chapter 9) is available to those who cannot be maintained in the family environment or do not have a social network that can be organized to act as a temporary caregiver; and
3. The identified patient is not a *battle scarred veteran* of the mental health wars ("chronic") who is so attached to (the idea of) hospitals that he/she or the family is unwilling to accept treatment that does not include hospitalization.

These same three conditions must also be met if psychotropic drug treatment is to be avoided or minimized (see Chapter 5).

BACKGROUND

In the United States hospitals have for a century and a half been *the places* where serious mental illness is to be treated. While in European countries traditional psychiatric hospitals are frequently converted leprosaria (Galzigna & Terzian, 1980), in the United States a whole new set of institutions were created, principally because of the crusading efforts of Dorothea Dix, to care for the insane.

The character of traditional psychiatric institutions changed on both sides of the Atlantic during the 1960s. Basically, they shifted from being custodial long-stay asylums to being places with an active treatment orientation. Initially this resulted in higher turnover rates, i.e., a rise in the number of admissions, shorter lengths of stay, and modest declines in total patients in residence. In the late '60s and early '70s state hospitals in the U.S. discharged large numbers of patients, mostly because of federal support through health insurance (Medicare/Medicaid) and disability pensions (SSI, SSDI). Deinstitutionalization was the order of the day. Simultaneously, psychiatric wards began to proliferate in general hospitals in the U.S. This shift in the site of care was propelled by a preferential availability of health insurance payment for treatment in general hospitals rather than in large psychiatric institutions. But the result was the same—an emphasis on institutional care.

What, it may legitimately be asked, is so wrong with treating disturbed and disturbing persons in hospitals? Several things:

First, when the person is removed from his usual physical and interpersonal environment, a process of decontextualization is initiated.

Second, by enforcing regimentation and dependency, the hospital routine violates the person's senses of individuality, autonomy, and self-control. A process of dehistorification is begun.

Third, because the diagnostic process focuses on symptoms, pays little attention to the influence of context on behavior, and transforms "the problem" (something a person can feel responsible for) into a "disease" that becomes the doctor's responsibility, the patient becomes further decontextualized.

Fourth, the treatment process is based on a set of negative attributions that patients must *disprove* in order to show themselves to be getting better. Common sense tells us that operating in a field of negative attributions will likely have a negative effect on self-esteem and self-confidence and hence maintain or worsen, rather than alleviate, the problem (disease).

Although we single out hospitals in our criticism, we recognize that any setting in which the processes we describe above go on is open to the same criticism. Hospitals are extreme examples of the operation of these processes because of their size, hierarchy, medical authority, and very distressed clientele, who see themselves as being without options. We've seen many community residential programs that differed only in degree from hospitals on these variables.

AN EXAMPLE

Rather than rely only on our prose and experience to support our views of hospital wards, even "good" ones in general hospitals, we will present the findings of 120 hours of participant observation on a 30-bed public (county) community hospital psychiatric ward that served as the control treatment setting in the Soteria project (Mosher, 1977; Mosher & Menn, 1978; Wilson, 1975). (See Chapter 9.)

The general hospital ward, affiliated with a university medical center's psychiatric training program, has 30 beds and an average length of stay of 15 days. The dispatching process is described by Wilson (1983) as follows:

1. *Patching-fixing.* Staff's initial contact with patients often revolves around the imposition of a variety of behavioral controls such as use of seclusion rooms, mechanical restraints, verbal instructions, and particularly heavy doses of psychotropic medications such as Haldol, Prolixin, or Thorazine. In essence, violent, out of control, or inappropriately bizarre patients are patched together by subduing their socially unacceptable symptoms as quickly as possible.

2. *Medical screening.* Because the psychiatric dispatching process (a term used to encompass the multiple, complex operations employed for "processing patients through" a clearing house model of care) takes place in a "medical" setting under the direction of physicians for the most part, a standardized routine of physical testing and diagnostic procedures is immediately initiated for all new admissions. These procedures include a physical exam, blood work, urinalysis, E.E.G., and a selected variety of others. Such screening also serves as an information gathering strategy in that on occasion a patient's psychiatric problem is discovered to be a consequence of a medical or physiological disorder. Properties of this process of screening are that it is extremely time-consuming for staff, that it requires accurate and proper completion of a multitude of requisitions and forms, and that it is rigidly imposed, even though a patient who is readmitted may have undergone the same screening process within the same week.

3. *Piecing together a story.* Proportionately speaking, the most staff time and energy is devoted to this dimension of the dispatching process. In order to make subsequent decisions about distributing a patient to the appropriate aftercare placement, as well as the more immediate decision of which course of medications to begin, a diagnosis must be made. Thus, information gathering and intelligence operations consume staff's focus during the first 72 hours of a patient's confinement. The interaction of staff attempting to sleuth out and uncover information about a patient in order to engage in fate-making decisions, with patients who are attempting to cover up what they believe is damaging data about themselves, constitutes another key focus for staff/patient contact. The major modalities for this contact are the "Group Intake Interview" wherein a newly admitted patient is confronted by a group of staff in an interview room and questioned, and the "Second-hand Report" where bits and pieces of data are passed along from shift to shift verbally and on

the patient's chart and then used to make generalizations about the patient. Properties of this process are its preconceived tendency, a reliance on speculations which easily become "truth," and the trickery involved in "finding things out."

4. *Labeling and sorting.* Once there is sufficient data to justify some decisions, patients are stamped with a psychiatric label. For the most part, patients in the study setting fell into the following diagnostic categories: schizophrenic, manic-depressive, alcohol or drug abuse, or violent character disorder of some type. Labeling acts as a key in deciding which medications to order and which aftercare placements to begin exploring. It also provides staff with an additional source of control in their dealings with patients, for with diagnosis comes an increased sense of being able to predict patient behavior and the ability to deal with patient communications and behaviors as typifications—"That's her hysterical personality coming out; those are just delusions, etc."

5. *Distributing.* The official goal of Community Mental Health legislation in California also includes a goal of moving mentally ill persons back into "the community" as rapidly as possible. Yet, psychiatric professionals in the study setting are constantly balancing this mandate against their perceived mandate to act as protectors of society and their patients. Consequently, staff act as fate-makers by distributing their "charges" to one of a variety of placement options for follow-up and aftercare. A property of the distributing stage of dispatching is its revolving door nature. Many of the setting's patients are "old familiars," who periodically rotate through the study setting and back out again. A number of patients are tracked by community liaison workers which contributes additional data taken into account when distributing decisions are made. Reports include that one aftercare facility or another "won't take her back again" so the options become limited by virtue of exhausting some of them over time.

The above conceptualization of "usual psychiatric care" in the study setting conveys, I hope, the complex nature of the psychiatric decision making and deposition process that goes on. Consequences of these operations include: (1) A very hectic and busy pace of work for staff while the hours "drift by" for patients. (2) A low accessibility of staff for patients—sitting and talking with patients has very low priority in view of all the tasks that must be accomplished. (3) A substitution of technology for potential face-to-face contacts (e.g., there's a mechanical cigarette lighter on the wall to discourage patients from bothering busy staff for lights, medications are announced over a loudspeaker instead of passed out by a nurse who seeks out patients around the ward, etc.). (4) Staff spend the majority of their time in interaction with other staff—in report, team meetings, intake interviews, and other meetings. (This observation differed on the two wards with more staff/patient contact on Ward 1, in ritualized formats such as "anger group," "feelings group," etc., but these contacts were low on spontaneity, low on openness, and high on superficiality and control.) (5) Staff are the constants on the units with patients only passing through; thus a lot of energy is devoted to intrastaff conflict, problems, and the distribution of labor. (6) Most staff have a lot of integrity about their work—their value systems are relatively congruent with conventional psychiatric and medical model explanations of madness. (Wilson, 1975)

As Wilson notes, today's psychiatric hospital wards are used mostly for social control — removal of problem behavior from public view and containment of it through force and medication. Therefore, use of the word "treatment" with regard to what goes on in them is basically a mystification. The relative absence of a real psychosocial treatment orientation is in part the result of economic pressures. Patients are allowed to stay in these very expensive locked jail/hotels for only a short time. Time and bureaucratic constraints also make it difficult for the type hospital environment described here to be a therapeutic milieu. In particular, these wards offer little real support, socialization, validation, stimulus control, collaboration, or respite, six of the ten functions necessary for a milieu to be therapeutic (see Chapter 9, p. 121).

HOSPITALS AND ECONOMICS

Medicalization of ordinary human problems is driven by economic considerations. Health insurance will pay for care on psychiatric wards in general hospitals; consequently, that is where disturbed individuals find themselves. What began in the 1840s as humanitarian reform was first perverted into custodial segregation (1870–1960) and then into a dehumanizing, decontextualizing growth industry in the 1970s. In the '60s and '70s wards for adults proliferated; in the '80s it has been places for adolescents. The industry is thriving on its new adolescent fodder. Middle- and upper-middle-class family problems come to roost in the person of the defective individual adolescent. The psychiatric system has joined parents in reframing a difficult, problematic, or embarrassing behavior as "illness." However, the less palatable juvenile justice system is avoided; that system is left to deal with the basically similar problems of less economically powerful poor families.

Unfortunately, no one seems particularly concerned about the consequences of inducting a new group of adolescents into patienthood: (1) creation of a new generation of institutionalized persons who will filter down into the *public mental health system*, and (2) further erosion of the basic fabric of American family life. Psychiatry's message to the American family is clear: "We know how to raise your offspring better than you do. Send them to our just opened adolescent ward (if you're insured or wealthy) and we'll return them 'fixed'." It is more effective and cheaper to intervene with these families in their homes or the clinic. If an adolescent has to be removed, it should be either to a nearby family-like residential setting or to a boarding school in his or her own community. Community programs should establish as the highest priority a policy of non-institutionalization of children and adolescents. They must be protected from the known adverse consequences of hospitalization.

REASONS TO AVOID USE OF HOSPITALS

Reducing our reliance on inpatient hospital care is justified on a number of grounds:

1. *Humanitarian*. Because these institutions treat persons as objects, basic human qualities like individuality, autonomy, independence, and sense of personal responsibility are undermined. Reducing their use will prevent this process of dehumanization.
2. *Moral*. Hospitals are known to cause the iatrogenic disease "institutionalism" (Barton, 1959; Wing & Brown, 1970) or social breakdown syndrome (Gruenberg, Snow, & Bennett, 1969). Not using them will keep the prevalence of these syndromes to a minimum.
3. *Economic*. Because inpatient care consumes 70% of mental health dollars, reducing its use will allow support of badly needed, more effective, and more normalizing community programs.
4. *Scientific*. Nineteen of 20 studies comparing inpatient psychiatric hospitalization with a variety of alternative forms of care found the alternatives as effective, or more so, and less costly (when measured) (Straw, 1982). These studies also found hospitals to be habit-forming; hospital-treated patients tended to recycle through the hospital whereas alternatively treated clients did not.

Despite all the problems with hospital care, for a variety of historical, political, economic, cultural, and professional reasons it has not been possible to disrupt the intimate association of madness and hospitals. The mental health professions, especially their most powerful and prestigious members, psychiatrists, have entered into an agreement with society to help it rid itself of troublesome members. Even Italy's radical reform of a mental health system retained hospital-based treatment as a major (and sometimes, unfortunately, only) component of the new system. Its retention, the result of a political compromise, illustrates the power of the hospital/madness associative link.

INDICATIONS FOR INPATIENT HOSPITAL USE

While we abhor today's overreliance on inpatient care, we acknowledge a continuing need for about 10 hospital beds per 100,000 population (the U.S. has just over 300,000 psychiatric beds, or about 130 per 100,000!). This estimate assumes that an additional 10 beds will be available in residential alternatives to hospitalization. When would these expensive hospital beds be used? Basically, we believe they should be used only when those functions offered *only* in places called hospitals are required by a particular client. These include:

1. Complex, technologically sophisticated, diagnostic processes that require frequent observation by specially trained personnel available only in hospitals (e.g., special infusions, PET, CAT, or MRI scans). In fact, in most instances these can be done on an outpatient basis.
2. Initiation of a treatment process with risks that need to be monitored over a period of time by specially trained personnel (e.g., preplanned drug detoxification, beginning lithium or neuroleptic drugs in persons with complicating medical problems).
3. Medical treatment of a person sufficiently disturbed or suicidal or homicidal so as to render care elsewhere too difficult for the staff, other patients, families, or significant others.
4. Treatment of acute intoxicated states (alcohol, PCP, cocaine).
5. Management of agitated, overactive, acutely psychotic persons who leave open settings and are a serious danger to themselves because of confusion and disorganization.

These five indications for hospitalization represent those in an "ideal" system.

In addition to these few hospital beds, easy access to an emergency room is required as backup for community crisis intervention teams when, for example, they are uncertain of the proper disposition for an individual seen in the community or the clinic. The emergency room can provide experienced consultants, rapid medical diagnostic tests (e.g., for drugs), a longer period in which to evaluate the patient, and time to test whether or not a positive response will occur to removal from the site of the original crisis. To allow this we recommend that there be one or two crisis beds, available for up to 48 hours, in the emergency room. Basically, the emergency room should serve as a second triage point (after initial triage by the community team) for a selected subset of difficult cases.

CHAPTER 5

Is Psychotropic Drug Dependence Really Necessary?

CURRENT COMMUNITY MENTAL HEALTH PRACTICE with regard to psychotropic drugs is an accurate reflection of the wider culture: Quick, even magical, relief is sought from a pill. Nonprescription legal drugs like alcohol are widely used and abused; prescription drugs like Valium are widely used and abused; illegal drugs like marijuana are widely used and abused. Why then do we propose to violate our normalization principle and attempt to curb psychotropic drug use in community programs? Simply put, why, if everyone else is doing drugs, don't we? Five reasons come to mind:

1. Because many psychotropics separate persons from their experience of themselves. This intra-individual decontextualization (fragmentation) may actually make what might have been a temporary disorganization into a permanent split—one that may be immune to the psychosocial change methods we espouse.
2. Because a number of these drugs, especially the neuroleptics, have very serious short- and long-term side effects and toxicities. One of them, tardive dyskinesia, causes cosmetic disfigurement that makes community work more difficult because of the instant stigmatization it engenders.
3. Because the drugs are given in situations in which clients have little real choice about taking them or not. Doctor power is enormous

and not usually a topic for discussion. Taking drugs puts the power to help in someone else's hands. Options and the power to make one's own decisions are vital ingredients to good community programs.

4. Because they are major contributors to today's individual-defect, biologic zeitgeist. This zeitgeist is accompanied by hierarchical relationships and linear causality; both stand in contradistinction to the psychosocially oriented open systems view we believe is important for ongoing community-based work.

5. Because they seem to foster oversimplistic, reductionist thinking, such as the currently fashionable dopamine theory of schizophrenia: Neuroleptics are useful in schizophrenia; neuroleptics affect dopamine metabolism; therefore, schizophrenia is a neuroleptic deficiency disorder. Try this one: Digitalis is useful for heart failure; digitalis affects heart muscle contraction; therefore, heart failure is a digitalis deficiency disorder.

Since only M.D.'s can prescribe drugs, one might think that this should leave non M.D.'s in community programs free to be open-minded and innovative — both important staff characteristics (see Chapter 10). Unfortunately, in our experience this is not usually the case. M.D.'s tend to view themselves as being superior to the non M.D.'s, in part because they control an efficacious treatment. Over time, the non M.D.'s comply with this expectation and implicitly see their work as possible only because of the simultaneous use of psychotropics. Teamness (because the M.D.'s are set apart), innovation, and staff empowerment suffer as a consequence.

What never ceases to amaze us is the degree of collusion that goes on around the use of psychotropics between psychiatrists, non-M.D. staff, most clients, and the wider community. All seem tacitly to have agreed that pills are "the answer" to the problem of disturbed and disturbing behavior. There appears to be a shared need to have this belief be true despite the scientific evidence with regard to the limitations of drug treatment.

For example, if neuroleptics are the answer to the type of disturbed and disturbing behavior labeled "schizophrenia," *why do about half of such persons relapse within two years despite being maintained on neuroleptics* (Davis, 1980)? Why has the long-term prognosis for this group been unaffected by neuroleptics (Bleuler, 1968; Ciompi, 1980; Harding et al., 1987a,b; Huber et al., 1980; Niskanen & Achte, 1972)?

One might imagine that part of psychiatry's current preoccupation with being scientific would be serious attention to the implications of this (and other similar) evidence. Our perception is that data that don't fit current dogma are either completely disregarded or invalidated by ad hominem arguments regarding exclusivity (e.g., only in lower Slobovia is that so) or methodology (e.g., they weren't *really* schizophrenic). Investigators who persist in producing such deviant data are at high risk for marginalization, usually by highlighting a personal peccadillo (e.g., "you know he's a womanizer, don't you?").

THE PSYCHOLOGY OF PRESCRIBING

Over the years we've made several interesting sociopsychological observations about drug-prescribing practices among psychiatrists. We don't pretend that they're universally true; however, they are of some relevance here.

The drug treatment of schizophrenia seems to be subject to the greatest intensity of *dogmatism*. That is, for a variety of difficult (for us) to understand reasons, withholding neuroleptics from persons with this label is extraordinarily difficult. Attempts to do so are greeted with raised eyebrows, quizzical looks, "do you think they might?" or "what if?" questions from non-M.D. staff, and allusions to malpractice from other M.D.'s.

We must wonder if the dogmatism so prevalent with regard to maintaining schizophrenics on neuroleptic drugs really stems from psychiatrists' desire to keep a safe distance from these oftentimes difficult persons. Very short "medication visits" do not lend themselves to the development of the type of trusting, collaborative therapeutic relationships required if neuroleptics are to be used only when symptomatic exacerbations occur.

The party line that schizophrenia is a chronic biologic illness treatable only with medication has the field firmly in its grasp. What is labeled bipolar disorder is also subject to serious dogmatism around the issue of treatment with lithium. However, in our experience this disorder is viewed less negatively than schizophrenia, probably because of the notion that some persons with it may be quite creative. Hence, it is somewhat easier to hold open-minded discussions regarding medication of manic-depressives than of "schizophrenics."

Drug treatment of less disturbed and disturbing persons (i.e., neurotics and some personality disorders) tends to be less doctrinaire. The minor tranquilizers (e.g., benzodiazepines) and the antidepressants are used with them on a trial-and-error basis. There is no serious "party line" about their use, in part because the evidence for their efficacy is less clear. In addition, these lesser psychopathologic states have not achieved "disease" status in the minds of many psychiatrists. Psychiatry has less trouble acknowledging that this group of potential clients can be treated by others than is true for the four most serious categories—schizophrenia, bipolar, and major depressive "disease"—which are seen as the real "property" of psychiatry.

Despite this rhetoric and territorial imperative, most American psychiatrists don't like to deal with persons labeled schizophrenic—a point made previously by us and by Torrey (1983). They're difficult, time-consuming, unresponsive, and unlikely to pay their bills. In fact, in the U.S., they are often without any means of paying for care. As a consequence, they are the largest single diagnostic group in the public mental health system. Bipolars and depressives are more attractive. They get better relatively rapidly, usually speak no language of social protest, have families who care about them, pay their bills, and can be pillars of society.

PRESCRIBING PRINCIPLES

Although we are concerned about the overuse and misuse of psychopharmacologic agents, they are, unfortunately, a fact of current community mental health practice. The degree of shared fantasy (in keeping with the dogmatism) around their efficacy makes it unlikely that the situation will soon change. Drugs are just too easy to use and too consistent with prevailing cultural norms to be given up easily. Nonetheless, we want to present principles that intelligent mental health workers and clients can use to make informed judgments about the psychopharmacologic practices of the group within which they are embedded. That non M.D.'s cannot write prescriptions is no excuse for their not being well informed, thoughtful, and critical of what is being done to their clients.

Furthermore, it is our hope that better informed clinicians will be drawn to conclusions similar to ours—that madness is all too understandable, and that it can be effectively treated by psychosocial methods, especially when the situation has not already been muddied by a course of psychotropic drug treatment. It must be pointed out in this context that the successful psychosocial treatment of very disturbed and disturbing behavior requires either a very supportive natural social network augmented by mental health staff or a properly organized, intensely supportive, residential therapeutic community designed specifically for this purpose.

Our principles are described below.

1. "A Well-Educated Consumer Is Our Best Customer"

Clients/users/customers/patients must have *knowledge about the chemicals they're being asked to ingest* (as well as about other treatments). One *cannot* rely on M.D.'s to provide this information in a way that will be heard and taken in by the disturbed person. Community mental health workers should know about the therapeutic and side effects of various *classes* of drugs.

A discussion of psychotropic agents does not have to be, and will usually not be, initiated by a doctor. Hence, workers at all levels should be familiar with what the five classes of psychotropic drugs do, and be able to outline phenomenologically what the experiences their clients are likely to have as a result of taking them. Appendix A (Medications for Mental Illness) should be studied and well learned by community mental health workers and users. The portions of it relevant to a particular patient's drug treatment regime should be given to him and discussed until clearly understood. These discussions should focus on what is to be expected, how the effects can be understood, and what other options there might be.

2. Power to the People

A crucial ingredient of responsible community care, one that distinguishes it sharply from more dependency-inducing care that occurs in hospitals, is that it *maintains individuals' power to be in control of their lives*. Preservation of personal power, or reempowering if it has been eroded by a treatment system, is a sine qua non of successful community treatment. Psychotropic drugs must be dealt with in this context. How do you maintain a patient's power while giving him an agent that exerts powerful effects on his physiology, his self-perceptions, and his sense of who and what he is? We have found that the following paradigm, if well presented, and carried out honestly, will preserve most patients' power over their own bodies and make them partners in the treatment process. The example is drawn from giving a person labeled schizophrenic a major neuroleptic (e.g., haloperidol, chlorpromazine):

I would like you to take a medicine that many persons with your type of problem(s) have found helpful in dealing with them. There is, of course, no guarantee that it will work. That's why it's so important that you regard your taking it as an *experiment* on yourself. By that I mean I'd like you to look at how you feel in terms of your emotional state, your sense of self, your perceptions of your body, your level of energy and overall comfort *before* you start the medicine. Then, beginning with the first pill, I'd like you to record, in writing, on at least a daily basis, changes in how you feel along all those parameters. I'll see you in one week and I want you to bring your diary into me. Based on that, and our discussion of how you feel at that time, we'll adjust the amount of drug you're taking. Between now and then, I'd like you to take the drug in the amount I've prescribed. If you begin to feel faint, weak and sweaty, stop the drug and call me. If you feel as if you must always keep moving, stop the drug and call me. If you feel spasms in your muscles, especially around the neck and shoulders, call me.

We will sit down again in two weeks to assess what, if anything, the drug has done for you by that point in time. I will discuss your diary with you from my professional point of view and will ask you to tell me about your experience of the drug. I will also seek the opinions of those with whom you live about its effects on you. If the overall experience is positive, I will adjust the dosage and encourage you to continue the drug for a period of time. If the composite overall picture is negative, we'll stop and *may* try another. I cannot predict now. Remember, however, that it is your body that this drug is affecting. Pay close attention. I cannot force you to take the drug. But it should be given a fair trial. Only you can do that. We must work as a team. In the end the decision will be yours. I would like it to be a responsible one based on your experience with this drug.

Although the description of possible effects will vary with the drug, the basic "experiment on yourself" paradigm is the same for all drugs. In these discussions it is useful to find a drug the patient has previously taken — alcohol being the most common — and use it as a teaching example. This drug-taking process, because it involves very powerful and potentially toxic substances, must be addressed seriously; most critical is that the clinician take seriously the client's experience and questions. *Compliance is usually a relationship issue.* Properly handled, drug-taking should not be a serious problem between clinician and patient. If it becomes so, the clinician should look at what he is doing that has undermined the focus of a common goal: helping the client get his life back on track.

3. Have Available Psychosocial Intervention Alternatives

Without other options drug treatment is almost inevitable. In particular, because long-term maintenance on the major neuroleptics is not usually warranted by the risk/benefit ratio, a variety of strategies and services need to be developed to serve in the place of neuroleptics. This is true of the other psychotropics as well, even though their long-term toxicities do not appear to be as severe as those of the major neuroleptics.

USE OF THE MAJOR NEUROLEPTICS

Our views on this subject are at variance with the predominant ethos in community mental health today, in which psychopharmacologic agents, especially neuroleptics for schizophrenia, are seen as *necessary* to the practice of community mental health. Their known and mythical effects are listed in Tables 5.1 and 5.2. Because tardive dyskinesia is an extraordinarily difficult and destructive iatrogenic disorder, *if* a proper social environment can be provided, every *newly* identified psychotic deserves several opportunities to recover without the use of neuroleptics. The evidence is reasonably clear that the vast majority of *newly* diagnosed psychotics *can recover without neuroleptics* (Bleuler, 1968; Huber et al., 1980; Mosher & Menn, 1978). The challenge is to organize and present an appropriate intentional

TABLE 5.1
Neuroleptic Drugs: Known Effects

1. Reduce "positive" symptoms
2. Shorten hospital stays
3. Reduce readmission rates
4. Produce tardive dyskinesia
5. Revitalized interest in schizophrenia
6. Produced large corporate profits

social environment. This type of environment, as well as its planning, organization, and implementation, is described in Chapter 9, p. 118ff). If, because an adequate therapeutic community is not available, clinicians are forced to use neuroleptics with newly identified clients, they should be used in as low a dose as possible for as short a time as possible. This may also be done with clients who have not responded to a fair trial of psychosocial treatment. This is actually a paradigm for the use of psychotropics in general: *first a trial of psychosocial treatment,* then *a drug trial.*

We do not believe in routine maintenance neuroleptic drug treatment for persons labeled schizophrenic. Basically, our argument against maintenance neuroleptic drugs runs as follows: Two-year relapse rates in random assignment double-blind studies of orally administered major neuroleptics run about 70–80% for placebo-treated patients and 40–50% for neuroleptic-maintained patients (Davis, 1980). In addition, the *annual* incidence of tardive dyskinesia in neuroleptic-maintained patients is about 5%. That is, by five years, about 25% of a neuroleptic-maintained cohort of newly treated patients will exhibit tardive dyskinesia (Kane et al., 1984). Based on these data, the risk/benefit ratio would seem *not* to favor long-term maintenance.

These 40–50% two-year relapse rates among drug-maintained patients

TABLE 5.2
Neuroleptic Drugs: Mythical Effects

1. Cleared out psychiatric hospitals
2. Changed the long-term social recovery rates of schizophrenia
3. Enhance learning of coping skills
4. Address schizophrenia's specific etiology
5. Can reduce readmissions to nearly zero if drug compliance is assured

have been attributed by many to noncompliance with medication. Certainly this is a reasonable position. The test of the noncompliance theory of relapse is the comparison of patients randomly assigned injectable neuroleptic or oral medication. If medication compliance is the critical variable, injectably treated patients should have substantially lower relapse rates than the orally treated ones. Four large-scale collaborative studies of this question have been carried out, the two most elegantly designed being Hogarty, Schooler, Ulrich, Mussare, Ferro, and Herron (1979) and Rifkin, Quitkin, Rabiner, and Klein (1977). The results of all four are extraordinarily similar. Relapse rates among orally maintained patients are no different from those of patients maintained on injectable neuroleptics, where compliance was assured. In addition, injectable neuroleptics had more unpleasant side effects than oral medication. What are the clinical implications of these studies?

1. For the 40–50% of patients already in the system who relapse *despite* maintenance neuroleptics, it is irresponsible to progressively increase their risk for tardive dyskinesia by progressively increasing the medication or by persisting in a search for another and another medication. They obviously need attention to their social environments so that stress can be reduced or avoided, thereby reducing the risk of relapse. For example, it has now been amply documented that offspring living in families with high levels of hostility, criticism, and overinvolvement relapse far more frequently than those living in families low on these characteristics (Leff & Vaughn, 1980, 1987; Vaughn, Snyder, Jones, Freeman, & Falloon, 1984). A client living in such an environment could be encouraged and helped to move out, or a known effective family intervention (Falloon, Boyd, McGill, Razani, Moss, & Gilderman, 1982; Hogarty, Anderson, Reiss, Kornblith, Greenwald, Javna, & Madonia, 1986; Leff, Kuipers, Berkowitz, Vries, & Sturgeon, 1982) could be initiated to help reduce these stress-inducing characteristics, or he/she could be provided with an activity that reduces face-to-face contact with the family to a minimum. *Thoughtful attention to the social environments of all clients, however labeled, should provide mental health workers with clues for the development of individualized psychosocial intervention strategies that will allow drug treatment to be avoided altogether, or at least kept to a minimum.*

2. Patients who are not on maintenance medication but are at risk for relapse should be involved in therapeutic relationships in which their particular patterns of evolution of madness can be described and discussed. If the relationship is in order, clients will be able to tell their therapists if, and why, they're about to go crazy. At that point options can be discussed, only one of which should be institution of neuroleptic drug treatment.

When drug treatment is the only viable option, a "targeted" drug strategy (i.e., treatment of symptom exacerbations only) should be chosen. This results in negligibly higher rates of relapse than long-term maintenance with neuroleptics (Carpenter, Heinrichs & Hanlon, 1987; Carpenter, Hanlon, Heinrichs, Summerfelt, Kirkpatrick, Levine, & Buchanan, 1990). Even more importantly, it appears that persons who have not been maintained on neuroleptics respond more quickly (than do maintained patients) when drugs are reintroduced; i.e., they spend less time in the hospital if they have to be rehospitalized (Carpenter et al., 1990). Carpenter has also recently shown that this "targeted" drug treatment strategy substantially reduces the risk of developing tardive dyskinesia, even though his "targeted" patients were on drugs roughly 50% of the time. *The targeted drug strategy is also supported by the clinical and research observation that madness waxes and wanes. Common sense tells us that treating people with very powerful drugs during intervals of "wellness" is unwise.*

3. If psychosocial programs are not available and clients are frequently rehospitalized despite the targeted drug approach, maintenance on as low a dose of neuroleptic as possible can be tried. Several investigators (Kane, 1983, 1984, 1987; and Marder, Van Putten, Mintz, Lebell, McKenzie, & May, 1987) have shown that this strategy is nearly as effective in preventing relapse as usual doses, has far fewer side effects, and is much better tolerated by patients.

We have found it very difficult to wean even relatively stable community-based patients completely off neuroleptics if they have been on them continuously for several years. We're not sure whether it's because their dopamine receptors are starving or because of a real addiction-like withdrawal syndrome, but ten days to two weeks after stopping most patients have what *looks like* the beginning of an exacerbation of psychosis (Chouinard, Bradwejn, Jones & Ross-Chouinard, 1984; Gardos, Cole & Torey, 1978; Luchons, Freed & Wyatt, 1980). To avoid the consequences of a serious crisis to the person from his community-based social field, we've pretty much given up trying to get clients *completely* off neuroleptics. Instead, we try to get them down to the vicinity of 25 mg. Thorazine equivalent a day. That usually keeps dopamine receptors happy enough (i.e., the levels of insomnia, anxiety, and restlessness experienced are tolerable) if it's the end point of a prolonged weaning process and levels of social stress are kept modest.

USE OF LITHIUM AND THE ANTIDEPRESSANTS

Recent data (Prien, Kupfer, Mansky, Small, Tuason, Voss, & Johnson, 1984) indicate that, despite combined lithium and imipramine maintenance, 62% of bipolar patients relapsed and were regarded as treatment failures during a 16-week minimum maintenance period. Furthermore, only 25%

were considered "treatment successes." Unipolar patients, receiving the same drug regimen, had a 51% failure and a 36% maintenance success rate. In addition, a recent meta-analysis of 22 studies in which two antidepressants were compared with placebo, hence enhancing the possibility of true "blindness" to drug condition, found medications little better than placebo. Using only patient rated outcome there was no advantage over placebo for either newer (e.g., fluoxetine) or standard antidepressants (e.g., imipramine) (Greenberg, Bernstein, Greenberg, & Fisher, 1992). This, taken in conjunction with lithium's known renal toxicity and the lethality of the tricyclics when used for self-destructive purposes, may indicate a need to reevaluate the practice of routine lithium maintenance in bipolar patients and the less common practice of routine tricyclic antidepressant maintenance in unipolar depressed patients. Illustrative of the divergence in points of view about the usefulness of antidepressants, their long-term use is now being advocated by some for relapse prevention (Kupfer, Frank, Perel, Cornes, Mallinger, Thase, McEachran, Grochocinski, 1992). However, because of their lesser toxicity (as compared with neuroleptics), we will not take a strong position against such use of lithium and antidepressants. Whether the new generation of less potentially lethal antidepressants, principally the serotonin reuptake inhibitors like fluoxetine (Prozac), will affect practice and recovery rates remains to be seen. However, use of any of these chemicals can create the kinds of problems enunciated on pages 38 and 39.

CONCLUSIONS

Drugs and psychosocial interventions, when properly construed, need not be either/or interventions. Drugs will be more effective when given in a positive context rather than an antagonistic one. However, in many situations psychosocial interventions can be as effective as, or more effective than, drug interventions, *if properly organized*. See, for example, the recent studies of the cognitive-behavioral and interpersonal treatment of depression (Beck, Rush, Shaw & Emery, 1979; Klerman, Weissman, Rounsaville & Chevron, 1984; Murphy, Simons, Wetzel, & Lustman, 1984). The problem is that pills are easy to give, while psychosocial interventions dealing with particular types of problems are much more complicated, expensive to arrange, and difficult to sustain; However, if the patient were one of us, a relative, or close friend, a psychosocial intervention would be preferable, given the known toxicities of the chemicals.

Community mental health is psychosocial. The position we espouse is a psychosocial one. Psychotropic drugs are probably here to stay, so they must be contextualized in the overall approach. They should not be oversold and overrelied upon as they are so often today. Nonphysicians tend to accept their use far too uncritically because of the authority of M.D.eities. To place them in proper context, non-M.D. community mental health workers must know both their value and limitations. They must know how to ask questions that call the prescribing practices of M.D.'s into question.

Community mental health workers must be very concerned about how much more difficult their work is when their clients have tardive dyskinesia or are experiencing the akinesic (demotivating) effects of neuroleptics. Community work must pay very careful attention to everything that makes the work easier or more difficult — drugs, families, stigma, etc. Leaving the drugs to the exclusive purview of M.D.'s is a common failing; on the other hand, physicians tend to overfocus on the drugs, leaving the psychosocial components to everyone else. The clients are the ones who suffer from this fragmentation in points of view.

Psychosocial Intervention

CHAPTER 6

Interviewing: Making All the Right Moves

IT IS NOT POSSIBLE TO DO EFFECTIVE community mental health without being able to establish and maintain a positive relationship between mental health worker and user. This chapter provides guidelines as to how this is best done and hence serves as the foundation for what follows. It should be read, reread and put into practice until it becomes instinctive.

INTERVIEWING

Every major mental health textbook contains a pro forma chapter on interviewing. There are entire books on the subject. With rare exception they emphasize history-taking, assessment of psychopathology, and the mental status exam, with the goal of enabling the student to make an accurate *DSM-III-R* diagnosis. In turn, this will purportedly allow an accurate treatment prescription (usually medication).

By way of contrast, the approach described here has as its principal emphasis the *relationship* between worker and user. We view making initial contact, building rapport, and establishing a collaborative working relationship as central to the work. In addition, we believe that our problem-focused, relationally oriented, contextualizing approach to the story the user brings, preserves, and enhances client self-control and power. Thus, the critical *therapeutic* process of remoralization is begun immediately.

We abhor today's trend to compartmentalize, and hence decontextualize, certain parts of assessment interviews. For example, one of us recently interviewed a 46-year-old chronically depressed, suicidal, unkempt, overweight man who had been confined to a wheelchair for several years since an auto accident. The interview focused on what kinds of things made him more or less suicidal, what, if anything, he had to live for, and events related to his most recent serious suicide attempt. It was only after the exploration of a number of areas in his life that we were able to agree upon something that presented a ray of hope for this otherwise hopeless, demoralized man. We agreed that he was lonesome for female company. He had let his personal appearance deteriorate because he didn't think he could ever again find a woman who would care for him (his last suicide attempt came after his then woman friend had left him). The discussion then focused on courting behavior, using his courtship of his ex-wife as an example. The interview concluded by our defining a number of specific things (e.g., lose weight, shave) he needed to accomplish before embarking on a new courtship. He looked revitalized. In the post-interview discussion, his worker remarked that she was afraid the interview would include a "real" suicide assessment! She obviously had been taught a format for such a decontextualized assessment. The interview, focused on suicide *in the context of events* in this man's life, didn't fit her format, hence didn't qualify as a "real" suicide assessment. For us there can be *no* valid assessment independent of context.

It is our position that mental health workers from several disciplines can be effective psychosocial change agents with very disturbed and disturbing clients. In our experience, the ability to implement a psychosocial intervention depends on a shared understanding of the client's current situation, of the life experiences involved in its development, and of the resources available for dealing with the problem, as defined by the client. The evaluative process should lead client and therapist to a shared, organized understanding of the client's world, which in turn will allow both players to act on a known and meaningful scenario. This sense of feeling understood is remarkably relationship-enhancing. Although the type, duration, and site of the intervention will vary, the evaluation process can be the similar across clients. Ideally, the evaluation will allow the development of a relatively specific plan in close collaboration with the client. *No actions should be taken until both parties understand* what is going on *in the particular situation.*

We are much more certain about the common nonspecific aspects of psychosocial treatments than we are about the applicability of specific types of treatments to particular patients. Although the type of interview we espouse is designed to result in maximizing the usefulness of these nonspecific factors, the techniques we describe to facilitate this process are quite specific in aim, content, and desired effect.

MAKING INITIAL CONTACT

One of the defining characteristics of persons coming for psychiatric help is difficulty establishing and maintaining interpersonal relationships. The extent of the difficulty and the reasons for this vary widely. However, very few persons labeled "chronically psychotic" will have an easy time beginning or sustaining a meaningful relationship—with a therapist or anyone else. Remember though—*everyone deserves a fresh look and another chance.* Thus, in approaching the assessment of a new client, the first and most critical task is to establish at least a thread of rapport. This can be achieved in a variety of ways. However, care must be exercised by interviewers so that their expectations are not unrealistic; otherwise they are likely to be disappointed. Approaching clients with a "what can I get out of them" attitude is likely to generate an unwinnable tug of war. Do not come on as a rescuer. Very often clients would rather "drown" than allow themselves to be rescued, with all the obligations (real or fantasied) engendered by the rescue process. Remember, the likelihood of your being the first person to try and save these clients is remote. They know, all too well, that disappointed rescuers usually give up when they find the rescuee is "uncooperative" or "unmotivated."

What are the elements in the interview that should be attended to? First, in order to be most effective you need to be as comfortable as possible. This means, for example, that you should do your evaluations in a setting in which you feel comfortable. Comfortable chairs, proper temperature, and uninterrupted quiet are essential. These *ecological variables* not only contribute to comfort but they also facilitate the rapport-establishing process by minimizing distractors and enabling the interviewer and the client to focus solely on the task at hand. Public settings tend not to take such ecological variables seriously. We do. You should be assertive with supervisors and colleagues about the need to be properly equipped.

What we describe here is what goes on when an evaluation takes place in your office; this is the setting where beginning interviewers feel most comfortable. With training and experience the contexts within which you feel comfortable should expand so that you feel comfortable working in other people's territories. Remember, the context in which an interview takes place affects both the content and evaluative process (Mosher, 1978). Metaphorically, your office is the zoo and the client's living place is the jungle; behavior may vary considerably across these contexts. We recommend in-home interviews when the client's living group plays a role in the problem and when the clinician wants to experience the situation first hand. There are, of course, realistic constraints on the frequency with which in home interviewing can be done. However, "it's too time-consuming" is an insufficient excuse if the real issue is lack of interviewer comfort with out-of-office contexts (see Burti & Mosher, 1986, for an example of the helpfulness of non-office-based interventions).

Setting the Context

It is important that you attempt to put yourself in your clients' shoes from the very beginning of your contact, i.e., the introduction (see Table 6.1). So, remember that they are bound to be nervous, unsure of what to expect, and hesitant—especially when seen in your office. Their interpersonal anxiety is often based on fear of rejection on the one hand and fear of being overwhelmed on the other. The interviewer must steer a course between these extremes; paying absolute attention to what clients say and do without being intrusive is a good guideline to follow. One way you can put yourself into the client's frame of mind is by thinking about times in your life when you've gone to a party in someone's home where you've never met the host or hostess and must introduce yourself. For us, this social context is analogous to the experience of the new client in an evaluator's office. So, like a good host or hostess, you should go out of your way to make the new guest comfortable. In psychologic terms this process can be called "active empathy." A warm hello, a firm, inviting-in handshake and a few words of small talk go a long way toward putting a new client at ease.

It is good practice to introduce yourself with your full name and ask the client for his. Call the client Mr., Mrs., or Ms. Jones and then ask him *how he would like to be addressed* in the interview—formally (Mr. Jones), by his first name, e.g., Richard, or by a contraction or nickname, e.g., "Dick" or "Rich." Too often a busy mental health worker will skip this process, introduce himself as "Dr. So and So" and addressing the client by his first name or nickname without first clearly showing respect by addressing him formally. Asking clients how they would like to be called, in addition to conveying respect, gives them some power and control in a still relatively undefined setting. There are sufficient power and status differences built into the situation without your contributing to them with the condescension implied when you don't feel obliged to follow usual social conventions. Clients are often very sensitive to this demeaning behavior on the part of mental health workers; in fact, a "veteran" (long-term system user) may be quite taken aback by being treated as a person entitled to the usual social amenities. It is also useful to answer clients' initial questions about the interviewer in a direct, honest, straightforward manner. It is important to remember that insofar as possible you want to treat clients as potential partners and attempt to recruit them into a collaborative relationship. Attention to these interpersonal nuances will facilitate this process.

For office-based evaluations we recommend directing the client to a particular chair as a means of providing anxiety-relieving structure. When on their territory clients should be allowed to determine the seating arrangement. If possible, use two similar comfortable swivel armchairs placed at a 90° angle. This allows both client and evaluator to change distance and degree of openness by turning the chairs from side to side and sitting forward or back (Figure 6.1). Similarity of the chairs is another way to avoid reinforcing power and status differences. All too often the evaluator has a large, soft, comfortable chair while the evaluatee is seated in a straightback or metal fold-up chair. This makes it very clear who is in charge in that context.

Assessing the Initial Relationship

Early in an initial interview distance will be defined mainly by the *physical* distance the client maintains. Psychological distance will be defined after initial rapport has been established.

Early distance assessment begins with clients' response to the initial handshake. Try not to vary your handshake. It should be firm and used to lead clients into the room. If their response is soft and their hand withdrawn quickly, you have an immediate clue that, at least in the beginning, they want to keep their distance. You may expect them to be rather passive. Initial eye contact is another good guide. Look new clients directly in the eye while you shake hands. If they respond by maintaining eye contact or looking you over, you'll know they are willing to engage you, at least

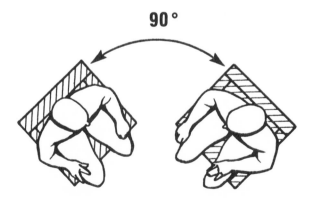

FIGURE 6.1
Interviewing: Optimal Seating Arrangement

initially. If the eyes do one thing and the hand another, you can presume that they're not really sure of how they're going to deal with you.

The few steps necessary between the handshake and the chair provide a good opportunity to get some sense of clients' physical presentation to the world. Do they carry themselves with head up and shoulders back and walk goal-directedly to the chair indicated, or do they move hesitantly, looking at the floor? Is the movement of their arms and legs free or do their joints seem to be filled with molasses? These physical movements are excellent indicators of such things as degree of situational intimidation, overall self-confidence, motor coordination, medication status, and passivity. Medication-influenced motor behavior is particularly relevant to an assessment of clients' ability to blend in with the rest of the people in the community. A grimacing, stoop-shouldered person with a shuffling gait typically evokes in others, including the interviewer, a response of "unusual," "odd," "peculiar," or "bizarre." Persons thus labeled are often avoided, if not actively rejected. Interviewers should be able to recognize and empathize with the client's position and not react as the client may have come to expect.

How persons seat themselves can also offer valuable clues to the amount of initial distance they require to be comfortable. Clients may sit as far away as possible in the chair or actually move it away. Others sit rigidly erect, equidistant from all sides. Others lean forward on the chair arms.

In addition to the physical (and by implication interpersonal) distance clients seek, it is very important to evaluate their initial degree of openness from their body language. Clients who sit far away, turned away, with their legs and arms tightly crossed, are giving a clear closed distant message. There are all kinds of variations on the open-closed, close-distant continua that should be assessed early on in the interview. These body movement variables provide an excellent nonverbal assessment of rapport parameters. Someone with whom you've been successful in establishing a relationship can go, in the course of an interview, from looking like a wilted plant to being firm, upright, and open. If they leave as wilted as when they came in, you've probably not been successful in establishing positive rapport. There are, of course, a number of clients with whom many contacts may occur before a relationship can be established.

In the beginning, it is important to respect clients' need for distance so as to avoid their feeling intruded upon and overwhelmed. For example, we recommend that with standoffish clients you push your chair back, lean back, and stare at the ceiling while beginning the interview with neutral, innocuous small talk about the weather or some similar topic. As the interview proceeds you can move in progressively with your chair, lean forward, and attempt to increase the amount of eye-to-eye contact as a test of the limits of their ability to tolerate closeness. When you get too close they will begin to withdraw. After a relationship has been established, their need to distance themselves can be commented on and the reasons for it questioned.

The "Joiner"

Joining is a technique whereby interviewers attempt to meet clients where they are, to share something about their world that is common to both. As part of interviewers' efforts to put themselves into clients' shoes, it is a good way to show active empathy.

Generally speaking, an informal, casual but respectful, open, interested, nonjudgmental, and *totally* attentive attitude is best. Informality will help undercut clients' attributions of extraordinary status and power to the interviewer. Attentiveness will both facilitate rapport-building and, in many instances, surprise clients. They may have gotten used to the all-too-common perfunctory "helper knows best" approach. Openness will allow you to meet clients empathetically, with a "fresh" eye.

Despite your very best efforts to begin a relationship, the client may still be wary of involvement. This can be a product of previous disappointment with "helpers," a lifelong need to maintain distance, or both. When you sense wariness (via the body movement patterns described above and a paucity of verbal response), it may be useful to begin the interview (while leaning back, staring at the ceiling) with a question focused on the client's geographical origins or recreational interests. These kinds of questions are usually nonthreatening and provide the interviewer access to an experience of the client's that he may, in at least an indirect way, share. In our experience even the most wary, almost mute clients will respond to a properly chosen joiner (although not always the first one).

> For example, one of us (LRM) opened an interview with a withdrawn, depressed 24-year-old woman with an obvious Texas accent by asking where she'd grown up (Houston) and then about the changes she'd seen there. She spoke of the high activity, boom-town, disorganized quality of the city and the interviewer replied that he'd experienced the same thing (with attendant discomfort) when he visited there some months earlier.

> In another interview a muscular, acutely psychotic 21-year-old man was asked if he like sports. He said he'd played football in high school and still followed the game. The interviewer acknowledged that he liked and followed football and then went on to discuss the ups and downs of the local professional team.

These seemingly mundane exchanges often prove to be remarkably facilitative to the rapport-establishing process. They involve limited self-
disclosure by focusing on an experience the interviewer can acknowledge as
having shared with the client. "Joiners" also serve to minimize status and
power differences inherent to the context. Finally, "joiners" tend to coun-
teract initial distortions and projections on the client's part by shifting
the focus of attention to a shared, here-and-now, less threatening reality.
Although these exchanges can be extraordinarily helpful, they should only
be used when necessary and should not be used to provide the interviewer
with a self-disclosure lecture format!

Another type of "joiner" found to be helpful in developing and maintaining rapport in an early interview is the use of the interviewees *exact* phrase-
ology when clarification or additional information is sought.

> During a discussion of a 24-year-old male client's views on death and
> afterlife he said, "There's no way to know when your card will be pulled . . .
> it could be today or 50 years from now." The interviewer, following his lead,
> inquired, "When you let your imagination run free, when do you *think* your
> card will be pulled?"

Persistent attention to using the client's own language provides ongoing
"joiners," keeps you on the client's level of expression and provides the
client with an immediate, real experience of having been listened to carefully, and perhaps cared about. Clients surveyed at the end of successful
psychotherapeutic relationships frequently report that what was most important to them was someone who *really* listened (i.e., understood their
experience).

Minimizing Distortions and False Attributions

No matter how able you are to approach users with an open mind and a
"fresh eye" (the phenomenological attitude), it is not likely that you will be
accorded similar treatment by clients. They will come to your interview
with varying amounts of baggage (i.e., unrealistic expectations, projections, false attributions, transference, misconceptions, preconceptions,
etc.). One important aspect of the evaluation process is understanding the
baggage but not letting it get in the way. To do this you must realize that
clients will, to varying degrees, distort how you believe you are presenting
yourself.

The type and amount of distortion will be a product of what both interviewer and client bring to the situation. Sullivan was especially eloquent
when he described therapists' need to understand what they bring to the
interview.

The psychiatrist must be alert to learn, insofar as possible, the immediate impression of him which is created in a stranger. It is useful for the therapist to review these details with great care at the start of his career, gradually catching on to what phenomena have made what impression on him; correspondingly, by observing the larger context of what the other person has done after the formal beginning of the interview, he can begin to develop dependable impressions of how he himself must have affected that person. . . . Throughout the inception of the interview, the psychiatrist certainly, and any interviewer in some measure, should "know how he acts"—that is, he should have learned from experience the *usual* impression obtained of him in the particular circumstances of encountering the sort of stranger that the interviewee at first glance *seems* to be. In other words, the psychiatrist should have some idea of how he affects the stranger and how he facilitates or retards certain things that the stranger may have thought of doing. (Sullivan, 1970, p. 67)

It is sometimes helpful in attempting to understand one's self-presentation for a relatively inexperienced interviewer to review, for herself, how she "comes across" to strangers of various types in social situations. In general, we recommend review of self-presentation to younger and older males and females, to persons perceived to be authorities (by virtue of age, intellect, or power), to persons of very different cultural backgrounds, and to persons with some obvious handicap (e.g., blind, amputee). For inexperienced interviewers a review of their self-presentation can be accomplished with other trainees and supervisors, perhaps utilizing role-playing to enhance the reality of the situation. This process is a very important element in the evolving context of the interview. How it is dealt with will affect the nature of the relationship that is (or is not) established.

How can you deal with in-interview distortions effectively? First, we recommend that interviewers solicit clients' understanding of the reasons for and expectations of the interview. After affording clients enough time to explicate and clarify their understanding of it, interviewers should honestly and straightforwardly explain their own understanding of the reason(s) for the interview, about how long it will take and what the patient might reasonably expect from it. "I've been asked to see you with regard to the problems that resulted in your seeking (or being brought for) help. We'll spend 45 or so minutes discussing them, with the hope that we can evolve a plan together that may begin to address and solve some of them."

Although it is important not to fuel unrealistic expectations on the client's part, the interviewer should also not approach the interview with unduly low expectations, as these will only contribute to the demoralized state of the client. Under these circumstances, a dose of optimism tempered with reality can be extremely useful. For example, it may be helpful to say something like the following: "I don't know enough about you yet to say for sure that I can help you, but I will try and I believe that together we may be able to improve your situation. I wouldn't be here if I didn't believe that, even if you don't." For the demoralized veteran of the system, this sort of faith and optimism can be sustaining and mobilizing. It also establishes a precedent of honesty and openness that is likely to be experienced as reassuring and refreshing.

Above all, it is important to acknowledge the client's experiential basis for misattributions to the interviewer. This is another example of a crucial aspect of dealing with psychotic clients—*validating their experience*. A common problem with inexperienced interviewers dealing with psychotic clients is that they try to *convince* clients they are trustworthy. Clients' mistrust is based on experience. Hence, to try to convince them otherwise is to invalidate their experience. It's better to acknowledge their experience and advise them not to trust you until they know you well enough to warrant it. At this point it is often useful to inquire about clients' previous experiences with therapists.

> A 25-year-old college graduate living at home with his parents after a year's hospitalization for schizophrenia was moved from the midwest to the east coast (at his parents', especially his father's, behest) to the city where his brother lived. During the initial interview, a major focus was what the client was going to do to get money. Each time the therapist mentioned going to work, the client would produce a litany of reasons why he couldn't. The therapist presumed, especially after having talked on the phone with the workaholic businessman father, that this was an attribution to him of the father's tremendous pressure on the client to "stop being so goddam lazy and go out and get a job." The therapist acknowledged the client's experience of his father's pressure about work and how that could certainly make him angry enough to resist. In fact, he hypothesized, the harder the father pushed, the stronger the resistance. The therapist also acknowledged that, since he'd been hired by the father, the client had *good reason* to believe the therapist would do the father's bidding, i.e., demand the client-son go to work immediately, if not sooner. At this point, the therapist returned to a previously agreed-upon goal—the client wanted to have his own source of support. The interviewer stated that how, when, and what the client did to get money was his responsibility, but that work was certainly the most common way in this culture. With that, the client began to focus on the types of jobs for which he might be qualified that might be available.

A second useful technique for dealing with in-interview projections is to shift the focus of discourse.

> For example, a young woman who had made a suicide attempt by slitting her wrists came to the interview preoccupied with whether or not the therapist could ever see her as anything but a woman with an ugly scar on her wrist. Acknowledging her experience of her family's and friends' rejection-laden

responses to her scar didn't defuse her preoccupation. She wanted to know the therapist's position. Did she "have any redeeming social value with a scarred wrist?" The therapist chose to use the client's metaphor — redeeming social value — and focus on it in its more usual context, that is, in the judgment of obscenity and pornography. This shifted the focus from an individual accept/reject response by the therapist to one of community acceptance of something it fears, but also "gets off on" by looking at. In discussing the application of this metaphor to her situation, the therapist placed himself in the position of an ordinary community member of his age and status and responded that, in fact, he was sorry but he probably wouldn't even notice the scar. Her plea for acceptance/approval, reassurance, and need to be special to the therapist was first shifted to the metaphor, then diffused and normalized within the reality context of community.

It is our intention to focus the interviewer's attention on the inevitable distortions that will occur in the interpersonal field with clients. As with so many other aspects of clienthood, the longer they've been in the system, the more hospitalizations they've experienced, and the larger the number of would-be rescuers they've seen, the more extensive and firmly held will be the projections. This is part of what causes so-called "chronic" patients to be viewed as very difficult and hence to be avoided if at all possible.

Avoiding Stereotypes

A preliminary, important aspect of a first interview is identifying the real "customer" of the intervention. In fact, in contrast to private office practice, where most patients go on their own, in public psychiatry, the patient often is brought to the attention of an agency by others or has been pushed by others: The patient is not the customer of the intervention.

This split in roles may be clear, as in the case of involuntary commitments. Often it is blurred or hidden and has to be actively looked for. It sometimes happens that a patient pretends to be cooperative but keeps being vague, generic, evasive, subtly "resistant." Usually this is because he only reluctantly agreed to see a mental health professional as a result of pressure from a spouse, a parent, or family doctor. In these cases the context is *not* therapeutic because there is no engagement. *Pretending to do therapy is nonsense.* It is advisable, instead, to conduct the interview in a way that brings to the surface how the patient has come to the attention of a provider, to show sincere understanding of his resistances and deal overtly with them, and to explain that therapy by force does not exist. However, we are available to treat him if he is willing. Sometimes, if motivation, however minimal, exists, it is possible to engage him. Also, paradoxically refusing to treat him may be the only therapeutic intervention possible.

In the case of involuntary commitments, it is hoped that every effort was already made to obtain the patient's consent. However, when a person has been committed involuntarily, it is still useful and necessary to explain to the patient the course of events that brought the therapist or some colleague, unwilling and compelled by the circumstances, to commit him. One explains that part of one's role as a responsible mental health professional is to do commitments and points out which behaviors of his were the most disturbing. A honest and realistic attitude may uncover in the patient an unpredicted awareness of the social disturbance he provoked and open the possibility for his cooperation in the treatment.

There may also be multiple layers of "customers," in which case one has to be concerned about who the ultimate purchaser of the intervention is; he will be considered to be "the" customer. A good way to recognize the real customer is to ask oneself: Who is most interested in the intervention? The inquiry about the customer may be complicated further if an institution is involved, for example, when a worker of another agency refers a case.

In the South-Verona (Italy) Psychiatric Register there is space to record who is the "customer" of each intervention. Alternatives provided are the following:

1. Patient
2. Relatives
3. Neighbor
4. Ourselves
5. Police
6. Family doctor
7. Psychiatrist
8. Other specialist
9. Agencies, other

There is also a very general "must" at the outset of any interview (or contact in general): *Never take anything for granted.* Information has to be probed in order to discriminate facts from assumptions and stereotypes, which tend to perpetuate problems and replicate the same answers and, therefore, make any change impossible.

For example, a common request in a case of someone who has had multiple previous hospitalizations is the following: "Come pick up Mr. X Y because he has gone crazy, just like the other time!" There are two important presuppositions (based on previous *institutional* practice) in a request worded like this: that X Y (1) actually has a mental illness, and therefore (2) actually needs hospitalization. No alternative is left to the mental health worker. He is regarded not as a professional, but as a mere executor. A request like this: "Come and see X Y because he does this and that — strange things!" does not require a higher level of sophistication; however, it is posed in a correct format.

An accurate inquiry has to be made right from the beginning, even over the phone. Proper questions include:

- What happened exactly?
- Who said it?
- From whom did you learn that?
- When did it happen?
- How long did it last?
- Who was there, etc.?

In general, facts in a context have to be collected. The classical 5 W's (who, what, where, when and why) are of help in guiding the inquiry. However, it should be kept in mind that *why* elicits an opinion and therefore is less reliable than *after what* is.

Collecting Information in the Initial Interview

In our view interviewing skills are better learned from clinical practice than from a book. However, some dos and don'ts to serve as broad, nonrestrictive guidelines can be helpful.

To reiterate, the initial segment of the interview should be aimed at maximizing comfort by use of active empathy, providing structure by setting the context, determining and respecting the amount of distance the client requires, facilitating rapport via small talk and "joiners," and defusing projections. Having done that you are ready to proceed.

Process Techniques: An interview is usefully separated into process and content elements. The latter will be described shortly. In terms of process, there are several ways by which an interviewer can both enhance the quantity and quality of it and have a positive therapeutic impact. These techniques also allow for the testing of client responsiveness to an interpersonal intervention.

Basically, we have found that it is useful for the interviewer to supply what is missing or underrespond to what is in oversupply in the interview. Three different variables — distance (relationship), verbal output (cognition), and body activity (affect) — should be observed and appropriate responses made based on these observations. Thus, when dealing with quiet, withdrawn, low energy (usually depressed) clients, interviewers should gradually change positions to sidle in closer, speak animatedly using lots of hand gestures (if it's comfortable to do so), while leaving plenty of time and space open to client response by asking open-ended questions and patiently waiting and gently prompting for responses. It is as if the interviewer is supplying the fuel for a stalled automobile with the expectation it will start as a result.

With an overactive, fast-talking, intrusive, but rather disorganized client the interviewer should exert control by moving in to meet the client face-to-face, by structuring the interview with short, focused, slowly and simply stated questions, by not allowing the client to respond tangentially, and by taking the stance of a firm, strong, and non-verbose person. The interviewer, once he has gotten in a face-to-face position, should move as little as possible and maintain as much eye-to-eye contact as possible while speaking slowly, quietly, and firmly. This is basically a containment technique using a highly structured interpersonal relationship.

With a withdrawn, quiet, frightened client, whose initial verbal responses are disorganized and contextually inappropriate, the interviewer's verbal behavior should be very structuring (simple, measured, quiet, focused), as with the overactive, intrusive client. However, the distance the client has established should be gradually decreased *only after* she has become less disorganized in response to the verbal structuring of the interview. Moving in too quickly will likely be experienced as overwhelming and lead to further disorganization and distancing.

What would be considered a positive response from each of these clients? From the first, depressed client we would look for more, and more animated, verbal output, increased motor activity, and an overall energized appearance. For the hypomanic person, a positive response to the interview would include decreased motor activity and intrusiveness and increased ability to stay on a subject without tangentiality or the intrusion of irrelevancies. The client should finish the interview in a much more mellow frame of mind. In the case of the disorganized acute psychotic, a positive response would include responding more promptly to the interviewer's questions and coherent speech that is clearly responsive to the questions asked (hence contextually appropriate). Finally, increased closeness will be tolerated without disorganization.

These interview process techniques are best learned through live supervision. However, an easy way to summarize what changing your in-interview behavior will do is to remember that greater structuring of the interview will result in greater organization and control but can also have the effect of dampening overall responsiveness and frightening clients who fear being controlled.

CONTENT – WHAT TO ASSESS

To begin with, it is important to acknowledge that your assessment must be somewhat limited and that it will change over time as your relationship with the client evolves. Since you can't do everything at once, priorities must be set. In general we recommend an overarching approach to assessment that focuses of what's *right* that can be expanded upon, rather than on what's wrong. Growth, development, learning, and competence are of greater interest to us than disease, disfunction and disability.

We recommend that answers to four questions be sought:

1. Why are you here? or, What is the problem? ("chief complaint")
2. What happened in your life that might relate to the development of the problem? ("precipitating events") (See Brown, 1981; Brown & Birley, 1968; Canton & Santonastoso, 1984; Day et al., 1987; Dohrenwend, 1975; Paykel, 1978; Rabkin & Struening, 1976; Schwartz & Myers, 1977; Steinberg & Durrell, 1968 for research support of the importance of stressful life events in the precipitation of illness.)
3. What do you want? (What needs to happen to change things for the better?)
4. How can I help you get it?

Interviewers should be careful that they don't get so caught up obtaining a detailed history that they lose sight of the last two questions. The focus on client-defined needs is crucial to the preservation and enhancement of clients' control and power. In addition, it provides direct acknowledgment that they have a critical role to play in the resolution of the problem.

Question 4 explicitly states the interviewer's position that the interviewer and the client will be working collaboratively, following, insofar as possible, the client's lead. Questions 3 and 4 are *not* meant to invite the interviewer to suspend his judgment and common sense. Totally unrealistic needs or problem solutions should be labeled as such and the questions readdressed. We also find it useful to attempt to look for a client's sense of humor. This does at least two things: provides another way to build the relationship, and assesses the depth of the client's demoralization. It's always a hopeful sign, as well as a helpful intervention, if interviewer and interviewee can share a good laugh.

The answers to some or all of these four questions may not be clear immediately; however, they should continue to be focused on as the relationship evolves over time.

The first two questions are usually easier to address with clients who have not had long careers as patients. The further clients get from the initial episode that required mental health care, especially if it was serious psychosis requiring impatient care, the harder it is to unravel the events that precipitated this original dramatic occurrence. However, even for long-term system veterans there is usually some event, however trivial it may seem to us, that precipitated a new need for "care." Focusing on the emotions associated with this event will both help establish empathic rapport and provide an opportunity to assess the degree to which the client is able to acknowledge and accept, rather than keep out of awareness, his feelings. Remember, the degree of difficulty encountered in attempting to establish a relationship and the degree to which content must be dissociated from the associated feelings will provide valuable clues as to how difficult it is going to be to involve the client in an ongoing therapeutic relationship. *Psychosocial interventions require relatedness.*

System veterans (the so-called "chronically mentally ill") are often distinguished by the degree of interpersonal scarring they manifest via active interpersonal distancing or passive disinterest in the interview. These interpersonal maneuvers are felt, by them, to be crucial to the prevention of further injury. Hence, they must be respected and approached with great care. The client's message is usually clear if we take the time to hear it: "I've been wounded and scarred too many times before by encounters like this one. Understand and respect my position." Inexperienced interviewers frequently make the mistake of trying to go too fast, of being pushy and unduly intrusive. Try to remember that it took a long time for clients to get where they are; you need not be in a hurry to unravel the story (heaven forbid that you even *think* of helping!). Instead say something like, "You don't have to talk now about things that make you uncomfortable or that you don't want to talk about. I hope that eventually you will." This usually enhances the patient's sense of control and autonomy and communicates respect. Clients have likely encountered many previous would-be rescuers; resist the urge to grab your lance and mount your white charger for the attack. The damsel has probably been at the dragon's mercy for a long time; nothing very serious is likely to result from waiting. *A tip:* we find it helpful to remember that when you begin to feel that you must *do* something, especially controlling action, something in the interaction is causing *you* to be nervous.

Another fantasy that commonly causes therapists problems (in addition to the rescue fantasy) is that something they do will cause irreparable damage to the weak, helpless client. This bit of omnipotence can be easily reality-tested by remembering something a great teacher, Dr. Elvin Semrad, said: "If you think schizophrenics are weak, try and change one."

However, there are times with very withdrawn "veterans" where no response at all can be elicited, despite various attempts. Waiting brings nothing. Providers, while not yielding to therapeutic furor, nevertheless have to become active, take the initiative, find their way through resistances, and seduce the patient into activity. Playing a two-person game or running errands together are examples of techniques that can be used. It often takes a long period of hard work before the patient becomes involved.

In other cases, especially with a person going through a psychotic experience, the patient may act out during the interview or overtly exhibit either disturbing behaviors or delusional ideas. To avoid being caught off balance, the interviewer should be aware of this possibility and remain tolerant while trying to understand the message hidden behind the behavior. It is a common observation that psychiatric patients produce more symptoms in the presence of the psychiatrist: How could it be different? How can a patient be helped by a mental health professional if he doesn't present what he is expected to, i.e., psychiatric symptoms? When he needs help, he simply plays his role as mental patient.

This concept may be better explained with an example:

> One day Piero and Maria show up for an appointment at the South Verona Community Center. They live in the territory; however, in spite of the fact that he is clearly a chronic schizophrenic, he is unknown to the register. So I ask why they come now; they explain that he needs a doctor from the public system to file a certificate for the renewal of his disability pension. Then he ventures into a stormy show of all psychotic behaviors he is able to perform, quite enough to result in an emergency admission if I (LB) had not the spirit to shout that I would sign the certificate right away. As if by magic, the show stopped; he did not need to play schizophrenic anymore.

An interpretation commonly made by professionals is that the patient, feeling uneasy and disturbed, unconsciously asks with his grossly disturbed and disturbing behavior to be stopped, controlled, sedated. We believe that this twisted interpretation serves only to relieve the conscience of the worker who resorts to such a drastic measure to deal with the crisis. More simply, we believe it is logical that a seriously disorganized person in great distress will communicate an urgent, dramatic need for help in a disorganized, "psychotic" way. The risk is to give the standard, institutional answer the patient expects or, as we think, reasonably fears: massive medication, seclusion, and the like. These answers reinforce withdrawal and dependency and miss the point of finding the reason for the crisis, an issue of tremendous importance for the patient. Taking measures to control him reinforces the idea that the crisis has come out of the blue, is beyond his control, and requires external means to be solved. In a relatively short period of time the person becomes unable to recognize any connection at all between events, feelings, and acts. Decontextualization has occurred.

> Lilly, a woman of 50, is a long-term patient in the South Verona community services. She has spent 15 years in various institutions. She is intelligent and capable of crystal clear speech but she usually utters a word salad; in

her accounts facts and persons of her life history are mixed up and used interchangeably. From time to time she has tantrums; sometimes she hits people. Asked why she does this, she denies ever hitting anybody. When confronted with the victim she protests that the "pope" or the "government"* must have hit that person, not her. An interested and careful questioning *always* reveals that a real frustration occurred before the "crisis" ensued and that she had *good reasons* for being upset. However, she is unable to recognize the correlation between being upset and acting-out.

In the course of piecing together the client's story, you should try to learn about certain historical and current aspects of his competence, both interpersonal and instrumental. These two related areas are critical for evaluations for psychosocial treatment because all such therapies involve at least two human beings interacting and usually have as an overarching goal the promotion of competence; that is, (1) the ability to be involved in a relationship (interpersonal competence); and (2) real world accomplishments (instrumental competence).

The initial aspects of interpersonal competence assessment have already been described in the section on Connecting in Initial Interview. These concern the in-interview experiential (in contrast to the historical) aspect of the evaluative process. The experiential assessment is perhaps more critical than the historical one in terms of one's potential to be helpful to a particular client. That is, clients may describe a litany of prior unsuccessful therapeutic endeavors; yet, if it is possible to establish rapport, a collaborative process, and a positive in-interview response from the client in an initial interview, the history of previous failures can be acknowledged but then set aside, for the time being at least.

Interpersonal Competence

It has now been amply documented (Cauce, 1986; Cohen & Syme, 1985; Dean & Lin, 1977; Gottlieb, 1985; Greenblatt, Becerra & Serafetinides, 1982; Hammer, 1981, 1983; Kaplan, Cassel & Gore, 1977; Potasnik & Nelson, 1984) that the availability of a supportive social network is the single most important environmental factor in preventing the occurrence of physical and psychological disorders, in reducing related morbidity, and in promoting rehabilitation. As explicated elsewhere (Chapter 9), the social

---

*These are the two villains of her life: Catholic, she married a Protestant, an American soldier. She was pregnant and had to resort to a civilian wedding, a scandal in her times, because of delays in getting special permission from religious authorities. She believes it was a handicap that hampered the marriage (later disrupted) from the beginning. By definition the "government" represents the total institution.

network can be "treated" or used as an adjunct to other psychosocial interventions; therefore, assessment of the social network is critical.

First and foremost, the size and quality of the person's *current* social network need to be assessed. A historical account will tell you whether past and present are similar and something about the vicissitudes of the client's social involvements. However, this is of secondary importance to the present status evaluation. We look for information about the size of the network ("How many people do you know with whom you have at least occasional contact?"), about its composition ("Of these people, how many are parental family generation, how many are your generation, and how many are unrelated peers?"), and about the intensity ("Whom do you see most frequently? How do you usually feel after seeing Joe, Jane, etc.?"). Seeing the entire family together, if possible, can expedite this social network assessment process.

The social network analysis will supplement and usually validate the information derived from the in-interview experience with regard to the person's ability to form relationships. For example, it is likely that someone with whom it is difficult to establish rapport will have a small, principally biologically-based network. If clients report a good-sized, positively evaluated social network and you are not able to establish rapport with them, you should examine your conduct of the interview for unrecognized problems. If that does not resolve the discrepancy between the historical and experiential information, you may wish to question the validity of the customer's reports.

Next we consider clients' level of independence. Assessment of this aspect of *current* psychosocial competence is relatively straightforward: Where is the person currently residing and how does that compare with the norms for his or her age, social class, and ethnic group? Because a number of clients may be living at home with their parents or in some other nonindependent setting (e.g., halfway house), it is worthwhile to establish their best-ever level of independent functioning: Did they ever live alone or with nonfamily peers? If so, when and for how long?

Great care must be exercised to properly factor in cultural, religious, ethnic, and gender differences relevant to the assessment of independence. The interviewer's standards must take a back seat to factors relevant to the particular individual being seen. For example, in cultures where leaving home is not expected, the assessment can focus on the degree to which there is reciprocal versus exploitative dependency. In the former the participants each make a voluntary contribution to the common good; in the latter there is a usually covert agreement that each participant make a required, usually disliked, contribution. Another example of potential problems with this assessment can occur when a male is evaluating a female; he must remember that affiliation is more important than autonomy to many women and not judge living with parents as necessarily indicative of psychopathology.

A tip: this evaluation will allow you to set a current anchor point and a past best-ever one. The effectiveness of your efforts to facilitate independence (if this becomes an agreed upon goal) can be judged vis-à-vis these two anchor points.

Ideally, interpersonal and instrumental competencies are combined in sexual accomplishments. That is, having a loving sexual relationship demands the ability both to make a friend and to perform sexually. Wide variation is, of course, expected — from minimally sexual but very loving relationships to almost purely sexual and minimally loving ones. The important questions are:

1. Does the client have now, or did he/she have in the past, relationships where sex and affection were combined? If so, how many and for how long? When was the last one? What happened?
2. What was the nature of the relationships where sex and affection were not combined? Follow with other questions as above.

Needless to say, if the client is married it is important to know about that relationship. If possible, especially when the spouse is described as part of the problem, we recommend that the client and spouse be seen together. This can be very helpful for getting a different perspective on the problem (from the spouse) and for finding a way to address it at the level at which it developed. In fact, insofar as feasible, all problems brought in by customers should be addressed at the level at which they developed (e.g., the peer network, the family, the living group).

Generally speaking, the issue of suicide or violence to others will be assessed in the context of the client's various relationships. Except when drug intoxication is involved, it is usually a change in or threatened or real loss of relationships that causes persons to consider violence to themselves or others. If clients present as currently suicidal, this should be discussed in detail: How long have they felt this way? Have they made plans? What has to change in order to feel differently about killing themselves? How have they resolved their suicidal intentions previously? What has kept them from killing themselves so far? If they have made previous attempts what means were used? (Violent attempts — cutting, stabbing, hanging, shooting — should be taken *very* seriously.) To prevent the therapist from becoming subject to manipulation, it may be helpful to acknowledge that clients have ultimate control over their lives. *If they really want to kill themselves badly enough, no one can stop them—even though the interviewer thinks it's a pretty dumb idea.* Discussion of suicide should be matter-of-fact and detailed; otherwise the therapist's anxiety about it will probably be transmitted to the client. This will, in turn, make it more difficult to define and implement a helpful intervention.

Instrumental Competence

Basically, determining instrumental competence involves a rather straightforward assessment of clients' educational, vocational and recreational accomplishments. How far did they go in school? What kind of grades did they get? Why did they stop? What jobs have they held, for how long, and paid how much? Why did they leave? If currently unemployed, for how long? What do they do with their spare time?

This domain will allow you to derive, in concert with clients, reasonable expectations for their future educational and/or vocational goals. Remember, proven ability to hold a job is the best predictor of successful employment. This also applies to friendships and sex. Although these are useful generalizations, they should not be so overvalued as to prevent the setting of future goals that surpass past accomplishments. Here, phenomenologic openness tempered by knowledge and experience can be very helpful.

So-Called "Special Cases"

Some persons introduce themselves as "special cases" from the outset, for a variety of reasons (e.g., an important person has referred them; they are friends; they have special characteristics). This beginning is generally a handicap because important steps of a routine procedure may be skipped.

For instance, during a team meeting one of the professional nurses speaks of a case he just referred to one of us (LB), the "doctor," after an unusually quick first interview. The patient, a teacher, had introduced himself as being "too dependent upon my mother" and extensively quoted Freud. The nurse, a born helper and an experienced counselor, had been caught off balance. He considered the case a "special" one, beyond his culture and therefore beyond his skills. He had even forgotten to fill out the register intake form. The author (LB) commented that considering a case as "special" exposes one to the risk of skipping important steps, as had actually happened. He also added that Freudian patients must receive the same treatment as all others—no more, no less—and suggested that the nurse see the teacher again and fill out the intake form.

The author saw the patient two weeks later; he said he had come *only* to keep the appointment because he had already recognized and solved his presenting problem talking with the nurse. He added that he had been elected principal in his school and had gone through a period of disorganization in dealing with the new tasks. This had come out during the intake questioning; the nurse had seen him two more times and given very good, effective suggestions. As often happens, a reality orientation, together with the sincere interest of an experienced counseler, was effective in mobilizing the resources of the patient, without having to use a fancy psychotherapeutic technique.

STOCKTAKING AND CLOSING THE INTERVIEW

Although this discussion of the stocktaking process occurs near the end of this chapter, this is an activity that should be conducted throughout the interview. We presume that interviewers have by now learned to monitor clients' responses more or less continuously. It is just as important, but not always as easy, for interviewers to be aware of their responses to clients. It is virtually impossible not to respond affectively to clients. These responses are normal expressions of interviewers' humanity. Clients will excite, depress, turn on, turn off, anger, dismay, bore, frighten, perplex, amaze, stimulate, and confuse interviewers. Experiencing such feelings is not usually a problem — except when they are not recognized and acknowledged or are acted on without awareness. Acting on such feelings generally occurs, in fact, *because* interviewers have failed to recognize and acknowledge them to themselves. *A tip:* generally speaking, acting on emotions generated in interviews will lead to either over- or underinvolvement with clients. In fact, this inappropriate level of involvement is a useful cue to supervisors for exploration of interviewer feelings toward clients. Keeping a watchful eye on one's own feelings, while simultaneously being totally attentive to the client, is something that can only be learned through experience and supervised client contact.

As is the case with clients, interviewers will have feelings generated both from the situation at hand (responses to the clients behavior) and from baggage they bring to the session from their own life experiences (countertransference, if you will). Earlier in this chapter we discussed the importance of knowing how you present yourself to various kinds of persons. It is also important that clinicians learn, over time, which kinds of clients consistently generate particular types of feelings in them.

For example, one of us (LRM) feels very sleepy, tired and bored when he interviews young men whose difficulties seem to stem from the lack of a well developed, functioning conscience. The response usually occurs within the first five minutes of an interview and is so predictable by now as to be a highly reliable indicator of a state of superegolessness. Clearly, these clients are not likely to be very positively regarded by this interviewer; acknowledging this helps avert problems by allowing anticipatory planning.

Basically, we advise inexperienced interviewers to ask themselves early in the interview whether or not they like the interviewee and/or find him/

her interesting. If the answer is *negative*, the interviewer should try to assess quickly whether the response is generated by the client's interview behavior or whether something about the client is distasteful because of previous experiences with similar clients or because of the interviewer's particular mood that day or because something about the client triggers feelings that come from his/her own life experiences. This is, of course, easier said than done while continuing to conduct an interview. However, sorting out client, interviewer, and situational contributions to responses is important for deriving the best possible understanding of the client and his/her potential amenability to psychosocial interventions.

Clinicians should not expect to be saints. No one likes everyone. They are not expected to be able to hit it off with every client. Problems don't come from not liking some clients — they come from not recognizing that you don't like them. As long as strongly negative or positive feelings are recognized and acknowledged they will not usually cause trouble.

In addition to unrecognized affective responses, the rescue fantasy and overintrusiveness, discussed earlier, are potential sources of in-interview difficulties. A final, not uncommon source of problems between clinicians and clients is clinicians' unfulfillable expectations *of* clients. People who choose to work in mental health often do so because they enjoy helping people. Wanting to be helpful is an excellent motivation so long as it doesn't contain a "you must respond as I think you should to my ministrations" clause. Clinicians should keep in mind that the life of the client they're trying to help belongs to the client, not to the clinician. Clients have to be allowed to do what they decide to do, even if clinicians believe it is a mistaken course of action (barring imminent danger, of course). Clinicians who have a strong investment in clients' living up to their expectations are bound to be frustrated, disappointed, and disillusioned over time. If their expectations are not easily lowered to more realistic levels, they'll likely withdraw, be inattentive, or leave the field. Luckily, most unrealistic expectations stem from inexperience. Tincture of time and supervision are very useful medicines for the treatment of such disorders of expectation.

At the end of an interview there should be a sense of closure for both interviewer and client. After enough basic information has been gathered, a collaborative problem resolution strategy developed, and the client's response limits tested (in terms of relationship, affect, and cognition), the interviewer should initiate closure. Closure should *not* be determined primarily by how much time has elapsed. In our experience, 40 to 60 minutes are necessary to do what we have laid out above. However, if at all possible about 75 minutes should be *allowed* for an initial interview. Allowing a time "cushion" will help dispel interviewer anxiety that occurs when time is running short and much remains to be done. Many times an interview can be satisfactorily conducted in 30 to 35 minutes. However, time pressure may lead to shortcuts, insufficient attention to critical content areas and important nonverbal cues, and misuse of clinician power in a way that will detract from the establishment of the essential collaborative relationship.

It is the clinician's responsibility to set the context. To do so when ending an interview it is helpful to say something such as, "We've talked about lots of things in this interview and I'm wondering if there's anything more you think I ought to know about you and your situation so I will have as complete a picture as possible?" This is *not* a pro forma exercise. The interviewer should wait quietly for a response. If there is none, the question should be rephrased, "Again, before we stop, are you sure we've discussed everything that's relevant to your problem and its potential for resolution?" The interviewer must patiently await a response, if any.

Next, the interviewer should review and summarize with clients the mutually agreed-upon goals, as well as the ways they have collaboratively identified to attain them. This summary should be a 1-2-3 simple one, with

TABLE 6.1
Making Initial Contact

1. Establishing rapport
   "the party"
   active empathy and respect
   understanding power and status differences
   condescension as a no-no
   partnership

2. Setting the context
   soliciting client expectations
   diffusion of projections
   providing structure
   defining the task

3. Assessing the initial relationship
   open–closed
   close–distant

4. The "Joiner"
   casualness
   commonality of experience
   exact replication of language

5. Dealing with distortions and false attributions

6. Avoiding stereotypes

TABLE 6.2
What to Assess

1. Critical Questions
   a. Why are you here?
   b. What happened that brought you here?
   c. What do you want?
   d. How can I help you get it?

2. Competence
   a. interpersonal
   b. instrumental

questions eliciting from clients their understanding of each: "Tell me as clearly as possible your understanding of. . . ."

Finally, the interviewer should attempt to elicit clients' explicit affective response to the interview and ask if they have any final questions to ask of the interviewer. Questions raised should be responded to honestly and straightforwardly. The client should be escorted to the door, the door opened by the worker, and the client's hand shaken while goodbyes are exchanged.

Departing from an effective initial interview, the client will likely look globally "better" — head held high, straight posture, firm stride and a smiling face.

TABLE 6.3
Stocktaking and Closing

1. Impact of your interview
   a. client response; physical and verbal
   b. your response

2. Sources of problems
   a. the rescue fantasy
   b. excessive intrusiveness
   c. unfulfilled expectations
   d. failure to recognize your response

3. And in conclusion . . .
   a. reset context
   b. summarize
   c. check affective response

This has been a long and complex, but important, chapter. Its content should be mastered through reading and dialogues with clients, coworkers and supervisors. Skillful interviewing is the bread and butter of effective psychosocial change agents. To aid the learning and review process we have provided, in summary outline form, the key elements that should be attended to in the course of an initial interview (Tables 6.1, 6.2, and 6.3).

CHAPTER 7

Ongoing Involvement

GOOD COMMUNITY MENTAL HEALTH PROGRAMS are characterized by their ability to offer clients long-term staff involvement *as needed* in the client's natural environments. This long process (and we mean *years*, if necessary) can be wearing on staff. In later chapters we describe how mental health programs are best organized to facilitate the development of these kinds of relationships (Chapter 8) and ways of detecting and dealing with staff burn-out (Chapter 10).

Here we describe particular ways of being involved in ongoing staff-client relationships that will facilitate change without wearing staff out unduly.

It is in the arena of continuing facilitative relationships that nonspecific factors identified as important in all types of psychosocial interventions (independent of theory or technique) assume special importance. Keeping them firmly in mind and attempting to maximize them will help clinicians maintain positive helping relationships over time. In this chapter we first define and elaborate upon common nonspecific factors in psychosocial interventions and then describe a corollary series of relational styles whose use will enhance the overall psychosocial intervention process.

NONSPECIFIC FACTORS IN PSYCHOSOCIAL TREATMENT

Originally elaborated by Frank (1971), nonspecific factors include:

1. *Healing context.* That is, the client perceives the helper, facility, or program as helping or as providing the context in which the client can help him/herself.
2. *Confiding relationship with a helper.* This critical variable was addressed in Chapter 6. It further encompasses the more recently described working alliance variables of client and therapist involvement, liking the process and defining it as helpful (e.g., Horowitz & Marmar, 1985).
3. *Plausible causal explanation.* Clinician and client should be able to evolve a shared definition of how and why the problem developed. Answers to the first two questions (What's the problem? What happened?) of the interview format described in Chapter 6, p. 000 should provide at least a preliminary working explanation. This in turn should lead to the development of agreed-upon goals and methods for achieving them. Recent work on the therapeutic alliance in psychotherapy has found a strong relationship between the goal and strategy consensus of therapist and client and good outcome (Bordin, 1979; Horvath & Greenberg, 1986). A goal and strategy consensus should evolve as the answers to questions three and four become clear (What do you want? How can I help you get it?). Having a shared, meaningful explanation for a phenomenon is useful for both client and worker and will help them sustain their work together over time.
4. *Therapist personal qualities generate positive expectations.* The relationally-focused, problem-solving approach, dosed with optimism, as described in Chapter 6, should enable clinicians to generate positive expectations over time. Clients almost always improve; this process can be facilitated by clear, consistent, realistic, positive expectations. *Expectations are powerful determiners of behavior.* Negative ones promote destructive behaviors and create negatively connoted definitions of contexts that can result in spiraling, destructive, self-fulfilling prophecies for clients and helpers. The personal qualities of hope and optimism displayed by staff via positive expectations can be critical for beginning the remoralization process needed by nearly all clients who seek psychological help. Indeed, realistic optimism is morale sustaining and enhancing for staff as well as clients.

5. *Provision of success experiences.* Low self-esteem and a lack of self-confidence, competence, and a sense of efficacy define the demoralized person. *It is a rare mental health system client who is not demoralized. The helping process can be viewed as one of remoralization, in which clients are given opportunities to develop options, solve problems, overcome obstacles, and accomplish goals.* To do this, clients and clinicians need to agree upon goals and strategies (Bordin, 1979) and then proceed to put them into practice. Even the smallest accomplishment—like sprucing up one's appearance—is important to the process. Sitting with clients while they arrange job interviews is a simple example of how to use the working alliance to provide a success experience. Ongoing attention to redefining goals and strategies (What do you want? How can I help you get it?) will allow clinicians to facilitate success experiences that will feed back positively into the process, so that the user will continue to like the process and find it helpful. A corollary of this is that *staff should never do anything for clients that they can do for themselves.* To do so promotes unnecessary dependency and prevents clients from assuming responsibility and developing competence via accomplishment.

RELATIONAL PRINCIPLES

The usefulness of these nonspecific therapeutic factors can be maximized if clinicians can also keep in mind certain relational styles in their day-to-day work with clients (see Table 7.1). Each relational principle will be paired with one or more of the nonspecific factors.

TABLE 7.1
Community Mental Health
Relational Principles

1. Atheoretical need to understand
2. Continuity across contexts
3. Response flexibility
4. "Being with," "standing by attentively"
5. Concrete problem focus
6. Consultation, facilitation
7. Partnership
8. Expectation of self-help

1. Atheoretical Need to Understand (Plausible Causal Explanation)

This is meant to encourage relationships that are open, nonjudgmental, tolerant, and respectful. The clinician tries to understand what's going on with clients while avoiding categorizations. Explanatory hypotheses may be collaboratively evolved to enhance shared understanding and meaningfulness, but these should be seen as always open to revision based on new information or new situations.

2. Continuity of Relationships (Confiding Relationship)

This is, in part, an administrative principle; unless a service is organized to allow and promote continuity, its implementation is difficult. Basically we propose that a *team* of three or more persons should be each client's primary therapeutic case manager/consultant. Thus, when a crisis arises that overwhelms the client's best self-help efforts, there will be someone with whom the person has an ongoing relationship available to help manage the situation. If a client is in some form of intensive residential care (e.g., alternative or hospital), the team's functions will be supplemented by facility staff. However, the team, in collaboration with the client and facility staff, will stay involved in an ongoing way. This can be accomplished in a number of ways, e.g., by team members' spending portions of their work day—in rotation—with the client in the facility. The team, or its representative, must be involved in all client-related meetings that might involve decisions.

3. Response Flexibility (Confiding Relationship, Success Experiences)

Basically this principle is intended to keep workers constantly alert and responsive to changes in the overall situation, in clients' clinical statuses and in their needs. It will be difficult to implement in hierarchical organizations, which tend to impair clinicians' abilities to respond to shifting situational demands, or in programs operating from a single theoretical perspective. It asks that facility rules and regulations be looked at in terms of their relevance to particular clients and requires that treatment plans be looked upon as guidelines rather than prescriptions. Absent bureaucratic or theoretical impediments, a plan will flow logically and easily from constant attention to and, as necessary, redefinition of the collaborative relationship established with the client. For example, it should allow the worker to recognize and implement a gradual shift from a predominantly "being with" interpersonal mode to a more down-to-earth, practical, problem-solving one as clients become more organized.

4. "Being With," "Standing by Attentively," "Letting Be" (Confiding Relationship)

This relational style will allow open nonjudgmental acceptance, empathic understanding, support, reassurance, validation, and containment *without* being overintrusive, overtalkative, or demanding, and without projecting unrealistic expectations. Its hallmark is a positive, attentive presence without an expectation of doing something *to* the client. It should be the major modus operandi with very fragmented, disorganized clients. As clients begin to reorganize, its use may be curtailed while practical problems are addressed. However, it should always be readily available to reorganizing clients, who will be facing increased levels of stress as they get their lives back on track. Remember, tincture of time is very powerful medicine.

5. Concrete Problem Focus (Success Experiences, Plausible Causal Explanation)

For many clients it will be difficult to begin addressing psychological and interpersonal issues until pressing financial, work, and housing issues are dealt with. It is not easy to approach a relational problem with someone who doesn't know how he's going to feed himself. Hence, the first priority in a problem-solving and relationship-building strategy should be practical, day-to-day issues. This approach will also provide opportunities for immediate successes that are remoralizing and self-esteem and confidence building. It will build a relationship because real needs are being acknowledged, addressed seriously and, we hope, filled. There's nothing like gratitude to help build a relationship! This can be viewed as a "doing with" relational mode. While activist, it still avoids the pitfalls associated with the "doing to" connotation of some forms of therapy.

In the course of accomplishing concrete tasks, a great deal will be learned about what has gone wrong. Staff will come to value "car therapy" highly. Much can be learned from a captive client audience while running errands. With this knowledge, devising a psychologically and interpersonally therapeutic program is much easier and will be more accurate (see below, The Spoken Word).

6. Consultation (Healing Context, Positive Expectations)

As pointed out by Wynne, McDaniel, and Weber (1986), consultation involves stock-taking, agenda-setting, collaboration between consultant and consultee, an emphasis on constructive coping, education and option development, and the expectation of involvement of at least three people.

Like family therapy, the kind of consultative relational mode we are proposing will be more open and public than is common to most doctor-patient, therapist-client relationships. These traditional two-party relationships usually have the expectation of exclusivity and confidentiality. In contrast, our approach, involving a variety of players, *cannot realistically guarantee complete confidentiality within the setting or program.* The advantages of consultative relationships over these two-party relationships are: (1) They tend to be focused on a return to functioning rather than a "cure"; (2) they tend to be collaborative, self-help, peer-oriented types of relationships rather than those in which the therapist sets the agenda and is "one up" on the client; (3) the principal focus is on the development of competence rather than on psychopathology and dysfunction.

> For example, John, a 30-year-old single man, has lived with his widowed mother for many years. He comes to the treatment team because his mother can no longer stand his disturbing behavior. This pattern has resulted in several previous hospital admissions. John acknowledges that his relationship with his mother is difficult but he believes he must return to her home because he can't see any other option.
> It is recommended that the staff acknowledge the problematic nature of the relationship and then offer to meet with John and his mother to obtain her view as well. In the meeting other options can be explored with both of them. If it appears that going home is what they both want, even ambivalently, the conditions for it can be agreed upon and additional meetings — to include significant others like sibs, other relatives and friends — scheduled. Although staff may view this arrangement as less than optimal (but not clearly destructive), they should not attempt to interfere if it is what John and his mother evolve as their solution.
> One way of addressing the situation is to involve the social network (if there is one). The notion here is that the network may defuse some of the intensity of the mother-son relationship. Also, staff might look for ways to help mother and son spend more time with peers. If this can be done there won't be as many opportunities for the development of conflicts that result in the son's being ejected from the home.
> In this example it would probably be wise for staff, acting as consultants to both mother and son, to schedule ongoing but relatively infrequent network meetings and to put them in touch with peer support groups (e.g., an AMI group for the mother and an ex-client group for the son).

7. Partnership (Success Experiences)

It is good practice for staff to approach clients in a humble frame of mind. Each encounter should be viewed as one from which they may learn something new or understand something better about the client or themselves. It is easier to convey these attitudes if staff approach clients as they would anyone, rather than approach them as if they are disturbed persons.

This relational style will enable staff to avoid many power struggles and attempts at manipulation. A partnership orientation does not necessarily mean equality or complete reciprocity of relationship. Both because of clients' inability to solve certain problems and staff's relevant life experience and special training, it is likely clients will usually get more than they give. Hence, the relationships will have in-built status and power differences. They cannot be avoided. To minimize their potentially deleterious effects, they should be recognized, acknowledged, and discussed. The aim is to develop relationships that can evolve into more or less reciprocal (friend-like) ones over time.

Proper use of this partnership orientation preserves client power, acknowledges the temporary nature of the need for help, and minimizes the staff's role as "experts." Staff can be usefully authoritative (e.g., by sharing what they've learned from their relevant life experiences) without being authoritarian. Temporary parent-like relationships are also fine, so long as they don't outlive their usefulness and become permanently established as *nonreciprocal*, dependent ones.

8. Expectation of Self-Help (Healing Context)

To promote personal problem-solving skills, responsibility, and client power and control, clients should be encouraged to evolve potential problem-solving strategies themselves and be helped, as necessary, to try them. They can be their own experts. Staff should intervene only when a strategy that is *clearly* destructive is about to be tried.

Self-help is really mutual help. A minimalist orientation will keep staff focused on how they can help expand clients' use of their own and other "folk" resources. Folk resources are naturally occurring ones (e.g., a church group) that do not involve a payer-payee component. The ultimate goal is to get clients out of the mental health system — even though it must be recognized that many may not leave or will return.

By displaying these relational modes in a clear and consistent manner, staff are more likely to become persons whom clients will seek to imitate and identify with over time. This generic learning process can result in substantial client change if there is sufficient exposure to staff qualities relevant to the person's needs and those of his family and network. How long "sufficient" is will vary considerably from client to client, depending on need, intensity, and duration of exposure. Hence, for a relatively competent, interpersonally unscarred person, a few interventions will suffice. By way of contrast, an 18-year-old, ninth grade dropout who has stayed with his madness in his bedroom since retreating there two years ago may require many months of intensive residential care for this process to be effective.

For this reason we believe that arbitrary length of treatment rules are unwise. Treatment should, of course, be only as long as absolutely necessary. However, how long that will be is difficult to predict in advance. Basically, when an initial set of goals is achieved, treatment should probably stop. If there are questions or disagreements about stopping, a supervisory process should be used to avoid idiosyncratic definitions of "optimal" being applied without opportunity for scrutiny by knowledgeable peers, clients, and significant others.

THE SPOKEN WORD (PSYCHOTHERAPY)

There are volumes written on psychotherapy — this is not one of them. We believe that a good community mental health program should offer and use network, family, group, and individual verbal and expressive therapies. They need to be integrated into the overall community system. They are critical to addressing many clients' psychological needs. However, they are no more or less important than clients' social and medical needs. There should not be a best or worst treatment hierarchy. This means, for example, that the most disturbed and disturbing persons (usually labeled schizophrenic) should be able to obtain intensive individual psychotherapy as readily as less disturbed (let's say neurotic) ones. A focus on needs of all types will result in a treatment plan that will attempt to fill as many of them as possible — including a need for psychotherapy.

The principles so far explicated are ones that describe relational orientations for staff vis-à-vis users. We have begun with and emphasized them because of our perception that verbal interchange tends to be overvalued compared to relational issues in many mental health settings. We do not wish to reinforce the community staff's becoming 50-minute hour, in-office psychotherapists — hence, the relegation of the use of talk to the end of this chapter. It should be obvious, of course, that the day-to-day practice of the various relational modes already outlined requires verbal exchange. *What we want to stress is that the interactional style (form or process) is every bit as important as what is said (content).*

What we describe now are *guidelines* and a *paradigm* (only) for having verbal discussions with clients in the context of a supportive relationship that may help them calm down, reorganize, behave in more socially acceptable ways, and identify new problem-solving options and strategies.

Based on our clinical experience, and supported by substantial research data (Mayer-Gross, 1920; McGlashan, Levy & Carpenter, 1975; Soskis & Bowers, 1969), we believe that clients who are able to fit a life disrupting episode of disturbed and disturbing behavior into the *continuity of their lives* will, over the long run, have better outcomes. Recovery and outcome are obviously not so simplistic as we're making them out to be here. For some persons, sealing over the disturbing events will be preferable. We believe that psychotherapy can be especially useful for the process of fitting an otherwise disjunctive experience into the continuity of a life. The process requires a relationship that can be sustained in difficult times. The quality of relationship needed may not be attainable with anyone in the client's immediate social field; hence, a therapist may be required.

Some clients, for a variety of reasons, are never able to make a good enough relationship to sustain a formal psychotherapeutic process. Psychotherapy is not everyone's cup of tea. However, staff should always keep in mind that insofar as possible every encounter and intervention should be therapeutic — and they usually will be if staff are focused on responding to needs.

Tables 7.2 and 7.3 contain an incomplete laundry list of generic psychosocial intervention techniques arranged by approximate degree of activism required to carry them out. Readers should by now know that we prefer the *least activist* techniques. Most are usable in almost any context, including formal psychotherapy. Insight is notable for its absence from the list; for us, it is overused, usually not well defined, and difficult to assess as to its presence or absence. Psychosocial interventions of whatever type, if properly conducted, should result in clients' acquiring new information and applying it to their lives. This defines a therapeutic process. It is eminently researchable. Hence, we do not use the less precise term "insight."

Our basic atheoretical operational paradigm — one that is relatively easy to teach (Table 7.4) — has the goal of helping clients fit an episode into the continuity of their lives. It begins by facilitating the connection of the emotions generated by a stressful life event to that event. The first step is

TABLE 7.2
Community Mental Health
Staff Intervention Techniques: I

Increasingly Activist	
	1. Meditation/relaxation
	2. Clarification
	3. Providing alternative viewpoint
	4. Giving permission
	5. Giving information
	6. Contextualizing
	7. Reframing to normalize
	8. Option development
	9. Reinforcing
	10. Suggestion/prescription

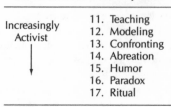

TABLE 7.3
Community Mental Health
Staff Intervention Techniques: II

Increasingly Activist	11. Teaching
	12. Modeling
	13. Confronting
	14. Abreation
	15. Humor
	16. Paradox
	17. Ritual

to help clients *acknowledge or recognize*, with the worker, its occurrence and the emotional responses to it. Once this is accomplished the verbal process should be focused on helping clients come to terms with the consequences of the event and their reactions to it. The event and the associated emotions may need to be repeatedly discussed, until clients can *bear or experience* them, in the context of the relationship, without undue distress.

The last step in the process is to help clients get some distance from—to *put into perspective* or to contextualize—these occurrences while at the same time finding a way to encompass them, as well as their consequences, into their now changed life courses (Semrad, 1966; Semrad & Zaslow, 1964). This part of the process is basically one of helping the client expand his observing ego so as to encompass this painful event. The outcome of this process should be observable along the same parameters as in the initial interview, i.e., changes in relationship, affect and cognition (see Chapter 6). Note that the nature of the life events, types of emotions generated, clients' reactions, and the way they will fit into their lives are unspecified. This is deliberate so as to recognize the vast number of combinations and

TABLE 7.4
Use of the Spoken Word:
A Paradigm

Fitting "the problem" into the continuity of one's life through a process of:
1. *acknowledging* the existence of the problem.
2. discussing it until it can be *borne*.
3. putting it into *perspective*.

permutations that can be manifest clinically. A paradigm for the *process* is spelled out but the content is unspecified. The specification of the content must occur from the ongoing application of an investigatory, atheoretical need to understand.

We chose to illustrate our psychotherapy with this example of a very disturbed person so readers could see its applicability to persons manifesting psychotic symptoms. It also illustrates how psychosis can recede in a matter of hours because of the application of a purely psychosocial intervention process. Finally, it illustrates how important an immediately responsive social environment is for dealing meaningfully with a crisis. Psychotherapy need not take place in an office for a specified amount of time.

A paradigm case: Susan, a 22-year-old psychotic woman in Soteria House.

It was almost 6 a.m.; the sun was just coming up. Susan, a resident, had just set her bed on fire, hoping to cremate herself. After the fire was extinguished, she and a staff member began talking. Here is the staff member's report:

"I asked her what was happening with her. She sat quietly and without any show of emotion told me she was the devil, that the radio and TV had been giving her messages to 'burn, baby burn,' to feel the fire of hell. She subsequently said she'd gone to a Puritan gas station and decided that since the Puritans burned witches, she was a witch, and that because Halloween was coming, she would burn.

"I told her that it seemed to me she was saying she was bad in some sense, that she'd done something wrong and her way of handling these very painful feelings was to see herself as the devil.

"I then inquired of her as to recent life events which might have resulted in her feeling like a 'bad person.' She then related at first in a very disorganized way something about having had a fight with her sister in L.A. I asked again about other recent events of note; she gave me, in a much more organized way and with some real sadness, the story of how she'd not gone to her maternal grandfather's funeral last May although her sister had called and asked her to. She said she'd not gone because she was afraid of funerals, didn't want to see her grandmother hurt and crying, and feared trying to deal with her mother and sister. Both descriptions were punctuated with occasional silly giggles, questions of me as to whether I thought she was the devil, and assertions that she *was*, in fact. I said it seemed to me she talked about being the devil whenever she began to experience the pain of her sadness and badness.

"In time we agreed between us that her delusional beliefs and ideas of reference did seem to come to the forefront when she was confronting the pain of her life; later we agreed that in fact this might be her way of avoiding the experience of that pain. I went into some detail with her about her relationship with her grandfather, how she'd lived with him when things were bad for her at home. We also went into some detail about the funeral she hadn't attended; she knew her grandfather had wanted to be cremated and wondered what in fact had happened to him.

"She said then that the fire had been no accident; she had quite intended to cremate herself and had placed the lit cigarette in the mattress, watched it catch fire, and allowed it to burn her hair before deciding that burning the place up would be unfair to everyone else there. Then she went to get Greg.

"Our chat then returned to her sister. The story unfolded with pictures and a very heart-rending letter about how a year ago her sister had required gynecological surgery and had lost all her pelvic organs. Sister's letter described how empty, depressed, unfeminine and hopeless she felt. Several remarks Susan made about her sister made me feel she was in a self-destructive, competitive relationship with her in which she, Susan, was always the "bad one," the "irresponsible one," the loser in the eyes of her mother and sister. This made me feel that burning herself also had something to do with destroying her femininity. At this point she unravelled a tale of sexual promiscuity that began with her sister's surgery.

"Around 9 a.m. we switched to the living room couch and as we focused on these events she began to cry quietly. When I got inattentive and sleepy, she would bring up radio and TV messages. They told her how bad she was— I suggested maybe they were Susan talking to Susan and brought up some of the events we'd discussed about which she felt so guilty. She really delighted in that and we shared it many times over the next several days. During our time together I would often tell her I thought she was really all right but recognized how bad a person *she* felt she was; when she asked me what was good about her I told her I thought she was bright, competent, and pretty, each of which she was. I held her hand, stroked her burnt hair, and made small talk. Often I found myself reaching out to her because she was so sad and I wanted to comfort her and let her know that I could stand to share it with her."

As to Susan's outcome, by 11:00 a.m. she was very much in touch with her feelings, both pleasant and unpleasant. Her face was now mobile, and appropriately expressive. Her psychotic disorganization, delusions and ideas of reference had receded almost completely. While she clearly could not be called happy, she was very much in touch with us and herself. She no longer had the deadened "catatonic" appearance which characterized her between 6:00 a.m. and 9:00 a.m.

Within the paradigm, any of the intervention techniques in Tables 7.2 and 7.3 might be applicable. It is expected that staff will be provided ongoing training and supervision around the proper use of these techniques. As this is best done in the context of ongoing clinical work, their use will not be discussed further here.

A Model for Effective Community Mental Health

CHAPTER 8

How to Organize a User Friendly System

THIS CHAPTER PRESENTS A DISTILLATE of the values, principles and practices we've found in one or more successful community mental health programs in the U.S. and Italy. In addition, we describe several administrative principles (horizontal authority and outcome-based bonuses) and three clinical ones which have not, to our knowledge, previously been explicitly applied to community mental health systems. For us, *these clinical principles capture, in summary form, the essence of good community mental health practice.* Because they will be set out without a specific geographic and administrative context, they may not all be applicable to a particular locale. They are meant to be modified and adapted to suit the needs and resources of a particular area. The distinction we've drawn between administrative and clinical principles is rather arbitrary; in practice they are complementary (see Tables 8.1 and 8.2).

PROGRAM VALUES

Community mental health practice is, by definition, labor intensive and rather low in technology. It is always interpersonal. Hence, a shared set of values to guide practice is an important ingredient to program functioning.

TABLE 8.1
Summary of the Treatment Principles of the Montgomery County
Department of Addiction, Victim, and Mental Health Services

As public servants, DAVMHS employees are charged to provide services that are responsive to the community, accessible, client-focused, and meet the highest level of professional and ethical standards.

DAVMHS Unity. DAVMHS is a *single* organization with *multiple* programs, each governed by the same philosophies of service.

Responsiveness to the Community. Priorities for service delivery are established within a broad sociopolitical, clinical, participatory process, which includes elected officials, funding and regulatory agencies, consumer and advocacy groups, providers and professionals, and individual care recipients. DAVMHS will ensure that its services and priorities reflect input from the identified groups.

Public Service Accountability. As a public agency, DAVMHS is accountable to the general public and to individual service recipients. This responsibility falls upon the agency as a whole and upon each staff member.

Service Environment. DAVMHS serves clients from diverse geographic, cultural, and socioeconomic backgrounds, and with diverse transportation, physical mobility, financial, scheduling, and age-related needs. This diversity will be considered in the design of programs and in the development of client treatment/service plans.

Client-Focused Services. Effective service delivery is a reciprocal process. Problem resolution requires a collaborative, mutually respectful effort involving client, clinician, family, and all other service providers. No treatment/service plan is useful if the client cannot or will not follow it, or if it is not coordinated across all services. DAVMHS will respect the rights of the client to make informed consent to service, to participate voluntarily within and to refuse a particular form of service.

Treatment Diversity. Treatment is an active, multidimensional therapeutic process. Treatment is not synonymous with psychotherapy or with medication; no single form of intervention will be uniformly considered superior to others. Every client contact is potentially therapeutic.

Family Participation. The client's family is an important element of the client's context. DAVMHS programs will relate to families in respectful and realistic ways. The strengths and resourcefulness of families will be supported and the difficulties families may have in dealing with the affected family member will be acknowledged. Families will be held accountable for their behavior when involved in the treatment process, just as are staff and the client.

Ecosystemic View. The context of problems—family, job, school, living arrangements, cultural, ethnic, and socioeconomic circumstances—contributes both to the expression of symptoms and to the resolution of problems.

Normalization. Services will enable users to live the most "normal" possible life, in terms of living arrangements, employment or education, leisure time, etc. Long-term service goals will focus on normalization rather than stabilization.

Medication. Medication is prescribed within the context of establishing and developing a collaborative, mutually respectfully therapeutic alliance.

Professional and Ethical Standards. Programs will be staffed by multidisciplinary treatment teams comprising qualified, well-trained professionals with a broad range of skills. All professionals will adhere to the standards of accepted practice in their particular fields, professional codes of ethics, and State and Federal laws governing human services.

1. Do no harm (from the Hippocratic oath all physicians take).
2. Do not unto others as you would not have done unto you (e.g., the same principles apply to clients and staff; everyone should treat each other with dignity and respect). (The Golden Rule)
3. Be flexible and responsive.
4. In general, the user knows best.
5. Choice, the right to refuse, informed consent, and voluntarism are essential to program functioning.
6. Anger, dependency, sexuality, and development of potential are acceptable and expected.
7. Whenever possible, legitimate needs should be filled.
8. Take risks; if you don't take chances nothing ever happens.
9. Make power relationships explicit.

In Montgomery County, Maryland, where the senior author works, these values were translated through input from all the stakeholders into 11 treatment principles that would govern the operation of the department's diverse, geographically scattered programs. These overlap to some extent with the three clinical principles to be described later in this chapter. Nevertheless, they are an example of how values can be translated into practical, down-to-earth, treatment guidelines (see Table 8.1).

ADMINISTRATIVE PRINCIPLES

1. Absolute Responsibility for a Catchment Area

The mental health center should be administratively responsible for a catchment area of modest size (roughly 100,000 people). All entry points into the system (e.g., clinics, emergency rooms, etc.) must be under its control (see Figure 8.1). Catchment area boundaries should be drawn, insofar as possible, in a way that conforms to preexisting natural community divisions — e.g., ethnic, religious, geographic. A 100,000-person catchment area will probably need to be divided into three or four subareas with a team assigned responsibility for each of these. As with the catchment area itself, these subareas should be drawn insofar as possible with boundaries that are natural to the existing sense of community. As the teams will be competing for a year-end bonus from the capitation payment that supports the services (see principle 8) the subareas should be fair in terms of mix of socioeconomic groups and quality of the social fabric. That is, it's not fair for one team to have an area that either consists primarily of all newly arrived residents who have not yet developed a sense of community and have the predictable problems of new immigrants or contains mainly lower

TABLE 8.2
Community Mental Health Administrative Principles

1. Catchmented responsibility.
2. Responsible teams.
3. Decentralized horizontal authority and responsibility.
4. Predictable, reliable funding
5. Use of existing community resources.
6. Multi-purpose mental health center.
7. Non-institutionalization.
8. Outcome based bonus system.
9. Citizen/consumer participation.

socioeconomic status residents with their known higher rates of all types of problems, including mental disorder. If natural boundary versus fairness of mix decisions must be made, we recommend that the former take precedence. The bonus calculation formula can be adjusted to compensate for socioeconomic differences.

2. Responsible Teams

Multidisciplinary teams of 3–5 workers should follow users from their point of initial system contact. The team should serve multiple functions for each client for whom it is responsible; crisis intervention and resolution, therapeutic case management, and formal psychotherapy (see also Chapter 9, Ongoing Outpatient Intervention). A multi-person group is required to allow continuity of *persons* across contexts (see Chapter 7, Relational Principles) despite departures, vacations and conflicting work demands. In addition, team members can provide each other support, consultation, and supervision with difficult cases. As noted below, they will function most effectively in a relatively non-hierarchical administrative structure that maximizes their autonomy.

3. Decentralized Horizontal Authority and Responsibility

Insofar as possible, authority and responsibility should reside at the lowest possible level within the hierarchy. As depicted in Figure 8.2, the system's organizational structure should be as flat as possible. Hence, only major overall policy decisions will need to involve the top administrative-clinical level. Each family-sized team or unit will make its own day-to-day clinical decisions. *This is the heart of the principle.* In this context small is indeed beautiful and normalizing (Table 8.2) (Schumacher, 1973). The

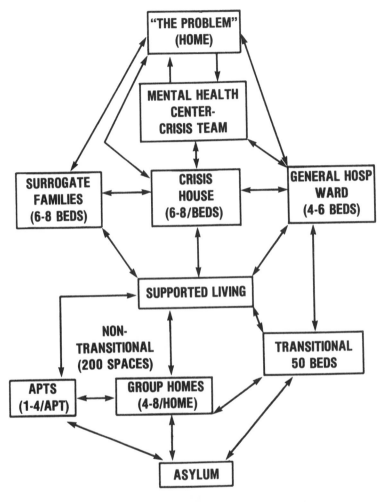

FIGURE 8.1
The Community Care System
Residential Care/100,000 Population

Morrisania program (see Chapter 12) operates in this way because of the theory its staff follows. When teams can't reach consensus, a consultant from the center's specialists (see Chapter 10) should be called in to help, either through the provision of a needed technical skill or information or

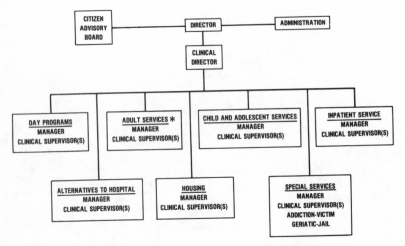

(The second service layer will more often be located away from the Mental Health Center
facility and may be operated on contract from the Mental Health Center rather than directly by it.)

*Includes: Emergency, community support, psychotherapies, medication

FIGURE 8.2
Organizational Chart
Model Community Mental Health Program

through group facilitation to resolve interpersonal issues that stand in the
way of consensus. Should this process fail, the team supervisor, in consultation with the clinical director, will make a decision.

The aim here is to be sure line clinicians are empowered (Rose, 1985) in
a meaningful way. The empowering process is enhanced by the fact that
decision-making authority and responsibility are kept at the team's level
while attempts are made to reach consensus. "Kicking something upstairs"
for a decision should be an unusual occurrence.

4. Predictable, Reliable Funding

According to our plan, the mental health center will receive at the beginning of each year a specified amount of money per resident in the catchment
area to cover all mental health related needs, ranging from educationally
oriented prevention to residential treatment and rehabilitation. In order to
be effective the system must have direct control of its resources. We esti-

TABLE 8.3
Community Mental Health
On Smallness

1. Small is beautiful.
2. Small is effective.
3. Small is tolerable.
4. Small is manageable.
5. Small is knowable.
6. Small is usual.
The bottom line: Small is normalizing.

mate this amount to be between 8% and 12% of the total health care budget. Each mental health center should have a minimum number of constraints, other than accounting ones, on how it decides to spend its money.

Although we espouse decentralized resource allocation and control—to each CMHC—this may be somewhat administratively unrealistic, as it would require duplicative management staffs for each 100,000-person catchment area. Also, although capitation payment, adjusted for local health status indicators, is desirable, there are other ways to provide support. The principle should be that the support is predictable and reliable, so that rational planning and implementation of programs can occur.

The Robert Wood Johnson Foundation's support for, and evaluation of, the development of Local Mental Health Authorities (also called Core Service Agencies) indicated that devolving needs assessment, service planning, resource allocation and management, program development and implementation, system co-ordination and outcome evaluation to existing local geopolitical entities, i.e., cities and counties, are both feasible and desirable (Goldman, Morrissey, Ridgely, Frank, Newman, & Kennedy, 1992). This arrangement uses existing governmental structures and functions while still being relatively decentralized.

5. Use of Existing Community Resources

The mental health center should not duplicate anything that can be accessed in the adjacent community, including vocational, school, athletic or recreational programs. In addition to being more cost-effective, this will help keep the mental health center remain firmly embedded in, and in constant communication with, the community, which is vitally important from our perspective. This requires an activist stance vis-à-vis the community in accessing its resources, while at the same time inviting the community to use the center's facilities as well.

6. Multi-Purpose Mental Health Center

The center should be a *multi-purpose* facility accessible from and to the community and open a major portion of the day, such as from 8 a.m. until 10 p.m. Although it can be located anywhere, having it on the grounds of an affiliated general hospital does offer some advantages to the staff, since in this plan the same staff will be responsible for patients wherever they are in the system. Consequently, when patients are in the hospital, the teams will be expected to provide staffing for the hospital in proportion to the numbers of patients they have there.

By "multi-purpose" we mean that the center can house both mental health services, e.g., outpatient, emergency, day treatment, *and* nonmental health community activities, such as evening classes, art exhibits, and recitals. If, for example, there is not an adequate library in the community, the center's library should be used for this purpose. The basic point is that the center should be in active communication with its catchment area. It must not allow itself to be segregated from it.

7. Non-Institutionalization

As the hospital beds in the system will be the most expensive single service, and since the capitation payment is fixed, this is the area where the greatest administrative attention must be paid to controlling costs. We have described in Chapter 4 the legitimate and appropriate use of hospital beds. When one of these criteria is felt to be met by the emergency services director or his/her designate, a patient can be admitted, absent an emergency. Thus, all non-emergency hospital admissions would require prior clearance. We define an emergency as a situation in which the responsible clinician has explored all the other available options and has found neither one that meets the client's needs nor one that is acceptable to the user. In practice, a candidate emergency for hospitalization is likely to be an agitated, overactive, acutely psychotic, new-to-the-system client.

From the Italian experience we have learned that once staff are firmly embedded in community work they quickly become disaffected with hospital-based work. Hence, requiring them to provide in-hospital staffing is, in and of itself, a great disincentive to hospitalization (see Chapter 11). Another disincentive is to make involuntary admission difficult and time-consuming, so that clinicians won't resort to it in the face of difficulty establishing rapport or persuading a patient that it is in his interest to go into some kind of residential care. Many observers believe this is the single most important factor in the dramatic decrease in involuntary commitment that took place in Italy after the reform of 1978 (see Chapter 11). Finally, the bonus system (see below) will provide a further disincentive by penalizing use of the hospital. We cannot emphasize enough that if a community system is to be cost-effective and comprehensive it must keep its use of hospital beds to a minimum. In this context, it should be remembered that at the present time about 70% of U.S. mental health dollars are spent on inpatient care.

8. Outcome Based Bonus System

We propose that mental health centers devise year-end bonus systems based on the clinical outcomes of patients treated by each team. Ultimately each locale will have to put together its own formula for determining what elements will be weighted in what way, but for the system to work use of hospital will need to be penalized. Elements that will need to be considered for inclusion are: number of hospital days; number of readmissions; use of psychotropic drugs; percentage of patients returned to work (including homemaking) or school functioning; percentage of patients living in places appropriate for their age and social status; percentage of patients conducting a normal social life; client satisfaction with the services; client satisfaction with their lives and number of patients successfully emancipated from the mental health system. We suggest that the variables to be included be decided on in discussions between the independent research team and line staff and users.

Program directors can modify the weighting of individual variables to encourage certain kinds of practices. For example, we recommend that medication use be penalized to encourage the use of drug-free trials or low doses or targeted neuroleptic drug strategies for the treatment of psychosis. At the same time psychosocial approaches to depression, anxiety, and phobic conditions might also be encouraged by the weighting of variables in the bonus formula.

Teams within each catchment area would be in competition with each other for parts of this year-end bonus. The bonus should be divided equally among team members regardless of educational background and experience. Giving all team members equal bonuses is a concrete means of reinforcing the notion of a nonhierarchical team with individuals on it having specialized functions based on education and experience (hence different base salary levels). The financial competition we envision may be offensive to some; in that instance we suggest that the most effective team and its clients share a properly ritualized ceremonial honor.

The bonus system we propose resembles those currently present in many HMO's in the U.S.A. However, it differs in two important ways. First, it is based more on actual client outcomes than on units of service. Second, it places greater value on more effective care rather than on less service of unknown quality. In HMO's, the incentive is to *not* serve. In our scheme the team that delivers the *most* units of service is likely to win the lion's share of the bonus.

Because our model is a "socialized" system, problems found in such systems are likely to occur: Employees may begin to see fewer patients for longer periods of time; they will try to select out the "easy" clients; and they can become so complacent as to appear institutionalized and hence non-innovative. Arranging the bonus system weighting of variables properly will help address these problems. This is a bonus system based on productivity, with productivity defined by client outcomes.

Finally, this bonus system will require an annual systematic program evaluation. As this research endeavor is directly relevant to clinicians' concerns, they will be highly motivated participants. Program evaluation, beyond units of service delivered, has historically been difficult to conduct in community mental health programs. The reasons for this are too many to detail here, but one of them is that it is difficult to convince clinicians of the relevance of research to their day-to-day clinical work. The type of careful research assessment needed to compute a bonus should both recruit them into the process and produce evidence that will validate (or not) their clinical practices. Thus, the bonus system provides an administrative mechanism that can be used to reinforce effective clinical practice.

In the 1990s there will continue to be increased consumer participation in program planning, development, implementation, and evaluation. The authors have developed a set of questions that clients might ask of their relationships to, and with, mental health programs as part of an evaluative process. These questions will provide detailed information to programs about consumer satisfaction that can be included in an outcome evaluation.

1. When you are dealing with a person who is designated a "helper" does that person, listen carefully to your wants/needs/problems so that she/he can repeat them back to you in your own words? Does she/he ask you to define how she/he can be of help?
2. When asking you for information relative to your needs/wants/problems, does he/she ask you the kinds of questions that would provide him/her with a sense of who and what you are and what your life has been like? Is the clinician interested in your unique story?
3. When discussing or developing a course of action (a "plan") to address your needs/wants/problems,

a. Does the helper ask you what you have already tried and what helped or worked and what did not?
b. Does he/she *really* involve you in the development of a plan?
c. Does the plan have options that you worked on together and do you understand what the possible positive and negative consequences of each option would be?
d. Do the options contain elements that seem pretty much down-to-earth, commonsensical, ordinary, and "normal"?
e. Are you asked whether or not your family should be involved? If yes, are you asked to help define the nature of their involvement?

4. When a plan is selected to be implemented does the clinician check back with you as to whether or not you are satisfied with it as a whole and each of its elements? Is the "plan" modified based on your responses to the inquiry about your satisfaction?

5. As you get to know the helper better, does she/he remember who you, as an individual, are? Does he/she continue to be interested in finding out more about you — both past and present?

6. Have you come to feel or believe that this clinician has come to understand and finds meaningful, in a way that can explain who and what you are, and why you do what you do?

9. Citizen/Consumer Participation

Most systems will have three, somewhat overlapping, types of public involvement: a citizens advisory board, consumer (user and ex-user) groups, and groups of involved others like parents and siblings.

The size, composition, and method of appointment to this Citizens Advisory Board will likely differ across locales. In general it should include representatives of local government, interested citizens, center staff, and consumers.

The board's function is to provide overall program policy and goals that will be translated into program activities by the center's directorship working with unit supervisors. Generally the board should not oversee the center's day-to-day operation. Rather, it should review it from congruence with expressed programatic policies and goals and quantity of resources available to put them into practice.

Several models for citizens boards have been developed and studied. Readers wishing more detailed information will find it in Bertelsen and Harris (1973), Bolman (1972), and Davis and Specht (1978).

Remembering again that the administrative/clinical distinctions we're drawing are somewhat arbitrary and that they operate in a complementary way in actual practice, we turn now to our clinical principles.

CLINICAL PRINCIPLES

There are three "umbrella" processes that must always be kept in mind by community mental health programs: (1) contextualization; (2) preservation and enhancement of personal power and control; and (3) normalization.

1. *Contextualization*. By this we mean keeping clients in as close contact with their usual surroundings, both geographic and interpersonal, as possible. In practice, the problem-focused approach explicated in Chapter 6 will serve to maintain persons in their context. To reiterate, we recommend that staff approach users so that they define the nature of the problem; then, staff can elucidate the environmental events temporally related to it, focus on clients' notions about problem solutions, and ask them what resources the team can help mobilize to deal with the problems. Validation of clients' subjective experience by the use of active empathy (see Chapter 6) will also help keep them in their context. The staff's job in this regard is to negotiate, over time, a compromise between the objective historical societal reality and the reality of clients' subjective experience. These two versions of reality need to be reconnected, since their disconnection has been part of the problem development. Contextualization is further facilitated by focusing on various aspects of clients' networks—their family and friends and the relevant professional network.

Even when clients are temporarily displaced from their usual surroundings—for example, by going into a transitional residential facility—staff must always keep their circumstances (context) in mind. Without this contextual thinking clients become difficult to understand and distant from staff. Implementation of the relational principles outlined in Chapter 7, pp. 00–00, depends on staff's being able to think contextually (also see Chapter 10).

2. *Preservation and enhancement of personal power and control*. Although we have used the term "empowerment" (Rose, 1985) in reference to staff, we prefer the clumsier term "preservation and enhancement of power," when discussing power in relation to users. Empowerment implies that one person holds something he can give to the other, that is, power. We think it is important to recognize that the mental health worker is not handing out power packages.

A major complaint we have with much of what goes on in today's mental health treatment is that the system immediately assumes the posture of knowing what is best for the users, especially if they are very disturbed and disturbing. This deprives clients of their power and undermines their sense of being in control of their lives—even though this is often a major feature of their problem. The system's job is to help them regain control over their lives or assert it for the first time — not to further erode their tenuous grasp on it. It's often easier to *do for* clients than to *help them with doing*. In our experience, unless this seductive process is kept under constant scrutiny, staff will soon create unnecessary dependency and deprive clients of opportunities to develop their own senses of autonomy and independence.

There are a number of ways that staff can enhance personal power: by providing information, helping to identify options, role playing and practicing scenarios, exercising advocacy, and most particularly, spending a great deal of time and energy keeping the client engaged in the entire helping process. The primary modus operandi in community mental health programs should be to serve as facilitators for clients' identification, definition, development, and expansion of their personal cognitive and emotional resources. *The ultimate goal is that of maximal self-help.* Hence, relationships evolved within a program will need to be collaborative, interdependent, reciprocal, and facilitative. They will usually be characterized by a "being with," rather than a more activist "doing to," interaction process. Adherence to this kind of process will maintain and enhance client power and diminish splitting and blaming. The staff should see their roles more as consultants (a less powerful and less *activist* position) than therapists (a term that implies "doing"). Activism per se is not the problem; in fact, we firmly believe in the importance of advocacy — a very activist function. However, the activism of "therapy" can be distorted in a way that aligns it with therapist, rather than client, goals or with adaptation to the status quo.

When necessary, staff need to actively demystify medical issues that arise. For example, how medications work, their effects and side effects, should be presented in ordinary language. Staff need to actively deinstitutionalize and destigmatize system veterans who have learned how to manipulate the mental health system to perpetuate unnecessary dependency. For example, they may need to call into question whether or not the particular function they are being asked to serve is necessary, and thus raise the possibility that clients could now do for themselves what, because of their previous training as patients, they have not previously seen themselves as being able to do.

Helpers must always keep a minimalist philosophy in mind. *The less they do, the better.* They should always be looking for ways to involve and support use of available nonmental-health network resources, e.g., friends, churches, Parents Without Partners. For clients with little previous experience in the mental health system, this orientation will help with critical aspects of normalization and maintenance of individuals in their natural contexts. This orientation will likely present problems for long-term patients who have evolved careers in the system and have come to expect that they will be taken care of by mental health workers. For them it is even more important that problem solutions be *evolved* from the client, not *prescribed* by a person in a high status role. Prescribing solutions results in a lack of personal responsibility on the part of the client for whom the solution is prescribed. Assumption of personal responsibility, and with it power and control, is a very important aspect of the deinstitutionalization process.

3. *Normalization (usualization)* (Wolfensberger, 1970). This principle overlaps to some extent with contextualization. However, they are distinguishable by time and reference frames: the process of contextualization includes an individualized longitudinal, historical point of view while normalization is principally a group cross-sectional, societal, or cultural norm perspective. That is, we mean there will always be times when clients are not able, by themselves, to generate the options they may need to solve a particular problem. It falls to the staff to help them develop options. In doing so, staff should think first of options that are most nearly normal. For example, if a client wants to work and has never really had the experience of finding a job, staff have at least two options: referring him to vocational rehabilitation or using the want ads. The preferred option is for staff to sit down with the client, discuss what kinds of things he might be interested in, and then go through the want ads with him. This option is preferable because this is the most normal or usual way of starting a job hunt. A referral to vocational rehabilitation is always possible if it becomes clear the user doesn't really know what he wants to do, or needs additional training, or isn't able to find and keep a job without extensive support.

Another good example of the application of the normalization principle concerns housing. For those users who cannot find, afford, or stay in housing without outside emotional support, community mental health systems have developed affiliated housing programs. Unfortunately, these are usually defined as transitional and "supervised." From our perspective it is preferable that they be *nontransitional* hence ascribing to clients the normal role of "tenant," and supported (something everyone needs) rather than supervised (a term connoting a non-normal dependent state on the part of the supervisee). The process of normalization will require a great deal of reframing, will exploit positive expectations, and will help enhance self-esteem and a sense of personal efficacy through real accomplishments, no matter how small, in a normal world.

In the following chapters we turn to a description of the smorgasbord of facilities and approaches needed to operate a good community mental health program. It will be seen, quite easily, that these facilities and our view of the way they should be organized flows from the administrative and clinical principles discussed above.

CHAPTER 9

A Community Services Smorgasbord

OUTPATIENT SERVICES

The Heart of the Matter: Mobile Crisis Intervention

WE BELIEVE THE 24-HOUR MOBILE CRISIS intervention team should be the center of every community mental health program. In most situations it will function as the gatekeeper to the system. Systematic research on the use of 24-hour mobile crisis teams has been shown that they reduce hospitalization by at least 50% (Hoult, 1986; Langsley & Kaplan, 1968; Test & Stein, 1978a & b). The experience in South Verona is that fully half of all patients labeled schizophrenic do not need residential care in any given year, principally because in-home crisis intervention is provided.

We expect that a substantial proportion of the work of the emergency services team will be done in the homes of the clients. This requires very good collaborative relationships with gatekeepers of different types: the living group, the general practitioner, the police, and the mental health system staff. A community mental health program that is well embedded in its community will not have great difficulty educating these groups.

Whenever possible the work of the crisis team should take place in the living unit, for the following reasons:

1. Using a battle fatigue or shell shock paradigm, in-home intervention will often prevent evacuation to an unfamiliar setting like hospital or alternative to hospitalization. Hence, the client will be able to remain in relationship to the natural, known support group.
2. It provides externally generated social support in the individual's own territory. Meeting new people on foreign territory is always more difficult than meeting people on one's own ground. As a result, observations made in the home are likely to reflect family reality more accurately than those made in the clinic.
3. Meeting with the in-residence living group (usually, but not always, the family) provides an opportunity for the clinical team to frame the intervention as a healing ritual experience to help alleviate the problem behavior. The usefulness of rituals in facilitating change in social networks has been highlighted by Imber-Black, Roberts, and Whiting (1988) and others (Selvini-Palazzoli, Boscolo, Cecchin & Prata, 1977).
4. The in-home context allows the crisis team to actively unlabel by use of positive reframing of "symptoms" or problem behaviors as normal, or at least understandable, responses to the stresses attendant to the particular situation.
5. By expecting the identified patient to be an ally/helper, maintenance of normal role functioning is promoted from the outset. This process helps preserve personal power and responsibility, goes on in the person's usual social context, and is framed in a normalizing way (see Chapter 8).

Basically, we believe that the in-home intervention paradigm mutes the potentially deleterious side effects of mental health system interventions by minimizing institutionalization and its inevitable decontextualization (even in community-based alternatives) of the individual. The process of repeated decontextualization and associated institutionalization—medicalization of an individual—is critical to the development of a view of that person, by the network and the system, as someone with a "chronic" illness. The disease-in-the-person view also provides the nidus around which the process of stigmatization forms; this process is a major culprit in the development and maintenance of "chronicity."

There are, of course, times when someone must be removed from a situation. Serious continued risk of violence or suicide, despite the family crisis intervention, requires that the situation be defused by removal of the person so disposed. This should be required in only a minority of instances.

We wish to draw readers' attention to the fact that, although for simplicity we label what the mobile team does as *"crisis intervention,"* whenever possible its work should be seen as involving *crisis resolution*. Crisis intervention is too frequently limited to assessment, triage and disposition. Our view is that the crisis team should continue to be involved until resolution occurs or an alternative course of action is clearly indicated.

There will also be situations in which the identified patient has already been taken out of the home and brought to an emergency room or some other intake point without the living group. In these instances it is often difficult to get the person back into the home and regroup the family or other persons in a way that will allow successful negotiation or settlement of the difficulties. However, approaching the problem from a systems perspective, even if it is not possible to send the patient home, will aid in the development of a plan that will facilitate returning there — or at least understanding of why it's not possible to do so. The availability of residential alternatives to hospitalization will allow a minimally decontextualizing response to the crisis; without alternatives, unwarranted institutionalization will take place.

Residential care must be considered when the person has no social network, when the person's social network is worn out physically and psychologically and in need of respite, when there is imminent danger to others, and when there is imminent danger to the self which clinicians judge cannot be successfully handled by a natural social network provided with mental health team support. A final indication for the use of residential care is when the in-home family crisis intervention has not led to a successful return of normal role functioning. Ergo, a situation in which the problem has not resolved or that continues to escalate despite the best ongoing efforts of the crisis intervention team necessitates the use of residential care. This response should be used infrequently.

The configuration of the crisis team will vary considerably across settings because of differences in geography, population density, manpower availability, and local regulations governing personnel use. One configuration used frequently in Italy is a four- or five-person team with two M.D.'s (staff and trainee), a nurse, and a social worker. Trainees from any other disciplines related to mental health may also be added to the team. A team configuration where psychiatric time is hard to find or very expensive and there are no M.D. trainees could be four non-M.D. mental health workers with psychiatric backup and consultation. However, each team should have at least *three* regular staff so as to provide continuity of persons, over time, for the clients.

Incoming calls are routed to the team responsible for the geographic area from which the call is coming. The call is then screened as to whether or not an immediate home visit is indicated. When it is unclear as to what the best response would be, we advise a home intervention. If a home visit is clearly not indicated, the case can be discussed in the team and a response made in a short period of time. This response can be anything from a call with some information to inviting the putative patient in for an individual or family evaluation.

If a home intervention is thought to be necessary the team *advises the caller of the plan and asks for his or her reaction.* If the plan is acceptable, the caller is asked to assemble the parties relevant to the problem and told that the team will arrive in about 15-20 minutes. If it is a call from police on site, they are asked to stay also.

A minimum of two team members, preferably a *male* and a *female*, should respond to in-home crises. A two-person response provides a feeling of safety and allows on-the-spot team consultation. On arrival the team evaluates the nature of the problem utilizing the interview techniques described in Chapter 6. If several people are present, the circular questioning style popularized by the Milan group (Selvini-Palazzoli, Boscolo, Cecchin, & Prata, 1980) can be utilized to evolve an interactional picture of the problem and possible options for its solution.

Home visits can vary greatly in length; the team should allow at least one and one-half hours in the home but have the flexibility to stay longer if needed. The actual intervention will utilize a variety of techniques previously described, e.g., positive expectations, reframing, support, reassurance, and ritual. The initial evaluation may be followed by daily visits, if necessary, to stabilize the situation. The principle to be kept in mind is that the *intervention should be tailored to the client's and family's needs—not to the needs of the mental health system.*

Ongoing Outpatient Intervention

In our view all line mental health center staff should be members of a crisis team. However, when not involved in crisis work they will carry out a variety of other functions:

Individuals, families and social networks will need to be seen on an ongoing basis, either in their own environments or in the clinic. This caseload is derived from the team's crisis work. We advise that the ongoing interventions with individual clients or families be the responsibility of *at least two members of a team.* Both need not be involved in every session. However, both should be up-to-date on developments. This arrangement will make continuity possible despite illness, vacations, departures, etc.

Specific therapies, such as cognitive-behavioral treatment of depression and behavioral approaches to phobias, can be provided by team members qualified to do so or by center "specialists" (see Chapter 10, p. 178). If a patient is referred to a specialist, the team should retain case responsibility. Specific interventions should be as focused and brief as possible. Group treatment should be highly valued and used to as great an extent as possible. It is in this part of the work that the relational principles and intervention techniques described in Chapters 6 and 7 will be used over and over again.

Case Managers Need to Be Therapeutic

The functions usually ascribed to case managers — case finding, assessment, service planning, linkage, coordination, monitoring, and advocacy — should, we believe, be the responsibility of the mental health center team with which a client makes initial contact. The reasoning behind our position is as follows:

1. Splitting out case management as a special role for one person outside the team complicates the situation unnecessarily and fragments responsibility for the client.
2. The role can be construed in such an activist doing-to way that the client becomes a bystander in the process. The development of competence and greater autonomy by the client via success experiences is very difficult when someone else takes care of everything. Institutional dependence can become case manager dependence.
3. As presently practiced, case managers are almost always individuals, not teams. What happens weekends, nights, and vacations? Clients will have a hard time finding someone they know and who knows them. In such situations, usually brought about by a crisis, a poor decision can be made. In addition to the problem with continuity of persons this engenders, a solo case manager has no peer support group with whom to discuss difficult clinical issues. Use of the generic mental health center team allows all of its members to know something about all the team's clients. Teams should have *no more than* about 20 active cases per member. Hence, a four-person team would have around 80 active cases, a manageable cognitive task for all team members.
4. The words planner, advocate, broker, monitor, and coordinator are not rife with connotations of support, empathy, and understanding. That is, as currently defined, case management does not explicitly acknowledge the importance of a therapeutic relationship to its work. We believe this is a serious omission because case managers will come to see themselves principally as brokers and conduits, lacking a meaningful therapeutic role with clients. However, if their role is defined as therapeutic they can then share the

morale boost a client gets from an accomplishment in which they have been involved. This will, in turn, help prevent burnout (see Chapter 10). Our point is that *no plan should be developed and acted on until a respectful mutual understanding of the problem needing to be addressed, in the context of a positive relationship, has been evolved.*

We also believe that case management can be more relationally focused if the mental health center has a designated concrete resources person(s). Thus, rather than many case managers having to know the ins and outs of all the relevant bureaucracies and the types of programs available, one person should be *very* knowledgeable on these matters and act as a consultant to the case managers and their clients. When relieved of the "doing for" task of identifying these resources, case managers can spend more of their time "doing with" clients, i.e., engaging in consultative activities that involve use of their collaborative relationships.

When mental health center teams are carrying out case management functions, we recommend they see themselves mainly as *consultants* to clients. Their consultative role should begin with a contextually valid empathic understanding of the problem(s) presented. Developing this kind of understanding will probably require team members to be with clients in several of their day-to-day activities. This down-to-earth orientation will also help dehierarchize consultant-client relationships so that they more nearly approximate our recommended partnership orientation. Insofar as these conditions are met, the client will not be made *unduly* dependent, the consultation will be therapeutic, and case management functions will be performed successfully.

COMMUNITY RESIDENTIAL PROGRAMS*

Community residential mental health system programs can be understood and compared by looking at three variables: (1) transitional versus nontransitional; (2) size; and (3) number of staff. For example, the Soteria/ Crossing Place alternative to hospitalization we'll describe is transitional, small (six to eight beds), and intensively staffed (1.3 staff per resident). By way of contrast, the halfway house model we espouse shares only transitionalness with the Soteria model, as it is rather large (20–25 beds) and lightly staffed (.3 or .4 staff per resident).

---

*Portions of the text in this chapter, titled Community Residential Programs/Alternatives to Hospitalization, appeared in Mosher (1989).

Alternatives to Hospitalization

In a properly designed and functioning community mental health *system* community residential treatment facilities should serve the vast majority of disturbed and disturbing individuals in need of intensive interpersonal care who cannot be adequately treated by in-home crisis intervention. Use of these small home-like facilities in conjunction with 24-hour mobile crisis intervention will dramatically reduce the need for psychiatric beds in hospitals (Hoult, 1986; Langsley, Pittman, & Swank, 1969; Mosher, 1982; Stein & Test, 1985). That is, a 100,000 population catchment area will need about ten adult beds on a ward in a general hospital. More than ten beds per 100,000 may be needed in urban areas into which many former long-term state hospital inmates have migrated. This estimate presumes the existence of separate facilities for children and adolescents, geriatric, and addictions cases. We also presume there will be *no* backup state hospital beds. This estimate also presumes that the system will have affordable transitional (halfway, quarterway houses) and nontransitional (group homes, Fairweather lodges, foster care, apartments, etc.) supported (supervised) and unsupported housing readily available for its clientele's use after the intensive care phase. Without adequate numbers of these facilities, users will get "stuck" at home, in the hospital, in alternatives, or in shelters. This is both clinically unwise and unnecessarily expensive.

In contrast to hospital-based interventions, where various treatments are administered to patients on wards, *residential alternative facilities are themselves the treatment*. That is, the total social environment (place and persons) is the healing intervention. In more traditional language these social environments are conceived of as "therapeutic communities" or "treatment milieus" (Gunderson, Will, & Mosher, 1983).

Research (Braun, Kochansky, Shapiro, Greenberg, Gudeman, Johnson, & Shore, 1981; Kiesler, 1982a,b; Straw, 1982; Stroul, 1987) and clinical experience have shown that approximately 90% of functional psychotics presently treated in hospital, can be equally well or better treated, at less cost, in intensive residential community care. Only patients who are seriously assaultive, uncontrollably overactive, acutely intoxicated, have complicating medical problems, insist on walking or running away, or need special monitoring or diagnostic procedures should be treated in places called hospitals (see Chapter 4).

Seriously disturbed and disturbing persons can be arbitrarily separated into two groups: those who have been recently identified and have not received much residential care (less than three months or so); and those who have been in the mental health system for a long time, usually more than two years, and have had more than three months of residential care (usually a year or more). For this latter group we prefer the term "veteran" (short for battle-scarred veteran of the mental health wars) to the more commonly used "chronic," as it has no illness association and is nonpejorative.

Community-based residential care is especially important for the first group. First, because these alternative facilities are minimally institutionalizing and maximally normalizing, they provide a means of preventing "institutionalism," a well-known iatrogenic disease (Barton, 1959; Wing & Brown, 1970) that contributes so much to what becomes labeled "chronicity." Second, because of their being relatively inexpensive (averaging about $130 a day), they provide a setting in which an adequate trial of a psychosocial treatment, with minimal or no use of neuroleptics, can be conducted. Low cost is important to a trial of treatment without antipsychotic drugs because the initial episode in residence will likely be longer than is generally allowed presently in hospitals for the treatment of acute psychoses. That is, given the current pressure to shorten hospital lengths of stay for economic (not clinical) reasons, use of neuroleptics becomes almost obligatory. In alternative care settings a three-month average initial length of stay (usually adequate to allow remission to occur) is not economically prohibitive. Thus, these environments allow an attempt to avoid two of today's most recalcitrant mental health problems: "chronicity" and tardive dyskinesia.

The design, implementation, and results of the use of residential alternative care without antipsychotic medication with newly diagnosed psychotic patients has been well researched in random assignment studies (Matthews, Roper, Mosher, & Menn, 1979; Mosher, Menn, & Matthews, 1975; Mosher & Menn, 1978; Mosher, Vallone, & Menn, 1992).

Of relevance to our recommendation of a drug-free psychosocial treatment trial are Soteria study data (Mosher, et al., 1992) from two separate cohorts of clients treated without neuroleptics that indicate that this psychosocial intervention was able to produce reductions in levels of psychopathology at 6 weeks post admission comparable to those found in the neuroleptic treated control group. The power of this milieu intervention to produce short term symptom change in newly diagnosed schizophrenics provides clear scientific support for a seemingly heretical recommendation. Interestingly, there is no random assignment study presently available to definitively support the usefulness of these types of facilities for "veteran" clients. However, there are a number of clinical studies (Kresky-Wolff, Matthews, Kalibat, & Mosher, 1984; Lamb & Lamb, 1984; Weisman, 1985a,b) that consistently demonstrate that these types of social environments can be successfully adapted for use with longer-term clients.

DEFINING THE SOCIAL ENVIRONMENTS

In our work with several types of residential alternatives to hospitalization that treat psychotic clients we have defined six milieu characteristics

TABLE 9.1
Residential Alternatives to Hospitalization:
Milieu Characteristics

Quiet
Stable
Predictable
Consistent
Clear
Accepting

(Table 9.1) and ten—five early and five later—milieu functions (Tables 9.2 and 9.3) that are critical to the promotion of recovery from psychosis.

The important characteristics are commonsensical to clinicians who have dealt extensively with psychosis. The environment should be quiet, stable, predictable, consistent, clear, and accepting. The milieu functions that should be emphasized early in the course of a person's stay in this type of environment are: (1) *control of stimulation* so as to prevent the person from being more overwhelmed by incoming stimuli; (2) provision of *respite or asylum*—that is, a place to be away from where the psychosis evolved; (3) *protection or containment* of poorly controlled behaviors engendered by the psychosis; (4) contact with people in touch with, and *supportive* of, the person's immediate experience; (5) early on, *validation* of the person's experience as real, even though it cannot be *consensually* validated. Hallucinations are all too real to the psychotic person. They should be acknowledged and respected as part of his/her experience, and an attempt should be made to understand them and how they are reflected in feelings and behavior. In no instance should they be labeled as "not real" or only "part of the illness." To do so would impede the development of a relationship, since it would affirm yet another disjunction between how the client experiences the world and how it is experienced by representatives of "reality." Bringing subjective experience and objective reality together takes time and

TABLE 9.2
Residential Alternatives to Hospitalization:
Early Milieu Functions

1. Control of stimulation
2. Respite or asylum
3. Protection or containment
4. Support
5. Validation

(Results in a quiet, safe, predictable environment)

TABLE 9.3
Residential Alternatives to Hospitalization:
Later Milieu Functions

1. Structure
2. Involvement
3. Socialization
4. Collaboration and negotiation
5. Planning

(Results in an activating, involving, future oriented environment)

can best be done in the context of a positive relationship. This relationship is best facilitated by planting oneself solidly in the client's shoes. This may call for a temporary suspension of one's own objective reality – an oft frightening experience. We encourage this stance because we've so often found it to be helpful. Try it, you might actually come to like it!

The five important functions of these social environments as psychosis is subsiding (Table 9.3) are more complex and require increased participation on the part of the client. By *structure* we mean close ongoing relationships with lots of feedback – *not* a highly organized program of daily activities. While sometimes useful, such prescriptive activities are not usually individualized, flexible, and responsive enough to suit the clientele's needs.

Involvement means setting the expectation that the client will begin to resume participation in her/his life, beginning with personal activities (doing laundry, setting appointments, etc.) and chores necessary for house maintenance (e.g., cooking, cleaning). *Socialization* includes gradually expanding the circle of people with whom the person relates, first within the setting, then outside. *Collaboration and negotiation* denote an interactive process that will begin to identify goals and strategies for achieving them. The result of this process will be a map for the future – a discharge *plan*, if you will.

Obviously many of these functions go on at the same time, and different ones will be more in evidence on different days. They should not be viewed as occurring in a stepwise progression.

The literature also provides differing descriptions of how milieus should be organized to deal with newly identified acutely disordered persons (Table 9.4) and with long-term "veterans" (Table 9.5) of the system. Basically, these descriptions provide more specific approaches that are to be carried out within the overall generic milieu functions listed above. The two types of effective milieus have a number of overlapping characteristics; however, they differ principally with regard to what should be done when. That is,

TABLE 9.4
Effective Milieus for Acute Psychosis

1. Small (6-10 patients)
2. High staff/patient ratio
3. High interaction
4. Real involvement of line staff and patients in decisions
5. Emphasis on autonomy
6. Focus on practical problems (e.g., living arrangements, money)
7. Positive expectations
8. Minimal hierarchy

From Mosher & Gunderson, 1979.

time needs to be allowed for the gross disorganization associated with acute psychosis to begin to recede before focusing on practical problems or decision-making processes. With system veterans this initial reorganization period may be either unnecessary or short and practical problems may be focused on almost immediately. For long-term clients we have found that often the presenting "acute" symptoms are really only a way of accessing help. Once help is assured by being admitted to residential care, these "symptoms" often recede quickly to the background.

If both acute and veteran clients are admitted to the same facility, staff will have to develop the skill necessary to distinguish between their differing needs. Of course, a number of clients will fall in a gray area between the two. Unfortunately, there are no research data and only limited clinical experience to address the issue of whether or not these two populations do better when mixed together or maintained in separate, more homogenous, groups. We believe, but can't prove, that a separate facility for newly identi-

TABLE 9.5
Effective Milieus for Hospitalization Veterans ("Chronic")

1. Clearly defined, specific behaviors requiring change
2. Action (not explanation) oriented, structured program
3. Reasonable, positive, *progressive*, practical expectations with increasing client responsibility
4. Continuation of residential treatment program into in-vivo community settings
5. Continuity of persons
6. Extensive use of groups to facilitate socialization and network-building

From Paul, 1969; Paul & Lentz, 1977.

fied psychotic persons would be the preferred arrangement. The issue will likely be decided on economic grounds; that is, are there enough newly identified clients deemed in need of hospitalization to keep 10 alternative beds (six in a surrogate peer facility and four in homes of surrogate parents) full in a catchment area of 100,000?

IMPLEMENTATION ISSUES

Given the substantial body of research that consistently favors alternative care over hospitalization, it can be legitimately asked why such care is not widely available. We have detailed some of the reasons for this:

> First and foremost, because all alternative care is by definition not given in a hospital it is classified by third-party payers as outpatient treatment. There are limitations on, and disincentives to, outpatient psychiatric care in nearly all health-insurance plans (including Medicare and Medicaid). Alternative care is usually intensive and may involve a residential (but nonhospital) component; outpatient coverage is rarely sufficient to cover professional fees and never covers residential care, because outpatient means nonresidential by definition. . . .
> Secondly, since early in our history American physicians, patients, and the public at large have come to expect that serious mental disorders will be dealt with in hospitals. After a century and a half or more, culturally sanctioned expectations are a powerful force and are not easily modified. An attitude of "out of mind, out of sight" is pervasive. Hence, alternatives to psychiatric hospitalization tend to be unacceptable because they run contrary to conventional wisdom.
> Thirdly, today's psychiatry prides itself on being scientific. The *Diagnostic and Statistical Manual* ("DSM") is the obsessional person's dream and the medical student's nightmare. Psychiatry's research on brain pathophysiology uses the latest biomedical technology. Its clinical research, especially into drug efficacy, uses highly sophisticated methods. Over the past several decades psychiatry has experienced a rapprochement with the rest of medicine, partly because of its scientific achievements. The growth of psychiatric wards in general hospitals has been part of this process. To ask psychiatry to move many of its therapeutic endeavors out of hospitals would be regarded as a disruption of its new relation with the rest of medicine. Hence, data about the effectiveness of alternatives are not greeted with great enthusiasm by the profession. (Mosher, 1983c, p. 1479)

In addition to the three reasons described above, alternatives to hospitalization have failed to be developed because of a combined training and critical mass problem. That is, those alternatives that exist are mainly in the public/community mental health system. Training in social work, psychology, and psychiatry tends to be focused on preparing students to be private practitioners. Community mental health, along with alternatives to hospitalization, is doubly afflicted; its clientele tends to be unattractive and few potential staff have training relevant to working with them.

This training issue is compounded in the case of residential alternatives to hospital; there are so few of them that it's impossible to provide training sites for more than a handful of students (the critical mass problem). Because there are so few of these facilities, there are not substantial numbers of experienced professionals available to organize, administer, and supervise these programs. This problem could be addressed if professional schools recognized the existence of the phenomenon of alternatives and began to include them in curricula. Over time a cadre of trained persons would be developed to provide the leadership and expertise necessary to implement these programs. We have described elsewhere a model for such community-based training (Burti & Mosher, 1986). Until this image and training issue is addressed it will be difficult to plan, develop, and implement the types of intensive residential community-based care described here.

CLINICAL MODELS

Two models of intensive community residential treatment have been extensively written about: the *surrogate parent model* developed in Southwest Denver (Polak & Kirby, 1976; Polak, Kirby, & Dietchman, 1979) and the Soteria/Crossing Place *surrogate peer model* developed by Mosher and coworkers (Mosher & Menn, 1977; Mosher & Menn, 1978; Mosher & Menn, 1979; Mosher & Menn, 1983; Wendt, Mosher, Matthews, & Menn, 1983). The Polak and Kirby model has not been formally researched in a random assignment study. The Soteria portion of the Soteria/Crossing Place model has been intensively and extensively studied in a random assignment two-year follow-up design. Crossing Place has published a clinical (i.e., nonrandom, no controls) short-term outcome study of its first 150 clients (Kresky-Wolff et al., 1984).

THE SURROGATE PARENT MODEL

The Southwest Denver model was developed in conjunction with the program's use of mobile in-home interventions as their major form of emergency service. They found, logically enough, that a certain percentage of in-home crisis interventions were not successful enough so that they felt safe in leaving all the parties at home. The program's leadership (principally Paul Polak) was moderately hospital phobic, so they devised their surrogate parent program to be used in those instances where someone needed to be temporarily taken out of the home.

The program's design capitalizes on the empty nest syndrome. By means of ads in local papers and word-of-mouth, the CMHC recruited families whose children had grown up and left home. In this mostly suburban part of Denver many couples had substantial homes with two or more empty bedrooms. Couples who responded to the ad were interviewed by CMHC staff and, if accepted, provided with a modest amount of information about, and training for dealing with, disturbed and disturbing persons. There were no hard and fast selection criteria, but they preferred to use couples with a previous record of some type of community service whose offspring were leading reasonably successful lives (i.e., not drug addicted, in jail, or the mental health system). Each couple was asked to set aside one or two bedrooms for use by CMHC clients. The rooms were paid for whether or not they were occupied.

The program's success (as it is judged by the CMHC and the families) was due to a variety of factors: First, the CMHC's mobile community team promised a 15-minute response time to any crisis that evolved in the surrogate parents' homes. Early in the program's life this availability was tested several times. As the parent couples became more comfortable with their roles, the need to call the backup team became quite rare.

Second, all acutely psychotic patients admitted to one of the homes were treated vigorously with neuroleptics, often via intramuscular "rapid neurolepticization." Hence, they attempted to minimize the occurrence of disruptive behavior through chemical restraint. Whether this type of high-dose neuroleptic treatment was still necessary when the parents became more experienced was never really tested.

Third, the parent couples who stayed with the program were natural healers. They approached their temporary children with a great deal of support, reassurance, and gentle firmness. As they got to know them, the parents began to involve themselves in helping clients with problem-solving. They gradually integrated clients into the family's ongoing life. Although there were no length-of-stay rules, most clients stayed two-to-three weeks and left gradually. Even after they were no longer sleeping in the surrogate parents' home, ex-clients would be invited to visit, to have dinner, or to share in a family event.

Fourth, the parent couples were highly respected by the CMHC staff. They were seen as an integral part of their program. They were identified and highlighted as the persons responsible for the CMHC's ability to use only one bed (on average) in the nearby state hospital—a statistic many people found astounding given a 75,000 person catchment area. Parent couples were sent to professional meetings to speak. They were visited by professionals, officials, and dignitaries of various types. All in all they felt themselves to be important contributors to a groundbreaking, innovative program. The parents became advocates for better community-based care.

Fifth, it provided the couples with a new career to be pursued during their retirement years. In addition, the predictable income from the program allowed many of them to keep and maintain family homes that otherwise might have had to have been sold.

In a sense the program provided preventive mental health care to the parent couples by refilling the empty nest. To us, the Polak and Kirby model is ideal for use in areas with low population density—i.e., semi-rural to rural areas. It is very economical even if the beds are not filled. Current replications provide stipends to the couples of $800-$900 per month per bed. With this model excellent care can be provided in the client's own, or a very nearby, community even in rural areas, thus minimizing disruption of ties with the natural support system. There are many rural areas where the nearest psychiatric impatient care is 100 or more miles away; in this context hospitalization is extremely disruptive for patient, family and network.

Although the surrogate parent model is particularly well suited to rural settings, we believe that urban and suburban community programs should have two or more (i.e., four beds) of these settings available per 100,000 population. Clinically, they would seem to best suited to the treatment of unemancipated psychotic persons, i.e., those in the 16–22-year-old age range with whom in-home family intervention has not been successful. Living in an alternate family environment affords many opportunities for these young people to experience, relate to, and learn from less highly emotionally charged parent figures. When properly planned, these settings can also provide the *client's parents* with an opportunity to share their difficulties with another set of parents, get support and understanding, and perhaps learn new ways of coping with their offspring from the surrogate parents' examples.

Utilizing empty nest parents allows the community program to actually address a problem of many seniors—feeling put out to pasture too soon and unnecessarily. These parents constitute a much underutilized natural resource—the experience, knowledge, and wisdom that accrues to people as they get older. Successful child-rearing capabilities should be a highly prized commodity. Yet, these qualities are rarely explicitly acknowledged and used for the benefit of others except grandchildren. This is an excellent illustration of a principle of good community psychiatry—using already available community resources. These include school and recreational programs, libraries, gyms, *and* personal skills.

SURROGATE PEER MODEL

The model developed by Mosher and coworkers has its roots in the era of moral treatment in psychiatry (Bockoven, 1963), in the psychoanalytic tradition of intensive interpersonal treatment (especially Sullivan, 1931;

Fromm-Reichmann, 1948), therapists who have described growth from psychosis (Perry, 1962), research on community-based treatment for schizophrenia (Fairweather, Sanders, Cressler, & Maynard, 1969) and to some extent in the so-called "antipsychiatry" movement (Laing, 1967). The Soteria project opened its first house in San Jose, California, in the fall of 1971. A replication house, Emanon, opened in another Northern California town in 1974. The original house closed because of lack of funding in October of 1983; the replication closed January 1980 for the same reason.

The basic notion behind the project was that the first treated psychotic episode was a critical intervention point. That is, the project's developers believed that the way the first episode of psychosis is dealt with will likely have great impact on long-term outcome. The project selected young, unmarried, newly diagnosed *DSM-II* schizophrenics because, statistically, the literature clearly indicated that they are the most likely to become disabled (Klorman, Strauss, & Kokes, 1977; Phillips, 1966; Rosen, Klein, & Gittelman-Klein, 1971). Hence, the project took clients with whom a successful intervention might save society a great deal of money over the long run in terms of hospital days, medications, and welfare costs.

An additional reason for taking only newly identified patients was our wish to avoid having to deal with the learned mental patient role that veteran patients have frequently acquired. Neuroleptics were not given for an initial six-week period so that a fair trial of a pure psychosocial intervention could take place. An additional reason for withholding antipsychotic drugs is that no, or minimal, neuroleptic treatment is the only certain way to prevent tardive dyskinesia.

Although the program's individual elements were not new, bringing them under a single roof in a 1915 vintage, six-bedroom house on a busy street in a suburban northern California town was. The program was designed to offer an alternative not only to hospitalization but also to neuroleptic drugs and professional staffing of intensive residential care. The program's psychiatrist, for example, was a consultant who did initial client interviews and staff training but had no ongoing contact with the clients. As the program matured, the psychiatrists came to be seen, and to see themselves, as mostly peripheral to it.

The 11 most important elements of the surrogate peer model we have identified are listed in Table 9.6. They are, for the most part, self-explanatory. However, a comment on the size issue appears warranted. We believe, based on our extensive experience, the Soteria data, the literature on extended families, communes, experimental psychology task groups, group therapy, and the Tavistock model, that for a community to be able to maximize its healing potential no more than eight to ten persons should

TABLE 9.6
Soteria and Crossing Place: Essential Characteristics

1. Small (6 clients), homelike
2. Ideologically uncommitted staff
3. Peer/fraternal relationship orientation
4. Preservation of personal power valued
5. Open social system (easy access and departure)
6. Participants responsible for house maintenance
7. Minimal role differentiation
8. Minimal hierarchy
9. Use of community resources encouraged
10. Postdischarge contacts allowed/encouraged
11. No formal in-house "therapy"

sleep under the same roof. Larger groups require more space than most ordinary houses provide; moreover, the interaction patterns and organizational governance needed are very different. Hence, economy of scale, i.e., facilities of 15 or more beds, is clinically unwise. Ideally, six clients, two staff, and one or two others (e.g., students, volunteers) should sleep in the facility at any one time. Eight clients can be accommodated, but this begins to tax the limits of the size of the social group and stretch staff availability if half or more of the clients are in acute distress. Actually, we believe that a 50–50 mix of disturbed and disturbing persons with nondisturbed persons is about ideal for the functioning of the house as a therapeutic community. This equation of six clients, two or three of whom have been in residence long enough to have reorganized sufficiently to appear relatively undisturbed, and two or three quasi-normal staff (including students) makes for an optimal mix.

There are a number of residential alternatives in existence that have 15 or so client beds (Lamb & Lamb, 1984; Weisman, 1985b). We believe that the home-like atmosphere is so absolutely crucial to the therapeutic functioning of community-based alternatives that we would *not* include such programs as examples of the Soteria/Crossing Place model. It is likely that when the NIMH or state departments of mental health get involved in the development of these facilities they will like the cost-savings of these larger units. However, it seems clear from recent research (Rappaport, Goldman, Thorton, Moltzen, Steener, Hall, Gurevitz, & Attkisson, 1987) that they sacrifice clinical effectiveness when they grow to the size of small hospital units, especially if they are located on hospital grounds. Their non-institutional character is compromised, and with it that compromise the treatment milieu is changed. To reiterate: to be family-like, their critical and unique characteristic, these facilities should have no more than six, or at most eight, client beds and must be real *community* homes – not institutional appendages.

Minimal role differentiation is a term that is sometimes misunderstood and responded to by comments like "what these clients need are examples of clear roles and boundaries." What we mean is that, for the most part, each line staff member will be able to do anything needed by a particular client. For example, the same staff member may accompany a client to apply for an apartment, go with him to the welfare office to see about SSI benefits, and meet with his family that evening. Only the program director and psychiatric consultants have different, and differentiated, roles. Having staff as generalists makes it easier to use the natural pairings that occur to accomplish particular client goals without having to assign a "special" staff member to the task.

A comment is also in order about the absence of formal in-house therapy. As noted previously, we view the entire facility "package" as providing the therapeutic social environment. Hence, everything that goes on in and out of it can be viewed as therapeutic. However, there are no time-limited in-office therapy sessions – individual, group or family – *in the facility*. We believe that because of this policy client fragmentation and community suspicion about what's going on behind closed doors are prevented and a treatment value hierarchy does not become established. That is, for the environment to be the treatment, the "real" treatment cannot be a one-to-one hour in the office with a therapist. Individual clients may be referred out, as indicated, to receive these types of therapy away from the setting itself. Having said there is no formal in-house therapy, we must go on to say that a great deal of therapeutic interaction takes place in dyads, in groups, and with families in the setting. Much of it is spontaneous, but not infrequently staff will take clients aside to discuss particular issues or behaviors.

Specific therapies can be made available in the house to persons living there as long as these therapies are invited in based on the approval of a majority of the participants and are made available to everyone who wishes to become involved. Hence, art therapy, bibliotherapy, yoga, massage, acupuncture, special diets, etc., have come and gone in the settings depending on the group's wishes and the therapies' availability.

Group meetings are also held. Some, like the house meeting, occur on a regularly scheduled basis. Others, like family meetings, usually occur soon after the client is admitted and on an as-needed basis thereafter. Morning "what are you doing today?" and evening "how was your day?" meetings occur regularly but are not formalized. The Crossing Place brochure describes the social environment that should characterize this type of intensive residential community care:

> The basic therapeutic modality is one-to-one, intensive interpersonal support. Specially selected and trained staff members are with the client for as long as intensive care and supervision are required. The staff members all have experience in crisis-care.
> The program's home-like environment is also an important therapeutic element: it minimizes the stress of going into residential care and re-entry into the community because it resembles the client's ordinary environment. Individuals focus on coping with their life-crisis in a real-life setting. In addition, the environment minimizes the potential for severe acting-out by being small, intimate, and rapidly responsive. This setting tends to elicit the best from clients by regarding them as responsible members of a temporary family.
> The staff members work closely with the director and psychiatrists to help individual clients formulate goals and plans. The entire staff meets regularly to discuss problems encountered in the helping process. The program director and psychiatrists are available to give individual attention to clients with particularly difficult situations.
> The length of stay varies from a few days to several months, depending on individual needs. Discharge is effected when the crisis has subsided and adequate plans have been worked out for important aspects of post-discharge living and treatment.

When we compare Soteria with its successor Crossing Place, we find a number of differences: Soteria House was a carefully designed research project that limited its intake to young, newly diagnosed schizophrenic patients. Crossing Place takes adult clients of all ages, diagnoses, and lengths of illness. Soteria House existed mostly outside the public treatment system in its city. Its clients came from only one entry point and were carefully screened to be sure they met the research criteria before being randomly assigned to Soteria House or to the hospital-treated control group. Because of its restrictive admission criteria (about three or four of 100 functional psychotic patients admitted per month met them), Soteria House was not seen as a real treatment resource within that system.

Crossing Place, on the other hand, is firmly embedded in the Washington, DC public mental health system. It was founded by Woodley House, a long-established private nonprofit agency whose programs include a 22-bed halfway house, a 50-bed supervised apartment program, and a thrift shop with a work support program. Because of contractual arrangements with the District of Columbia mental health system, Crossing Place accepts referrals from a variety of entry points. Its clients are primarily system veterans whose care is paid for by one of these contracts. Although it officially excludes only persons who have medical problems or whose primary problem is substance abuse, it has little control over the actual referral criteria used by a variety of clinicians.

Thus, in contrast to Soteria House, Crossing Place clientele are a less well-defined, more heterogeneous group. They *may* be less ill, violent, or suicidal (unfortunately it's not possible to know for sure) than those sent to St. Elizabeth's Hospital, the main residential treatment setting for public patients in Washington. Compared with Soteria subjects, Crossing Place clients are older (32 versus 21), are more frequently members of minority groups, and have extensive hospitalization experience (4.5 versus no admissions). Basic subject data comparing the two settings is shown in Table 9.7. Thus, although the characteristics of the Crossing Place client population are not as precisely known as those of the Soteria patients, the former group can be characterized as "veterans" ("chronic") and the latter as newly identified ("acute").

In their presentations to the world, Crossing Place is conventional and Soteria was unconventional. Despite this major difference, the actual in-house interpersonal interactions are similar in their informality, earthiness, honesty, and lack of professional jargon. These similarities arise partially

TABLE 9.7
Patient Demographic Data

	SOTERIA* (N = 75)	CROSSING PLACE* (N = 155)
Age	21	32
Marital status:		
unmarried	80%	96%
Education	13 years	12 years
Employment:		
any prior to admission	73%	47%
Diagnosis	All schizophrenic	62% schizophrenic
		26% affective psychosis
		17% nonpsychotic
Previous hospitalizations:		
percent of sample	34%	92%
average number	1	4.5
weeks hospitalized		
previous year	1	8
Initial length of stay	126 days	32 days
Neuroleptic drug Rx		
during initial admission	24%	96%

*Cohorts I (1971–76) and II (1976–82) combined

from the fact that neither program ascribes the usual patient role to the clientele. Both programs use male-female staff pairs who work 24- or 48-hour shifts.

Soteria's research funding viewed length of stay as a dependent research variable. This allowed it to vary according to the clinical needs of the newly diagnosed patients. The initial lengths of stay averaged just over four months. Crossing Place's contract contains length-of-stay standards (one to two months). Hence, the initial focus of the Crossing Place staff must be: What do the clients need to accomplish so they can resume living in the community as quickly as possible? This focus on personal responsibility is a technique that Woodley House has used successfully for many years. At Soteria, such questions were not ordinarily raised until the acutely psychotic state had subsided — usually four to six weeks after entry. This span exceeds the average length of stay at Crossing Place (32 days).

In part, the shorter average length of stay at Crossing Place is made possible by the almost routine use of neuroleptics to control the most flagrant symptoms of its clientele. At Soteria, neuroleptics were not usually used during the first six weeks of a patient's stay and were sometimes given thereafter. Time constraints also dictate that Crossing Place will have a more formalized social structure than Soteria. That is, when goals are identified rapidly, there must be a well organized social structure to allow them to be pursued expeditiously.

The two Crossing Place consulting psychiatrists evaluate each client on admission and each spends an hour a week with the staff reviewing each client's progress, addressing particularly difficult issues, and helping develop a consensus on initial and revised treatment plans. Soteria had a variety of meetings but averaged one client-staff meeting per week. The role of consulting psychiatrists was more peripheral at Soteria than at Crossing Place. They were not ordinarily involved in treatment planning and no regular treatment meeting was held.

In summary, compared to Soteria, Crossing Place is more organized, structured, and oriented toward practical goals. Expectations of Crossing Place staff members tend to be positive but more limited than those of Soteria staff members. At Crossing Place, psychosis is frequently talked *around* by staff members, while at Soteria the client's experience of acute psychosis was an important subject of interpersonal communication. At Crossing Place, the use of neuroleptics limits psychotic episodes. The immediate social problems of Crossing Place clients (secondary to being system veterans and having come from lower-class minority families) must be addressed quickly: no money, no place to live, no one with whom to talk. Basic survival is often the issue. Among the Soteria clients, because they came from less economically disadvantaged families, these problems were sometimes present but much less pressing. Basic survival was usually not an issue.

Crossing Place staff members spend a lot of time keeping other parts of the mental health community involved in the process of addressing client needs. Since the clients are known to many other players in the system, just contacting everyone with a role in the life of any given client can be an all-day process. In contrast, Soteria clients, being new to the system, had no such cadre of involved mental health workers. While in residence, Crossing Place clients continue their involvement with other programs. At Soteria, only the project director and house director dealt with the rest of the mental health system. At Crossing Place, all staff members negotiate with the system. The house director supervises this process and administers the house itself. Because of the shorter lengths of stay, the focus on immediate practical problem-solving, and the absence of most clients from the house during the daytime, Crossing Place tends to be less consistently intimate in feeling than Soteria. Still, individual relationships between staff members and clients can be very intimate at Crossing Place, especially with returning clients.

One aspect of the Crossing Place program that deserves special mention is the ex-residents' evening. It is based in part on the Soteria experience, but also grew out of the emphasis at Crossing Place and Woodley House on alumni involvement. An art therapist supervises the session, to which former and current residents are invited. Attendance varies considerably, but the formal time, place, and the nature of the activity make returning much easier for persons who might otherwise not be sure they are "really" welcome. The evening provides social contact, a place to find friends, and a chance to meet new people. Art seems to be an ideal medium around which to focus a meeting of long-term clients. Almost anyone can draw, and the critical comments of others can be easily deflected by saying, "Well, I've never drawn before." Although a large informal social network of clients existed around Soteria, the house never had a formal arrangement with ex-residents. Again, this program difference would appear to be best explained by differences in clientele.

Both Soteria and Crossing Place use non-degreed paraprofessionals as staff. Although some of the staff may, in fact, have college or graduate degrees, they are not required in the application process. These facilities seek staff who are interested, invested, and enthusiastic about the type of work they anticipate doing, independent of credentials. The down side of this practice is that there is often no career ladder available to them. Additional problems with using non-degreed paraprofessional staff are the generally low salaries paid them and a lack of recognition of their value in the professional mental health community. Hence, staff turnover is usually a consequence of returning to school to get graduate degrees, most frequently MSW's.

Our experience is that the more accurately the reality of the job is described, the less likely it is that a misfit between job and person will occur. Thus, we like to make very explicit exactly what will be expected of staff in ads and job descriptions provided to them. Our view is that the *self-selection process is the primary determinant of the quality of staff*. The requisite values and attitudes predate their employment; the setting only serves to reinforce and expand them.

The job description should contain sufficient substance to allow candidates to easily identify the major activities that will be part of their job. These include:

1. *Client assessment.* Staff are required to evaluate each client's strengths and weaknesses, with an emphasis on expandable areas of strength. The task is to respect and *understand*, in context, what's going on with the client. Psychopathology will be factored in, but in a manner that preserves the focus on health, positive assets, and normalization of functioning. This assessment will also include a future planning element, since in these transitional programs the *process of leaving begins at entry*.

2. *Relationships, "being with."* Staff will be expected to form some modest relationship with most clients. It is expected that they will form close relationships with a minority of clients. The relationships are expected to be peer-oriented, fraternal, nonexploitative, attentive but not intrusive, warm, nurturant, supportive, and responsive. Staff are not expected to like everyone, nor are they expected to have a close relationship with the majority of clients. They are not expected to see themselves as psychotherapists, even with those clients with whom they form close relationships. Quiet, attentive, nondemanding support is highly valued.

3. *Advocacy/empowerment.* Staff will work with clients on *their* goals. If this requires involvement with specialists or others outside the facility, they will be involved as required. Client goals are always primary, even if they require staff to go out of their way. Staff take clients and stay with them, if necessary, to the welfare, vocational, housing, socializing, and recreating systems. Their goal vis-à-vis the clients' goals is to facilitate the process of normalization and integration back into the mainstream of society. They are to view themselves as being clients' employees and should treat them as "the boss" insofar as their requests are at all reasonable. Even seemingly unreasonable requests (if not dangerous to anyone)

should be pursued. Staff are not to see themselves as necessarily knowing what is "best" for the client. A truly unreasonable request will likely be treated as such by the entire social environment. Hence, staff need not make it their responsibility to define this "reality." Also, they need not necessarily try to protect clients from the impact of pursuing their requests (absent real risk of serious harm). Doing so would deprive the client of an in-vivo learning experience.

Basically, staff should be able to put themselves, flexibly and nonjudgmentally, into the client's shoes. This ability will allow them to accept a variety of wishes, needs and goals from the client without a predetermined staff-derived hierarchical scale of importance or "rightness." This is why we try *not* to hire staff with a strong commitment to a particular mental health ideology — psychoanalytic, behaviorist or what-have-you. In our experience adherence to a particular theory inhibits the staff person's ability to be immediately and flexibly responsive.

What follows are three illustrative excerpts of staff-client interactions taken from the Soteria treatment manual (*Treatment at Soteria House: A manual for the practice of interpersonal phenomenology*, 1992, available from LRM). This document attempts to provide management guidelines and case examples of how Soteria staff dealt with various difficult behaviors and states of mind without using seclusion, restraints or medications. Major headings include: aggression, withdrawal, regression, sexuality, relationships, contagion, and leaving.

The first example illustrates the course of a series of interactions around a young woman's firmly held, but not consensually validatable, belief system. It is not uncommon for an individual staff member to spend entire shifts for weeks on end with one resident, often sleeping in the same room with him.

> For a long time it was Monday through Wednesday, which is my shift. I'd spend the whole time with Hope when she wasn't asleep. She went through a long period where she just didn't sleep at all at night, like, you know, we'd watch the sun come up every morning talking. Hope was an all-nighter — one of the most famous all-nighters.
>
> She was consumed by the devil in the beginning, but she wouldn't talk about it as much after a while because she knew that people would try to talk her out of it. Then when she really started to believe that there was something inside her besides the devil, and the closer she would come to figuring out things for herself, she would talk back to you a lot of times, really getting a lot of garbage out. She needed a sounding board. She'd suddenly become more and more rational. She would talk about how she really knew she wasn't

the devil, yet inside, she felt so awful. Sometimes I argued with her about it. She would talk about how she was the devil, then together we would find these coincidences that could prove that anybody was the devil or that she wasn't the devil. After a while, when she really became aware that nobody in the house believed that she was the devil, she was sort of pissed off. She really would try hard to prove it. Sometimes I'd get angry at her if she was really carrying on trying to prove she was the devil. I'd tell her about the parts of her that weren't the devil.

The next example is taken from the manual's section on regression:

I had had three hours of sleep, and even that had been broken sleep. Sleeping with and guarding Sara is not especially conducive to good resting. I was sleeping on the floor by the door so that I would waken if she tried to leave. She awakened at 6 o'clock demanding food. I got up and started to fix her breakfast. She was sitting at the table waiting more impatiently; she then urinated on the bench she was sitting on. I took her to the bathroom, changed her pants and we went back to the kitchen. I fed her at the table. She finished and sat quietly for about two minutes. Then she looked at me with a fearful expression on her face and asked me what day it was. I told her it was Sunday, and she said, "No, I mean what day is it *really*. *You* know what I mean!" I told her that it was Sunday, September 5th. I knew that it was Sara's birthday but for some reason I didn't want to deal with it then. I was tired, I was sad — it was Sara's 16th birthday, "Sweet 16." It was Sara's special day to celebrate, and there sat Sara in Soteria, soiling herself, terrified of dying, of being alone, of being with people, of spiders, of noises, of being loved, of being unloved. Happy Birthday, Sara — it was so goddamned sad.

Anyway, when I told her the date she was stunned. She sat completely still and stared at me. Then came the change — fear, anxiety, joy, little-girl pleasure, sorrow, and pain all flashed over her face in seconds. Then she started to cry, a slow, sad, and painful cry. And then she said, "It's my birthday, say 'Happy Birthday' to me." And I did. Then she got up and came over to me and sat down. She took my hand in both of hers and said, "Hold me!" I held her while she cried for a few minutes. Then she sat up and said, "Give me a present. Give me something. Give me anything. Give me something you don't want anymore. Give me something you hate. Just give me anything of yours and I'll love it forever." I told her that she would be getting birthday presents later in the day — that we hadn't forgotten her.

I was wearing a T-shirt that morning, one that Sara liked. She asked me then if I would wear her shirt and could she wear mine, just for her birthday. No one else in the house was awake — it was early and it was Sara's birthday — so we exchanged shirts.

Regression, while not induced, is allowed and tolerated when it occurs naturally. Staff feel that it is often an important step toward reintegration.

The last excerpt is a marvelous example of the concept of "being with," both physically and psychologically:

While we were talking he kept talking about how his father was Howard Hughes. And at this point he was just laying on the bed and I think I was sitting on the floor next to him. And he was saying he had to find out where his Lear Jet was parked. I asked him why he wanted it and he said he had to get back to Nevada to see his mother. He was saying his back was very sore, so I gave him a back massage. He talked more about his mother. He wanted to see his mother and bring her back here. He'd start crying a little bit. This went on for pretty close to an hour. Afterwards he said his back felt better. He said he could wait to go see his mother but he still wanted to find his Lear Jet. He thought it was parked on the driveway. So we went out to the driveway and it wasn't there. He said it must be at the airport. We came back in the house and we went to his room again. He was talking about things that happened in the war between him and Harly Bird. And then I wanted some coffee so we went over to Spivey's (a nearby restaurant). And I bought him a hamburger. He was telling me all about when he was a kid—the childhood he had and the paper routes and about school. About every two or three minutes he'd stop and laugh and say, "Well, this is silly for me to tell you; you're my father; you already know all this." As we were coming back, he stopped and said, "That was really nice. I knew you were going to take me out to dinner some night, Dad. And now we've done it." When we got back to the house he began telling me the Venutians were going to come down and visit him that night. He says "I can see them coming down now. They're going to be waiting for us." So then we went across the street under the stoplights, because he had to see the sun at the same time he saw Venus, and the sun was just coming up the other side. And he had to be between them for the Venutians to find him. So we were waiting there for maybe a half hour or 45 minutes, and he figured, well, they weren't going to come today, after all. It was getting light and Venus was disappearing from the sky, and they hadn't shown up yet, so he figured they weren't going to come. We came back to his room and it was maybe 5:30 or 6 in the morning by this time. He was talking about this belt that Harly Bird had given him that allowed him to go through space and time and it was a seat belt for the Lear Jet. Somewhere thereabouts he fell asleep, and I fell asleep too.

We hope these examples convey the flavor of the very unusual ways of dealing with madness that evolved at Soteria House. These descriptions should be compared with Dr. Holly Wilson's account of the treatment process on the ward where comparison group clients were sent (Chapter 4, pp. 41–42).

Systematic research comparison of the Soteria and Crossing Place treatment milieus has taken place. Moos' Community Oriented Program Environment Scale (COPES) (Moos, 1974, 1975), a 100-item true-false measure of participants' perceptions of their social environment, was administered at regular intervals to staff and clients in both programs. This measure has both "real" (i.e., "How do you see it?") and ideal (i.e., "How would you like it to be?") forms.

Although staff and client real and ideal data were collected, only staff real data are reported here (see Figure 9.1). According to these data, Crossing Place staff members, as compared with Soteria staff members, see their environment as three standard deviations higher in practical orientation and two standard deviations higher on order and organization and staff control. Both programs are one or more standard deviations lower than norms derived from other community-based programs on autonomy, prac-

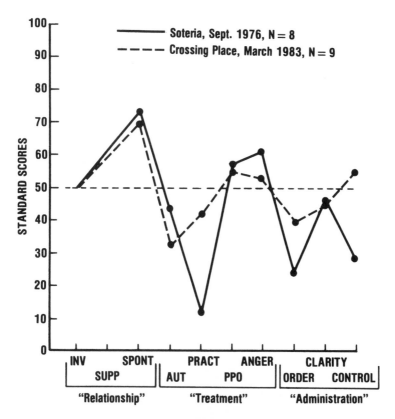

FIGURE 9.1
Program Comparisons: Staff
Soteria and Crossing Place

ticality, and order and organization. They are one or more standard deviations higher on the three psychotherapy variables—involvement, support, and spontaneity—and on the treatment variables of perceived personal problem orientation and staff tolerance of anger. The overall shapes of the two profiles have almost point-by-point correspondence on six variables and similar profile shapes on the other four. The congruence between clinical descriptive and standardized assessment findings is both noteworthy and gratifying (Mosher et al., 1986).

The two programs also conform well, by both clinical description and systematic assessment, to the literature-derived descriptions of effective therapeutic milieus for acute and "veteran" clients outlined earlier.

RESULTS OF THE SOTERIA PROJECT

A. *Cohort I (1971-76) (Soteria subjects N = 30, control subjects N = 33)*

Six-week and two-year outcome data from the subjects admitted between 1971 and 1976 have been reported in detail elsewhere (Mosher & Menn, 1978; Matthews et al., 1979.) Briefly summarized, the significant results from the initial, Soteria House only, cohort were:

1. Admission characteristics: Experimental and control subjects were remarkably similar on ten demographic, five psychopathology, seven prognostic, and seven psychosocial preadmission (independent) variables.
2. Six-week outcome: In terms of psychopathology, subjects in both groups improved significantly and comparably, despite Soteria subjects' not having received neuroleptics.
3. Community adjustment: Two psychopathology, three treatment, and seven psychosocial variables were analyzed. At two years post-admission, Soteria-treated subjects from the 1971-76 cohort were working at significantly higher occupational levels, more often living independently or with peers, and had fewer readmissions; 57% had never received a single dose of neuroleptic.
4. In the first cohort, despite the large differences in lengths of stay during the initial admissions (about one versus five months), the cost of the first six months of care for both groups was about $4,000.

B. *Cohort II (1976-82) (Soteria and Emanon subjects N = 45, control subjects N = 55)*

Admission, six-week, and milieu assessments replicate almost exactly the findings of the initial cohort. However, at two years there are no significant differences between the experimental and control groups in symptom levels, treatment received (including medication and rehospitalization), or global good versus poor outcomes. Consistent with the psychosocial outcomes in cohort I, cohort II experimental subjects, as compared with controls, had become more independent in their living arrangements at two years.

Interestingly, independent of treatment group, good or poor outcome is predicted by three measures of preadmission psychosocial competence: level of education (higher), living (independent), and work (successful) (Mosher, Vallone, & Menn, 1992). It was also associated with the presence of clear precipitating events in the six months prior to study entry. Good outcome was defined as having no more than mild symptoms *and* either living independently or working or going to school at both one- and two-year follow-up.

In summary:

1. It is possible to establish and maintain an interpersonally based therapeutic milieu that is as effective as neuroleptics in reducing the acute symptoms of psychosis in the short term (six weeks) in *newly diagnosed psychotics*.
2. The therapeutic community personnel did not require extensive mental health training and experience to be effective in the experimental context. They did, however, need to be sure that this was the type of work they wanted to do, be psychologically strong, tolerant and flexible, and positive and enthusiastic. Finally, they needed good on-the-job training and easily accessible supervision and backup.
3. Longer-term outcomes (two years) for the experimental groups were as good or better than those of the hospital treated control subjects.
4. Although it is difficult to confirm or dismiss from the data, it appears that the positive longer-term outcomes achieved by cohort I experimental subjects, as compared with cohort II, were at least in part due to the spontaneous growth of easily accessible social networks around the facilities. These informal networks provided interpersonal support, housing, jobs, friends and recreational activities on an as-needed basis to clients and staff. Unfortunately, these networks disintegrated as it became clear that the facilities would close. Hence, in contrast to cohort I, cohort II subjects did not receive as much of the *peer case management* provided by the social networks around the houses during their two-year follow-up.

Based on 12 years of experience in the Soteria project and 14 years and more than 1,400 clients in Crossing Place, we have identified what we consider to be the nine essential therapeutic ingredients of these special social environments. They are:

1. Positive expectations of recovery and learning from psychosis.
2. Flexibility of roles, relationships and responses.
3. Acceptance of psychotic persons' experience of themselves as real — even if not consensually validatable.
4. Staff's primary task is to *be with* the disorganized client; it must be specifically acknowledged that staff need not *do* anything.
5. Normalization and usualization of the experience of psychosis by contextualizing it, framing it in positive terms, and referring to it in everyday language.
6. Tolerance of extremes of human behavior without need to control it except when there is imminent danger.
7. Sufficient time in residence (one to three months) for development of surrogate family relationships that allow imitation and identification with positive characteristics of staff and other clients.
8. Sufficient exposure to positively valued role models to identify, experiment with, and internalize strategies for problem-solving that provide a new sense of efficacy, mastery and competence.
9. Readily available post-discharge peer-oriented social network with which contact is begun while in residence.

The reader will note that most of these have been previously described in Chapter 7.

Transitional Residential Programs ("Half-way Houses")

Transitional housing is a clear departure from usual living arrangements and therefore not optimally *normalizing*. Transitional facilities and programs should be arranged in a way that delivers the *"this is a temporary arrangement"* message clearly and consistently. In contrast to what we espouse for both alternatives to hospitalization and supported nontransitional housing, we believe that halfway houses should be somewhat institutional and have a social organization that expects, promotes, and reinforces independence in the context of support. Their social structure will produce the desired independence-promoting effect only if they are closely associated with supported nontransitional housing programs. Repeated separations from friends and family and housing instability are known to be associated with increased rates of psychiatric disorder. For these reasons, the thrust of transitional programs should be toward helping clients establish permanent housing and stable social networks.

What kind of "institutional" characteristics should such facilities have?

1. They should house more persons than an extended family. Hence, 15 to 25 clients is a good number of clients for such places.
2. Program rules should specify the independence-oriented behaviors desired:
   a. Length of stay should be limited.
   b. There should be few private rooms and clients should have only minimal say in roommate selection.
   c. Outside the house day-time activity should be required. Consistent school attendance or paid work should result in paying less rent.
   d. All therapy should take place outside the facility.
   e. Residents should be involved in the day-to-day running of the house as training and practice for their own living environment.
   f. Attendance at client-run in-house meetings focused on dividing up chores and planning educational, social, and recreational events should be required.
3. The program should be relatively lightly staffed so that staff are forced to focus on helping the client group develop into a reciprocal-help, peer-based support network. Foremost in each staff member's mind should be the question: "How can I foster groupness?" Ideally, instead of turning to staff for help, clients will use each other. Subsets of the networks that develop can be helped to move out together into the associated housing program.
4. The setting should be regarded by staff (and thence transmitted to clients) *as if* it were a college dormitory. The resident managers (not counselors or therapists) should be there after 4 p.m. and overnight and leave in the morning as clients are expected to do.

The rules should function to prevent settling in and the dependency it tends to foster. This is intended to help minimize problems with leaving. It is an intentional social environment focused on restricting in-house freedom for the sake of promoting out-of-house autonomy. It is meant to make the nontransitional housing program look very attractive by comparison. The program should provide individualized training to those who need it in cooking, cleaning, doing laundry, and personal care. This training can be continued as clients make the transition to new residences.

Halfway houses in the 15–25-bed range can also provide on site (if space is available) a variety of general health-oriented activities — aerobics, yoga, meditation, safe sex education, etc. The literature contains a number of specific models for these types of programs (Budson, 1978; Budson, Meehan & Barclay, 1974; Glasscote, Cumming, Rutman, Sussex & Glassman, 1971; Golomb & Kocsis, 1988; Jansen, 1970; Landy & Greenblatt, 1965; Purnell, Sachson & Wallace, 1982; Rausch & Rausch, 1968; Rothwell & Doniger, 1966; Spivak, 1974). Above we've attempted to provide flexible principles that can be adapted to fit local conditions.

A 100,000-person catchment area will need about 50 halfway house spaces. Their daily cost should be about $40 per client.

Supported Non-Transitional Housing

There are a number of contextual factors in the U.S. that make the inclusion of decent, affordable housing a critical element in an effective community mental health system. They are:

1. At the present time, because of its progressive nuclearization and frequent disorganization as a consequence of divorce, remarriage, and absent fathers, the American family is not a reliable source of housing for its adult children or the grandparental generation. In the U.S. fewer than half of community-based mental health clients live with their families. By way of contrast, about 80% of such clients in Italy live with their families.

2. Politicization of the homelessness problem has added fuel to the "irresponsible deinstitutionalization" fire surrounding mental health policies and programs. This attribution has further eroded public confidence in community mental health programs and resulted in a call for a return to institutional care. Mental health programs must become able to absorb into their programs those homeless individuals who are truly disturbed and disturbing and seek permanent housing. This is not only humane but good public relations for community mental health. It is worthwhile in this context to point out that Italy's closing of its large psychiatric institutions nearly 10 years ago has not resulted in a substantial increase in the homeless population in that country. This cross-cultural difference is probably due both to the strength of the Italian extended family and the system's focus on *preventing* institutionalization rather than on deinstitutionalization.

3. Users of the public system are almost by definition poor. SSI recipients receiving about $380 a month (the present Washington, DC rate) cannot, by themselves, afford housing in most urban areas.

By seeking housing in an ongoing way, a mental health program can find bargains, negotiate leases, guarantee payment and upkeep to landlords, and serve as housemate brokers for the clientele. Program staff can also develop the expertise necessary to access the local housing subsidy program on behalf of its users. There are, of course, other ways of assuring the availability of housing to mental health system users. In fact, setting aside a percentage of units in public housing programs is in many ways a more normalizing option and should be used if feasible. There are many ways to skin the housing cat; all should be tried.

We estimate that the average U.S. public psychiatry program will need about 200 supported independent living *spaces* (beds) for a 100,000-person catchment area. Clients should not have to pay more than about a third of their incomes for housing. Programs may add a modest consultation fee to the amount paid for rent (e.g., $20 per month) to help the program pay for itself. Doing so (assuming clients cover the rent one way or another) will result in a very economical housing program; the equivalent of six or seven full-time staff for 100 spaces will cost approximately $1500 per space per year after startup costs.

In keeping with the principle of normalization, we believe that community residences (group homes, apartments, Fairweather lodges) developed by mental health programs should be labeled *nontransitional*. This is designed to promote security, stability, predictability, and "ownership" in the lives of users. Persons seeking housing who are not mental health system clients are not ordinarily (assuming the terms of the lease are met) subject to arbitrary length-of-stay rules or required to leave places they've leased to make room for others who also need a place to live. So we believe it is best, *insofar as feasible*, for programs to make clear to clients that the program will turn over its lease to the clients in residence if they wish to remain there. It should also make clear that they are always free to leave to find a place of their own choosing. This policy most nearly approximates what ordinary citizens experience in the role of "tenant." This means that mental health programs will need to seek replacement housing units in an ongoing way. However, we also recognize that the transfer of a lease to a client group will probably not be the modal experience. It is just too difficult when groupings are formed at least in part based on program needs for a three-, four-, or five-person group to be compatible enough to remain together.

So *in practice* many units in housing programs will be transitional and thereby remain in the program. The important point is that if clients know there is no *programmatic* barrier to their making the unit into "home" it will tend to encourage them to take care of it as if it were theirs. Thus, an important normalizing expectation is facilitated by program policies. Creative program staff will attempt to be housing matchmakers; for example, when program users find friends in the group, staff should facilitate their efforts to move in together and eventually take over a lease.

Most community mental health experts agree that ghettoization of the mentally ill in community-based residences is just another form of segregation from so-called normal society. Hence, it is typically recommended that housing for clients be scattered in the community and only a minority of units in multi-unit apartment buildings be leased to them. We agree completely. However, is restricting the types of persons eligible for the housing to the mentally ill not also a form of segregation? We therefore recommend that community mental health housing programs attempt to make their units available to nonmental-health-program-related persons in need of housing. Although administratively cumbersome, having a mix of mental health clients and "normal" people in the housing has several things to recommend it:

1. It continues the process of desegregating the so-called mentally ill.
2. For a "normal" person it provides direct day-to-day experience with a person carrying a "mentally ill" label and vice versa. This is the most effective way to destigmatize mental health clients.
3. The "normals" provide role models clients can imitate and identify with and from whom they can learn various coping skills. The users provide the "normals" with access to life experiences they've likely never had.
4. It provides housing that some of the "normals" might not have been able to afford.

Where are such persons to be found? Students and persons on public housing waiting lists come immediately to mind. Actually, persons with limited incomes might be recruited via newspaper ads.

This mixing of populations may prove difficult to implement because of bureaucratic and administrative issues, but it does highlight a continuing problem with segregation of the mentally ill even in good community programs. It will need to be addressed before clients can be truly embedded in the community.

Having posited above that ghettoization of the mentally ill is not good practice, we must say that if one conceives of this clientele as a *subculture* that need not be mainstreamed into "normal" society another type of housing option becomes tenable. Pioneered by Mandiberg and Telles (1990), the notion of *clustered apartments* to encourage the development of a subculture, along with a *peer support* model, was demonstrated to be an effective option within a variety of supported nontransitional housing programs. To be viable, the model requires a closely located group of 60–100 clients and a respite apartment for clients who decompensate.

We like to apply our oft-used analogy of the smorgasbord to the types of living arrangements possible in housing programs. The nontransitional housing smorgasbord should vary widely along two continua: type of living arrangement (e.g., group home, apartment, Fairweather lodge) and amount of interpersonal *support* provided by the mental health system. We prefer the term "supported" independent housing to the more commonly used "supervised," as it has less of a child-like, dependency connotation. This is in keeping with the normalization principle; everyone needs support, whereas only specially designated groups, like children, need supervision. No living group should be larger than an extended family, i.e., six to eight persons. If possible, the group should decide whether or not it will be mixed or of one gender only.

Ideally, program support should be flexibly available to all living arrangements in the system, so that it is *brought to clients* when they need it—including those living at home with their families. This arrangement makes it possible for individual units to become independent of mental system support—a salutory development when it occurs. Having to move into a new living situation when more support is needed only adds the stress of moving to those already being experienced; hence, bringing support to the client to prevent this stress makes good clinical sense. Of course, if sufficient in-residence support can't be arranged or if the family or house or apartment mates are feeling no longer able to tolerate the crisis, then a move to a hospital alternative or some other intensively staffed transitional facility is warranted. One interesting way to structure a program is to have the staff consultants based in an apartment that can also be used as needed for temporary intensive respite care.

We recognize that a comprehensive housing program will need to include nontransitional settings that provide 24-hour on-site supervision and caretaking. Foster care, board and care, boarding houses, single room occupancy hotels, and nursing homes will be required to care for a subset of the population. Staff support should be available to clients and caregivers as needed. We have not highlighted these settings because we believe it's better to aim a bit high rather than too low with regard to the degree of independence clients are able to sustain in the community. However, clients should be free to trade some of their freedom and autonomy for reliable on-site caretaking if they so choose.

An array of support and intervention should be available in housing programs—family meetings, house meetings, single and multi-apartment group meetings. In-residence training sessions focused on cooking, cleaning, doing laundry, and personal appearance should be provided as needed, usually to clients new to the program. It must be remembered that what clients learned in other settings will not necessarily transfer to new ones. Staff should generally view themselves as consultants to *households* (i.e., the living group), not to individuals. This attitude will help foster collectivity in the group and self-help and independence on the part of the individuals. Staff should focus their efforts on helping clients learn to solve their own in-residence issues by modeling an approach that attempts to deal with problems at the level at which they occur. For example, a problem between two roommates should be dealt with by meeting with them (assuming they've already tried to solve it themselves), *excluding* others in the same apartment if they're not *directly* involved in the problem.

If housing program developers keep in mind the principles of normalization and preservation of power we've described, program policies should flow logically from them. Doing so will enable the program to avoid the oft-made mistake of creating mini total institutions in the community. For example, we are frequently asked what kind of rules should be made with regard to sex and alcohol in residences. Our response is that *insofar as feasible* the clients in each unit should make whatever rules are needed. We advise that program staff look at the issue from the perspective of their *own* group living experiences. Externally introduced (i.e., program) rules should be kept to the absolute minimum consistent with the program's functioning. Society's views on the particular issue should be used as guidelines in developing program rules. That is, society allows alcohol consumption, so a housing program should not have a *blanket* rule against it. However, individual units should be free to decide to not allow alcohol. Also, if a unit seems to be having a problem with alcohol that is unresolved after a series of staff consultations, a temporary, externally imposed (from staff) rule against it can be made. By way of contrast, we believe that housing programs affiliated with the mental health system should have an explicit rule against illegal drugs in their facilities.

Staff should remember that rules are easier to make than to do away with. Also, given the realities concerning the amount of staff time available to supported housing, staff's ability to enforce externally applied rules is limited. For example, in a discussion of a program's rule against having sex in its housing, a staff member wryly remarked, "Yes, they don't have sex in the house between 4 and 8 p. m. —when we're there!"

Many clients in these residences will have had long institutional experiences. A large part of their difficulties adjusting to the community will stem from their expectation that, if they agree to abide by a series of institutional rules governing their behavior, they will be totally taken care of. A good community program should not replicate this institutional experience in its housing. This is not to say that clients with long institutional experiences can be expected immediately to be individually self-governing and to participate appropriately in within-unit discussions. However, these should be overarching long-term goals to be pursued in collaborative relationships between staff and users. Deinstitutionalization should be an active process – not a state designated by the fact the clients are no longer in the hospital. Because the degree of institutionalism evident in clients will vary widely, it will take experience and good clinical acumen to be able to walk the ever shifting line between expecting too much and asking too little of individual clients.

Supported independent housing programs are fortunate that their rental units do not usually require a special permit or license that would bring their presence to the attention of the community. Halfway houses, because of the number of residents involved (e.g., 10–15), are not usually so fortunate. Community opposition to such facilities is a reality. What is needed is patience, strong backing from official agencies, good legal counsel, and good diplomacy with and responsible reassurance of the community by the program.

Discriminatory zoning regulations have been consistently struck down in the courts. Hence, the most frequent legal grounds used in support of community protest is not usually viable when court tested. In addition, evidence from the study of the implementation of the Willowbrook decision indicates that community fears were unfounded and quieted rapidly as group homes in the community were established and filled (Rothman, 1980). Hence, if programs can quietly and consistently maintain pressure they will eventually overcome opposition. Once in place they can actually begin to expect a rather neutral or even positive view of them by the community. This process is easier if the agency has a good reputation, if it does something that actually enhances property value (e.g., repair and renovation), and if staff are sensitive to the needs of the neighbors. Tincture of time seems once again to be a useful medicine, this time for dealing with community opposition to mental health clients living in its midst. The passage of the Fair Housing Amendments in 1988 and the Americans with Disabilities Act in 1992 provide new legal backing for the movement of clients into "normal" neighborhoods.

There are a number of mental health housing program models (Arce & Vergare, 1985b; Carling, 1984; Carpenter, 1978; Chien & Cole, 1973; Fairweather et al., 1969; Goldmeir, Shore, & Mannino, 1977; Kresky, Maeda, & Rothwell, 1976; Mannino, Ott, & Shore, 1977; Murphy, Engelsmann, & Tcheng-Laroche, 1976; Randolph, Lanx, & Carling, 1988; Segal, Baumohl, & Moyles, 1980; Solomon & Davis, 1984). Unfortunately (at least from our perspective), they are too often designated as "transitional" and "supervised." We believe that calling them *nontransitional* while expecting that most will in fact be used as transitional housing is preferable in terms of the expectations engendered. Readers interested in day-to-day implementation, administrative and program management issues can find that information in these publications.

In many locales bureaucratic regulations will make adherence to the principles outlined above difficult. However, they do set out relatively ideal program guidelines against which current program realities can be compared.

DAY AND EVENING PROGRAMS

The literature indicates that only 20–25% of all persons discharged from psychiatric hospitals are competitively employed (Anthony & Dion, 1986). Hence, the majority of mental health clients lack the organizing, structuring, expectant daytime environment associated with working. They also lack the rewards for accomplishment that flow from successful work.

Community-based day and evening programs should be focused on providing intentional social environments that address the interpersonal and instrumental competence deficiencies of the clientele. They should provide concrete vocational and social success experiences in the context of a supportive group. Optimally, these success experiences will come from learning the skills they lack, or are deficient in, and from flexible programmatic attention to their individual needs. The expectation should be one of making the transition, with proper training and support, to a more normal way of life (including a job) in the community.

While functioning as nonresidential alternatives to hospitalization, day programs should also be able to provide for clients who are either unwilling or unable to be involved in an organized, structured group exercise. That is, acutely disorganized clients using the program as an alternative often find the environment of a large, well-organized psychosocial rehabilitation center or day hospital just too stimulating, confusing, and overwhelming. This is also true of a number of clients recently discharged from intensive residential care (e.g., alternative or hospital). They will drop out or appear only irregularly. For these clients a low intensity, low demand, simple, casual, "drop in" social environment should be provided. This requires a sound-dampened room with soft, comfortable furniture and the availability of optional low-key activities like art, cards, checkers, VCR movies, community outings, and the like. The social interaction should be mostly dyadic or triadic. Staff should be patient, non-intrusive and nondemanding. Small groups discussing sports, the soaps, the VCR movie, etc., can be organized. We highlight this need because in our experience day programs do not often attend to the special needs of this subset of clients. This results in unnecessary utilization of the system's most expensive component – intensive residential care.

Two different types of day programs have proliferated over the past three decades and dominate the field: day hospitals and psychosocial rehabilitation centers based on the Fountain House Model. Both have been shown to be effective in shortening impatient stays and reducing relapse rates (to 10% a year as compared with an expected rate of 40% per year) among formerly hospitalized patients (Anthony, Buell, Sharratt, & Althoff, 1972; Beard, Malamud & Rossman, 1978; Bond, Witheridge, Setze, & Dincin, 1985). Day hospitals have, in addition, been shown to be an effective alternative to 24-hour impatient care for selected clients (usually those with involved families) (Herz, Endicott, Spitzer, & Mesnikoff, 1971; Washburn, Vannicelli, Longabaugh, & Scheff, 1976; Wilder, Levin, & Zwerling, 1966). Both seem to be ideal environments in which to implement the kinds of individual social skills and family intervention programs recently found to be effective in reducing relapse and enhancing community adjustment (Bellack, Turner, Hersen, & Luber, 1984; Falloon et al., 1982; Hogarty et al., 1986; Leff et al., 1982).

Although day hospitals and psychosocial rehabilitation centers grew out of different cultures (medical versus rehabilitation), the social environments they provide serve the generic milieu functions we describe in the chapter on residential alternatives for their clientele. Most day hospitals are what the name denotes: an eight-hour-a-day hospital staffed mostly by medical personnel. Their focus is on providing specific treatments (medications; individual, group, and family psychotherapy) in the context of a highly organized, structured program format. The usual medical hierarchy may be muted but M.D.'s are usually in charge. Psychosocial rehabilitation centers tend to have a practical down-to-earth focus, while day hospitals tend to focus on resolution of personal problems. Day hospitals tend to be smaller – 20–40 persons versus 75–150 in rehabilitation programs. Psychosocial rehabilitation centers frequently have their own housing programs; day hospitals usually do not. Day hospitals generally take patients with involved families; psychosocial programs take persons from any type of living arrangement.

Propelled by a key NIMH training grant, active involvement in the development of the NIMH Community Support Program (see Mosher, 1986, for a more complete explication), and the development of two centers focused on the rehabilitation of the mentally ill (at Boston University and the Thresholds Psychosocial Rehabilitation Center in Chicago), psychosocial rehabilitation programs have proliferated rapidly. At the present time there are about, 300 "clubhouses" attended by about 25,000 clients throughout the U.S. It is for this reason we are reprinting portions of the classic article on the Fountain House model of psychosocial rehabilitation—a model that dominates the field at the moment. It, or a variant, should be included in the smorgasbord of community-based facilities.

Because of day hospitals' medical/psychiatric/individual psychopathology focus, we are ambivalent about recommending their inclusion in a community array. If reframed as day centers and focused on family, network and systems interventions, they can provide a useful additional element in a community array. This is especially true if they are not in, or on, the grounds of a hospital. Day hospitals have often been established because they are sufficiently medical in their orientation, programming, and staffing to qualify for third-party reimbursement. To the authors this seems to be an example of penny wise and pound foolish. They usually cost $200–300 per day as compared with $30–40 per client per day for psychosocial rehabilitation centers. Unfortunately, there are no random assignment studies comparing outcomes of clients seen in psychosocial rehabilitation centers with those in day hospitals. Until the issue can be resolved empirically we advise program planners to chose the less costly option. Having said this, we suspect that day hospitals *may* be best suited to the treatment of a subset of clients: middle- and upper-class depressed persons with well established occupations as housewives or white collar workers and only temporary loss of social competence. For this group, something called "hospital" may be more legitimate and acceptable than a rehabilitation center, a term they tend to associate with serious physical disabilities.

We estimate that a catchment area of 100,000 persons will need about 100 or so day program spaces. This is a crude estimate that will need to be modified in areas that have large numbers of veteran clients.

THE FOUNTAIN HOUSE MODEL*

The Fountain House model is a social invention in community rehabilitation of the severely disabled psychiatric patient. Fountain House itself is an intentional community designed to create a restorative environment within which individuals who have been socially and vocationally disabled by mental illness can be helped to achieve or regain the confidence and skills necessary to lead vocationally productive and socially satisfying lives.

Fountain House conveys four profoundly important messages to every individual who chooses to become involved in its program:

*From Beard, J. H., Propst, R., & Malamud, T. J. (1982). The Fountain House Model of Psychiatric Rehabilitation. *Psychosocial Rehabilitation Journal, 5*, 1, 47–53. Reprinted with permission.

1. Fountain House is a club and, as in all clubs, it belongs to those who participate in it and who make it come alive. As with all clubs, participants in the programs at Fountain House are called, and are, members. The membership concept is considered a fundamental element of the Fountain House model. Membership, as opposed to patient status or client status, is regarded as a far more enabling designation, one that creates a sense of the participant's belonging, and especially of belonging to a vital and significant society to which one can make an important contribution and in which one can work together with fellow members in all of the activities that make up the clubhouse program.

2. All members are made to feel, on a daily basis, that their presence is expected, that someone actually anticipates their coming to the program each morning and that their coming makes a difference to someone, indeed to everyone, in the program. At the door each morning every member is greeted by staff and members of the house, and in all ways each member is made to feel welcome in coming to the clubhouse.

3. All program elements are constructed in such a way as to ensure that each member feels wanted as a contributor to the program. Each program is intentionally set up so that it will not work without the cooperation of the members; indeed, the entire program would collapse if members did not contribute. Every function of the program is shared by members working side by side with staff; staff never ask members to carry out functions which they do not also perform themselves.

   To create a climate in which each participant feels wanted by the program is the third intentional element in the Fountain House model. It is to be seen in stark and radical contrast to the atmosphere created in more traditional day programs, especially the attitude, almost universal in such programs, that persons coming to participate are doing so not because they are wanted by the program but because they are in need of the services provided to them by the program.

4. Following from the conscious design of the program to make each member feel *wanted* as a contributor is the intention to make every member feel *needed* in the program. All clerical functions, all food purchases and food service, all tours, all maintenance, and every other ongoing function of the clubhouse program are carried out jointly by the staff and members working together. Fountain House thus meets the profoundly human desire to be needed, to be felt as an important member of a meaningful group, and at the

same time conveys to each member the sense that each is concerned with all. Mutual support, mutually caring for the well-being, the success, and the celebration of every member is at the heart of the Fountain House concept and underlies everything that is done to ensure that every member feels needed in the program.

These four messages, then, of membership, of being expected, being wanted, and being needed constitute the heart and center of the Fountain House model.

Additionally the model is informed with four fundamental and closely related beliefs:

1. A belief in the potential productivity of the most severely disabled psychiatric client.
2. A belief that work, especially the opportunity to aspire to and achieve gainful employment, is a deeply generative and reintegrative force in the life of every human being; that work, therefore, must be a central ingredient of the Fountain House model; that work must underlie, pervade, and inform all of the activities that make up the lifeblood of the clubhouse.

   Thus, not only are all activities of the house carried out by members working alongside staff, but no opportunity is lost to convert every activity generated by the clubhouse into a potential productive contribution by members. Such involvement in the work of the clubhouse is a splendid preparation for and source of increased confidence in each member's ability to take gainful employment in the outside world.

   Further in support of this profoundly held belief, Fountain House guarantees to every member the opportunity to go to work in commerce and industry at regular wages in nonsubsidized jobs (see Transitional Employment Program, below). Indeed, Fountain House considers this guarantee part of the social contract that it makes with every member.
3. As a parallel concept to that of the importance of work and the opportunity to work is the belief that men and women require opportunities to be together socially. The clubhouse provides a place for social interchange, relaxation, and social support on evenings, weekends, and especially holidays, seven days a week, 365 days a year.
4. Finally, Fountain House believes that a program is incomplete if it offers a full set of vocational opportunities and a rich offering of social and recreational opportunities and yet neglects the circum-

stances in which its members live. It follows that the Fountain House model includes the development of an apartment program, which ensures that every member can live in adequate housing that is pleasant and affordable and that provides supportive companionship.

Program Components

The following program components of the Fountain House model will be seen to flow naturally and logically from the underlying concepts discussed above.

- the prevocational day program
- the transitional employment program (TEP)
- the evening and weekend program (seven days a week)
- the apartment program
- reach-out programs
- the thrift shop program
- clubhouse newspapers
- clubhouse name
- medication, psychiatric consultation, and health
- evaluation and clubhouse accountability

PREVOCATIONAL DAY PROGRAM

The psychiatric patient returning to the community faces extraordinary difficulties in achieving vocational objectives. Employment interviewers in industry do not look favorably on previous psychiatric hospitalization. The psychiatric patient often lacks self-confidence in his or her ability to perform a job and typically does not have the job references essential in securing employment. The Fountain House prevocational day program provides many opportunities for members to regain vocational skills and capacities.

All of the day program activities are performed by members and staff working together. What everyone does is clearly necessary to the operation of the clubhouse. In working side by side with members the staff become aware of each member's vocational and social potential and the Fountain House member begins to discover personal abilities and talents that can lead to greater social effectiveness and more meaningful work.

At Fountain House, as in other clubhouse settings, members view their daily participation in the prevocational day program as a "natural process" that is essential to the growth and well-being of all individuals. They are members of a club and voluntarily provide their help and assistance. They do not regard themselves as undergoing a formal rehabilitation process, in which something is being done to them. The goal is to establish a foundation of better work habits, enriched social skills, and a more helpful view of the future. Many discover that although they are viewed as disabled, there are many ways they can still be constructive, helpful, and needed.

In time, this newly discovered self-awareness can be translated into a more rewarding, nondisabling way of life, free of financial dependency and perpetual patienthood.

In brief, the prevocational day program provides a diversified range of clubhouse activities that clearly need to be performed and that, if reasonably well done over a period of time, will not only be personally rewarding to individual members but in a most fundamental sense will give them the self-confidence and awareness that they can successfully handle a job of their own or an entry-level job in the business community. These opportunities are guaranteed to all Fountain House members through the transitional employment program.

TRANSITIONAL EMPLOYMENT PROGRAM (TEP)

The Fountain House transitional employment program makes it possible for members to work at jobs that other members have held before them and that industry has made available specifically to Fountain House to facilitate the work adjustment of the vocationally disabled.

The major ingredients of the transitional employment program are as follows:

1. All job placements for the severely disabled mentally ill are located in *normal places of business*, ranging from large national corporations to small local firms employing only a few individuals.
2. All job placements are essentially *entry-level employment, requiring minimal training or job skills.*
3. The *prevailing wage rate is paid by all employers* for each job position, ranging from the minimum wage to considerably above minimum wage.
4. Almost all jobs are worked on a half-time basis so that one full-time job can serve two members. A few TEP placements, however, are available on a full-time basis.
5. *Most job positions are performed individually by a member in the presence of other workers or employees.* Some job responsibilities, however, are shared by a group of six, eight, or even ten individuals from a community-based rehabilitation facility. In that case members relate primarily to one another on the job.
6. *All placements*, both individual and group, *are temporary* or

"transitional" in design, providing employment for as little as three months to as long as nine months or a year.

7. TEP provides a guaranteed opportunity for disabled members to maintain temporary, entry-level employment through a series of TEP placements or to use such employment as a link or step to eventual full-time, independent employment.

8. *Job placements are maintained only if the individual member meets the work requirements of the employer.* No adjustment or lowering of work standards is made by employers.

9. *Job failures on a TEP placement are viewed as a legitimate and essential experience for most vocationally disabled members* in their effort to eventually achieve a successful work adjustment. In setting up a TEP with employers Fountain House agrees that if a member does not come to work, *another member or a staff person* will be selected to do the job. No matter what an individual member's vicissitudes may be, employers can count on the job assigned to Fountain House being done every day.

10. In the work experiences of normal or nondisabled individuals, failure or withdrawal from entry-level employment often occurs, and *TEP employers emphasize that job turnover rates are not typically greater for the vocationally disabled mentally ill on TEP placements than for the normal or nondisabled employee.*

11. *New TEP placements in the business community are always first performed by a staff worker for a few hours,* longer if necessary, so that an accurate assessment can be made of the requirements that must be met if the job is to be handled successfully by individual members. Staff initiating new TEP placements are also able to evaluate the work environment and its compatibility with the needs of the vocationally disabled individual.

12. Through direct familiarity with the work environment, staff have immediate access to a work site whenever vocational difficulties occur that require prompt evaluation and assessment of a member's performance.

13. All TEP placements are allocated to Fountain House by the employer and the selection process to fill TEP placements rests with Fountain House and the individual members its serves.

14. *No subsidy is provided to the employer* with respect to wages paid by the employer to a member on a TEP placement.

15. The unique collaboration or rehabilitation partnership between the business community and Fountain House is not a charitable act on the part of the employer. It is an agreed-upon arrangement that is of mutual benefit to the employer and the member who is

seeking a higher, more rewarding level of work adjustment through the vocational services of the TEP.

16. The TEP provides a unique opportunity to enrich and expand the evaluation process concerning vocational potential and work adjustment. Assessment is made through guaranteed positions in a normal work environment, one that only the business community can provide, rather than through evaluations based solely on an individual's past work adjustment, performance in sheltered environments, or personal interviews and psychological assessment.

17. *In the TEP it is not assumed that a member's prior history of vocational disability or handicap is necessarily indicative of his or her inability to successfully meet the minimal requirements of entry-level employment* provided as a primary service within the supportive, comprehensive delivery system of a community-based clubhouse.

18. TEP placements remove or circumvent barriers that typically preclude or diminish the possibility that psychiatric patients will seek and secure entry-level employment:

    a. A history of psychiatric hospitalization does not prevent the member from having the opportunity to secure entry-level employment.

    b. No attention is given to the duration of a member's hospitalization, which may frequently be as long as 20 or 30 years or more.

    c. The number of psychiatric hospitalizations is irrelevant to a member's opportunity to assume a TEP placement.

    d. The absence of a work history, the presence of an extremely poor work adjustment, or lack of, or very poor, job references does not prevent or serve as a barrier to TEP work opportunities.

    e. An individual's inability to pass a job interview is not viewed as a relevant to working on a TEP placement.

    f. A TEP job placement is an opportunity guaranteed to all clubhouse members. It is not a requirement, therefore, for the disabled member to have sufficient motivation to seek employment independently. In the TEP it is believed that the ability of a member to perform a TEP placement productively is not necessarily correlated to the individual's motivation to seek employment independently.

The presence of guaranteed part-time, entry-level work opportunities within the rehabilitative environment emphasizes to the members that *men-*

tal illness is not viewed as the sole or even primary explanation for vocational disability. It is, rather, a personal experience, one that typically prevented members from having normal opportunities to experience the real world of work and to develop capabilities to perform work productively and meet job requirements.

Transitional employment programs have been developed as a rehabilitative function of the normal work community. Although designed to meet the needs of the more severely disabled mentally ill, TEP placements have been integrated from the beginning with the work community rather than intentionally simulating the real world of work, yet clearly separate and apart, as in the case of the sheltered workshop.

THE EVENING AND WEEKEND PROGRAM

The evening, weekend, and holiday social-recreational programs offered by Fountain House are designed to meet the members' needs for companionship and socialization. Fountain House members can experience being with each other, taking part in art programs, photography, chess and other table games, dramatics, chorus singing — indeed, in a rich and varied program. In addition members have the opportunity to be participants in outside volunteer-led activities such as bowling, movies, tours, theater, and sporting events.

The evening and weekend program enables members to maintain longterm contact with the clubhouse after they have become fully employed, which is of primary importance to their adjustment in the community. Such contact enables the member to continue to benefit from the supportive relationships developed at Fountain House, as well as from specific services such as the educational and employment programs. Members must know that there is assistance and encouragement available to them in their efforts to obtain a better job or to pursue their educational aspirations.

The evening program is also helpful to members when difficulties arise, such as when a job is lost or there is a recurrence of illness. Through the evening program, staff and members become aware of such problems and are able to assist the member who is in difficulty. This might involve helping someone to get to a clinic for a change in medication, or to become hospitalized, or to return to full-time participation in the Fountain House day program.

THE APARTMENT PROGRAM

In an effort to provide less institutional, more normalized housing alternatives, Fountain House some years ago began to lease modestly priced apartments and to make them available to two or three members living together. It was felt that not only could Fountain House provide much more attractive apartments, furnishing them with contributions to the thrift shop, but that members living together could provide support, comfort, and understanding for each other. All apartments have kitchen facilities so that members may cook their own meals. Members pay their fair share of the rent and utilities.

Although the leases are initially held by Fountain house itself, it is entirely possible for a member or members to take on the lease once they have become stable and employed in the community. Apartments are located in various neighborhoods of New York City and many of them are located just across the street or in the immediate neighborhood of the clubhouse.

The apartments serve other important purposes. Resident members often host a new member who is still hospitalized and who is interested in exploring the kinds of living arrangements Fountain House provides as well as the activities of the clubhouse itself. With assistance from staff and other members, apartment residents have the opportunity to learn or relearn needed living skills, including housekeeping, cooking, budgeting, and getting along with a roommate.

Residence in a Fountain House apartment carries with it continuing active involvement in the clubhouse program as long as such participation facilitates the adjustment of the member. Fountain House does not provide apartments to individuals who are in need of housing but who are not at the same time seeking membership in the full Fountain House program.

REACH-OUT PROGRAMS

Often a member stops coming to Fountain House and it is not clear why he or she has done so. At other times a member requires rehospitalization. In both instances Fountain House feels that a reach-out effort from the clubhouse to the member is important, both to carry the message that the member is missed by fellow members and staff and to ascertain whether there is some way in which the clubhouse can help the member.

The reach-out function is intended to convey important messages to members—not that they must come back to the clubhouse, but that they are cared about, that they are missed when they don't come, and that Fountain House will try to supply whatever assistance they may require.

THE THRIFT SHOP PROGRAM

Many years ago Fountain House began to receive a number of telephone calls and written inquiries from people interested in its programs, some of whom expressed their willingness to make donations of goods they thought might be of value to Fountain House.

In response to these generous offers Fountain House established a thrift shop with several goals in mind. First, the shop makes possible the sale of donated goods at reasonable prices both to community residents and to members of Fountain House. The income from these sales converts donated goods into cash donations to the Fountain House program. Second, operation of the thrift shop provides opportunities for a variety of prevocational experiences for the members: warehousing, classifying, sorting and pricing merchandise, arranging merchandise attractively in the store, and meeting the public both as salespersons and as operators of the cash register. Volunteering in the thrift shop has been particularly appealing to, and effective for, older members.

CLUBHOUSE NEWSPAPERS

Some years ago it was felt that there should be a vehicle for alerting members of Fountain House to the activities available within it and to current news about fellow members and staff. A clubhouse newspaper was established that from the beginning was a cooperative effort of staff and members. The newspaper contributes to bringing the membership together, it provides a variety of work activities in the prevocational day program, and it also serves as a very powerful communicating tool that informs staff and members of other clubhouses about Fountain House activities.

Members have the freedom to say what they wish about the programs of Fountain House, about experiences in the house, about successes and failures, in articles that they are free to publish. This helps both the members who write articles and the members who read them to experience a deepening sense of participant contribution to and shared responsibility for the club that they and the staff bring to life and help to flourish.

CLUBHOUSE NAME

Fountain House believes that one of the very significant acts a clubhouse program can undertake is to establish its own name. In many instances — and there are many — when a clubhouse is a component of a larger mental health consortium, such as a community mental health center, it is critical that the clubhouse establish its own identity and a separate location in its own building. The name of the clubhouse thus comes to signify not only its identity but also its independence as a program. The name also can reflect the feeling the program is meant to convey. For example, The Green Door suggests a welcoming place; more traditional names of facilities are often not as suggestive.

MEDICATION, PSYCHIATRIC CONSULTATION, AND HEALTH

Fountain House plays an important role in helping members maintain themselves on prescribed medication and in ensuring that they get required psychiatric care. Most of the members view medication as both necessary and helpful in their adjustment and they are of significant assistance in reinforcing this attitude among other members. Staff and members become aware when other members seem to be suffering a relapse and often help the member in getting to the clinic or hospital for assistance. Part-time psychiatric consultation is also available at Fountain House in emergencies.

Members and staff also help other members utilize community health facilities. This is extremely important to members who do not have the financial and personal resources to secure such help independently. In this important sense, Fountain House plays a crucial family role in encouraging members to get the care they are entitled to and require.

EVALUATION AND CLUBHOUSE ACCOUNTABILITY

Fountain House believes it is imperative that a continuing effort be made to evaluate the effectiveness of its programs, a belief shared by responsible community-based day programs for chronically mentally ill patients living in the community. Characteristically, however, the justification for the necessity of evaluations has been the staff's need to know the effectiveness of programs. Fountain House believes that this central reason for evaluation must include the members' right and need to know what kinds of successes and failures each of the programs of Fountain House is contributing to in the lives of fellow members.

Fountain House considers it both natural and desirable that members themselves become significantly involved in the procedures that are utilized to evaluate program effectiveness. The major evaluation effort currently undertaken by Fountain House and other clubhouse programs, the Categories of Community Adjustment Study, is therefore to a very large extent being carried on by members of Fountain House with the assistance and guidance of staff.

* * *

In our view Fountain House type rehabilitation programs are especially well suited to persons with substantial institutional experience who are in the process of leaving, or have recently left, hospitals. Their comprehensiveness and steady, gentle tug toward community reintegration is responsible deinstitutionalization at its best. The potential problems with such programs have to do with their size, which invites hierarchization, and their sometimes doctrinaire commitment to *the* Fountain House Model. Also, in day-to-day operation they seem to have bought into the genetic-biologic-chronic-disease model of disturbed and disturbing behavior that's so fashionable among today's biologic psychiatrists and Alliance for the Mentally Ill members. This ideology runs counter to the program's push for true community integration of clients and makes us somewhat uncomfortable.

VOCATIONAL REHABILITATION

Transitional employment has been a feature of Fountain House Model programs for many years. This form of in-vivo paid work training and adjustment is clearly more normalizing than more traditional approaches centered on sheltered workshops and training for placement. In the U.S. there are presently 131 TEP programs, with 557 employers, providing over 1,360 jobs, yielding earnings of over five million dollars. The Fountain House research team recently surveyed the results of TEP programs, They found:

1. Following the start of a TE placement, the percentage of those who are independently employed steadily increases from 11% at the end of one year to 40% working on independent jobs at the end of three and a half years. Studies elsewhere report only 10–20% employment rates for similar populations.
2. Those who spent the longest period of time in Fountain House *prior* to entering the study also had the highest rate of independent employment—66%.
3. Length of time spent by individuals on TE was significantly related to the securing of subsequent independent employment.
4. The entire study sample represents the "target population"—severely vocationally disabled chronic psychiatric patients—and, in addition, no significant differences in background descriptive characteristics were found for those independently employed versus those who were not.
5. Psychiatric rehospitalizations following TE placement were both few (from 2 to 4% at any time) and of short duration (an average stay of only 26 days). Both of these figures represent a substantial change in pattern in the prior histories of the study sample. (Fountain House, 1985)

More recently, the rehabilitation field has begun to focus on "supported employment." This movement began in the early 1980s among the advocates and providers for the mentally retarded. By the mid-80s, after strong multiorganization lobbying efforts, the U.S. Congress passed a series of amendments to the Rehabilitation Act of 1973 that mandated supported work programs for persons with serious mental health problems. Supported work is of interest because, while overlapping with transitional employment, it is different from it in several more normalizing respects (Anthony & Blanch, 1987):

1. The trainees are involved in identifying work slots for themselves that are commensurate with their interests, abilities, career aspirations, and likes and dislikes. Hence, *non-entry-level jobs are possible.*
2. The jobs are sought via the usual application process (TEP's are usually given to programs). The difference between job complexity and job *stress* is factored into the process.
3. The reality of stigma is acknowledged and attempts to get around it are made. That is, for example, program support to the employee may not be given on the job site, and the employer may not know his employee has a history of mental health involvement. Support and a low stress environment during non-work hours are seen as critical.
4. The jobs are permanent and have, hopefully, career ladders.

For readers wishing more information, the entire October 1987 issue of *Psychosocial Rehabilitation* is devoted to supported work.

A brief note about several other work-oriented community-based rehabilitation programs is warranted:

The Fairweather Lodge program (Fairweather et at., 1969) provides a model that combines housing and work. It is a program that has been replicated many times across the U.S. As always, there are local variations, but the basic notion is to form a living group of mental health clients that will also sell their services in the open marketplace (e.g., maintenance, gardening, etc.).

In Italy, the cooperative is a common form of client-operated business. Prototypical cooperative activities are cleaning, gardening, and working in restaurants that feed both mental health clients and the public at large. Housing is not generally part of the arrangement.

The Boston Center for Psychiatric Rehabilitation, directed by William Anthony, Ph.D., has recently developed a new vocationally focused continuing education program that is both innovative and promising. Their brochure describes it as follows:

What is a Career Development Program?

A career development program is an innovative rehabilitation program that teaches young adults with psychiatric disabilities how to develop and implement a career plan. Students attend classes on a university campus to learn new skills that enable them to make decisions about choosing an occupation or additional education or training that leads to an occupation. With support from staff and other resources, students are helped to take the steps necessary to change their role from patient to student and worker.

Students learn how to develop a profile of themselves as workers and then to match these profiles to occupations. They develop short-term and long-term goals to begin the process of acquiring the occupations of their choice.

We have mentioned sheltered workshops only in passing for several reasons:

1. These traditional work programs are well-known and extensively used already (Bennett & Wing, 1963; Black, 1970; Wadsworth, Wells, & Scott, 1962; Wansbrough & Miles, 1968).
2. They are mostly nontransitional (in practice, if not theory), hence more dependency-producing and perpetuating than we like.
3. They violate our normalization principle. We would like their use to be kept to a minimum.

The Incentive Issue

Despite extensive experience with vocationally focused programs, there remains a major problem in the field around incentives. That is, at the present time most clients who successfully obtain work in entry-level jobs do not earn enough to make it worth their while to go off welfare principally because it usually comes with health insurance (Medicaid or Medicare). Mental-health-affiliated transitional employment programs basically train clients (when successful) to become members of the working poor. Whether this will also be true of supported work programs remains to be seen. The notion is only now really beginning to catch on. In many respects the working poor are the most disadvantaged group in American society; they usually can't afford decent housing, have no health insurance, and have jobs with no career ladders. The principal reward successful clients get is the satisfaction that comes from accomplishing the work task — but at the price of considerable security if they give up their welfare benefits.

Supported work and transitional employment programs are clearly preferable to sheltered workshops, "make work" in day programs, or long-term "employment" in clubhouse maintenance or volunteer work without prospects of eventually becoming paid. However, they have not yet solved the incentive conundrum described above. What appears to be needed now is a variety of experimental programs that focus on the issue of how to enable clients to get themselves out of the welfare-poverty-dependency cycle via truly rewarding work. Unfortunately, such programs have to operate within the United States' current welfare context. It is this context that makes it so difficult for clients to step out of the ranks of the poor and dependent. We wish we had a solution to offer to this very important problem but we do not. We hope that identifying and acknowledging it will begin a problem-solving process.

CHAPTER 10

Power to the People: Staffing

THE QUALITY OF PROGRAM STAFF, assuming a reasonable administration, is probably the single most important factor in creating a quality program. Staff qualities we will describe are, in our view, *generic* for clinicians working in community mental health programs. Hence, we believe a similar selection process can be used to hire staff for the mental health center team, adolescent and child and specialized addiction programs, and mental health affiliated housing.

We believe today's trend to train highly specialized "counselors" with limited range and flexibility of function is unwise. For example, persons trained in highly specialized alcoholism treatment programs who have only limited experience with other types of clients are likely to be very uncomfortable and unsure when attempting to deal with functionally psychotic persons. Staff who have learned to deal pretty much exclusively with mental health system "veterans" will likewise tend to feel at sea when the veteran has a simultaneous substance abuse problem; yet, at least among urban public sector long-term clients in the U. S., substance abuse is endemic — at least for the first few days of each month after an SSI check has been received.

In part because of a lack of breadth in training and experience among many front-line clinicians, the so-called "dually diagnosed" (mental illness and substance abuse) client may get short shrift in both systems. We believe there should be only *one system*, staffed mainly with broadly trained and experienced clinical generalists, to minimize the numbers of clients who are hard to serve because they don't "fit." This would represent a substantial improvement over the situation as it exists in most programs today. In our problem- and needs-oriented view, the same clinicians should be able to deal with substance abuse, depression or psychosis, especially since they not infrequently coexist or are serially present in the same client.

In our experience there is no necessary association between desirable attitudes and values and particular mental health relevant academic degrees. In fact, some of the characteristics of good staff (e.g., openmindedness, flexibility, and tolerance), are sometimes inversely related to the amount of formal training persons have received. This is particularly true of persons trained in institutions with a single dominant theoretical orientation. We recommend a staff selection process based more on competence than on degrees.

It is an unfortunate reality that pay is generally determined by training (i.e., type of degree) and experience using that degree. Time spent taking care of an ill relative or friend, being a volunteer community organizer, expanding one's personal strength and resources through reflective self-discipline (e.g., martial arts, psychotherapy) aren't usually rewarded with a higher salary. To develop an applicant pool that will contain properly degreed persons who also have such experiences, we advise that a wide advertising net be cast in terms of acceptable educational and experiential background. Selection can then take place from among a group of equally *formally* qualified candidates on the basis of the *informal* experiential and personality characteristics of known effective staff. A large net will also be more likely to produce an appropriate (i.e., to the particular locale) mix of socioeconomic strata of origin, race, ethnicity, and religion in the candidate pool.

We recommend that candidates be interviewed by as many persons as possible from the team they will join. In addition, the team manager (administrator), clinical supervisor, and the program's clinical director should see all viable candidates. Finally, if feasible, a representative of the consumer group associated with the center should be involved in the process. Final selection should be by consensus development among line team members and their immediate clinical supervisor. If the program director or consumer representative has a strong opinion that runs counter to the consensus selection, he must meet with this group to discuss his concerns; if his concerns are still unresolved after discussion, the team's selection should be hired. Note that this practice is in keeping with the principles of horizontal authority and responsibility, staff empowerment (Rose, 1985), and program unit independence we've already described.

We recommend that mental health center team staff also work on the associated 10-bed ward in a general hospital. This arrangement serves to

ensure continuity of persons and proper service coordination for hospitalized users. However, ward staff will need to be supplemented with additional staff, mostly nurses, to meet hospital staffing requirements, provide
continuity in the milieu, and allow mental health center staff to perform
their ongoing outpatient duties. Residential alternatives to hospitalization
and housing programs will need to have their own separate staffs with
coordination (a case management function) provided by the mental health
center's staff teams. Members of mental health center in-house teams will
need to be the most flexible and contextually thinking of all the staff.
Their job descriptions include in-residence and walk-in emergency crisis
assessment and intervention, case management, and in-office and in-home
psychotherapies. They provide the critical element of continuity of persons
for the clientele. In addition, some of the mental health center team staff
should have extensive experience with individual, group, and family therapy so they can supervise these therapeutic activities with less experienced
staff. These "renaissance" staff will require a great deal of morale attention,
through opportunities to interact with colleagues, live case supervision,
seminars, problem-focused groups, formal educational opportunities, and
the like.

Although most clinical supervisory personnel will have professional degrees and extensive experience, we see no reason why experienced, equally
competent, nondegreed persons should be excluded from these positions.
Unfortunately, community mental health programs are usually embedded
in city, county or state personnel systems that don't readily allow persons
with competence and experience, but without an advanced mental health
degree, to be eligible for supervisory positions (see, for example, the Morrisania experience, Chapter 12). The absence of a career advancement ladder can be very demoralizing for highly motivated, experienced, competent
nonprofessionals. If career ladders can't be erected for them, we recommend the development of mental-health-center-supported work-study programs leading to advanced degrees.

SELECTION

Based on the Soteria and Crossing Place experiences (Hirschfeld, Matthews, Mosher, & Menn, 1977; Mosher, Reifman, & Menn, 1973), the
literature on the characteristics of effective psychotherapists (Rogers, 1957;
Vandenbos & Karon, 1971; Newton, 1973; Schaffer, 1982; Strupp, Hadley,
& Gomes-Schwartz, 1977), and consulting experiences in a widely varied
array of community programs, we have been able to distill a set of personality attributes and life experiences of potential staff that should allow employers to be discriminating in their hiring practices. These attributes and

TABLE 10.1
Community Mental Health Staff Selection:
Desirable Personality Characteristics

1. Strong sense of self; comfort with uncertainty
2. Open minded, accepting, nonjudgmental
3. Patient and non-intrusive
4. Practical, problem-solving orientation
5. Flexible
6. Empathic
7. Optimistic and supportive
8. Gentle firmness
9. Humorous
10. Humble
11. Thinks contextually

experiences outlined in Tables 10.1, 10.2, and 10.3, are, we believe, relevant to the hiring process of all community mental health staff (including volunteers). They are guidelines, not recipes! They will need to be adapted to suit local hiring practices and work conditions.

We believe that self-selection, based on a complete and accurate job description, is probably the most important single factor in obtaining the right kind of staff for a particular program. We have found that most good staff bring the requisite values and attitudes with them. The program only provides a vehicle for their expression.

One reason we recommend that degree and relevant experience not be sole selection criteria for work in community mental health programs is the wish to avoid, as much as feasible, staff who have been taught tightly organized, overexplanatory theories of the etiology or treatment of dis-

TABLE 10.2
Staff Selection:
Relevant Experience

1. Dealt with real life problem
2. Lived with madpersons
3. Martial arts
4. Local community involvement
5. Training to look at and understand their reactions (e.g., psychotherapy, supervision)
6. Ex-consumer

TABLE 10.3
Staff Selection:
Deselection Characteristics

1. The rescue fantasy
2. Consistent distortion of information
3. Pessimistic outlook
4. Exploit clients for own needs
5. Overcontrolling and needing to *do* for others
6. Suspicious and blaming others

turbed and disturbing behavior. We believe it is easier to interact with individual mad persons from an interpersonal phenomenologic stance (i.e., open, accepting, without preconceptions) if previous learning does not have to be unlearned. It is also easier to learn and practice a family, network, and open systems point of view without a previously learned individual defect theory.

Hence, when interviewing potential staff it is useful to ask about their ideas about the nature and treatment of madness. Most people have some theory of madness. However, in our experience, tentative, open-minded, non-exclusive theoretical preconceptions do not create difficulties. However, doctrinaire adherence to *a* theory—no matter what its content—may create subsequent interactional difficulties. Research on harmful psychotherapists supports this clinically derived notion of ours (Grunebaum, 1986).

The characteristics that tend to make for effective staff are listed in Table 10.1. These attributes are clearly easier to list than to accurately assess in a pre-employment interview. Careful attention to applicants' in-interview language and behavior will usually allow the interviewer to evaluate their degree of self-confidence (#1). Asking interviewees their opinion of a hypothetical case of a person with a strong belief in a nontraditional religion or living an unorthodox lifestyle will often elicit information as to how open-minded and accepting they are (#2). Patience (#3) can be looked at in terms of persons' life histories; did they stay with jobs or family obligations that required them to postpone satisfying their own needs in favor of those of others? In relating information in this area their capacity to be empathic (#6) will also be assessable, because fulfilling other persons' needs requires empathic identification.

Number four—practical, down-to-earth, problem-solving orientation— can be assessed by asking the questions: How do you see your role with the clients? What will your overall orientation towards them be? We like to hear some version of a practical, problem-solving approach. Responses such as, "Those folks have real problems—maybe I can help them deal with them," or, "Life seems to have dealt them a bad hand—maybe I can help them learn to play their cards better," are used as positive selection criteria. Responses indicating a psychotherapy view of their role with clients, e.g., "I'd like to help them understand how they got that way," help to deselect potential staff persons.

Presenting a decontextualized case history and asking the candidate to generate an approach or a solution to the problem will allow contextual thinking (#11) to be evaluated by means of the kinds of additional information sought (if any) before answering. Flexibility (#5) can be looked at in terms of how a candidate can change from one possible problem solution to another when the interviewer arbitrarily designates the chosen one as a nonsolution. Firmness (#8) can be evaluated from the response to a child-rearing problem or from historical material. Sense of humor (#9) can be assessed by means of jokes inserted into the interview after a relationship has been established.

Braggarts (#10) will go out of their way to impress potential employers with their wonderfulness. After a great deal of experience with charismatic therapists and the mischief they can create, we've come to believe that humor and humility are very important characteristics. Good staff don't generally take themselves too seriously.

The six relevant experience variables (Table 10.2) are much easier to assess than the ones that have to do with personality. All one needs to do is ask candidates about their lives with these areas in mind. In terms of having dealt with a significant life problem, it has been our experience that persons who've had a modal American middle-class, suburban, intact, no-problem family upbringing don't generally make good staff.

In our original group of Soteria staff we found a surprisingly large number who had been invulnerable children in "vulnerable," problem-laden families. That is, they were frequently the rather neutrally regarded (by the problem parent in particular) caretaker child in the family. For example, one staff member was his fatherless family's principal housekeeper (at age nine) while his mother was nonfunctional because of an 18-month-long episode of unlabeled and untreated psychosis. His older brother, who was much closer to, and involved with, the mother, grew up with serious psychological difficulties, while our staff member developed into a highly competent person without serious problems.

We now look for this type of overcoming of serious adversity in the backgrounds of potential staff members. While obviously it is not always present, when it is we are more confident in our selection. We believe that the test-measured personality trait of high ego strength (Hirschfeld et al., 1977) we found in Soteria staff is also related to the process of successfully coping with these difficult life experiences. These experiences also seem to contribute to the responsiveness, flexibility, and tolerance needed to work in these settings. Without such experiences we found that staff had substantial difficulties relating to newly diagnosed, unmedicated psychotic clients for prolonged periods. At Crossing Place, with its "veteran" clientele, on-the-job development of the ability to "hang in there" can take place more easily than was the case at Soteria, because the amount of externally manifest madness is diminished, primarily because of the use of neuroleptics.

The attributes and experiences we've set out here must be taken with a grain of salt in the hiring process. They're helpful, but in no way exact. It is especially important to remember the context of the assessment interview — this situation can bring out the worst in some persons. We tend to believe that people who show up with a good understanding of the job, who are motivated out of real interest in doing what it entails, who have had difficulties in their lives, and whom we like will probably make good staff. It's probably unrealistic to expect them to exhibit a number of the personality characteristics we'd like to see in a short interview. These are better looked at in vivo, that is, on the job, over time. In our lighter moments we like to say that sainthood, i.e., having all these wonderful characteristics, call only become apparent after seeing someone actually working miracles.

Deselection

In terms of characteristics to watch out for (Table 10.3): The rescue fantasy (#1) can be tapped by asking applicants why they want to do this kind of work. Knights ready to grab their lances and mount their chargers will usually make themselves known by detailing an experience(s) that makes it vitally important for them to provide a better life for the clientele. However, we continue to be impressed by how many job applicants are truly motivated by altruism — a real interest in helping others, but without rescue fantasies.

Distortion (#2) can be picked up by asking candidates to convey their understanding of the job description to the interviewer. The last three variables on the list can be assessed by asking potential employees to describe their most and least successful interpersonal experiences or interventions with users. The "yes but" person is readily identified as a pessimist (#3). Overconcern with "what if" and liability issues generally indicate a rigid, frightened, moralistic person who won't be a good staff member.

MORALE MAINTENANCE

Burnout is a dysfunctional psychological state that seems to be most common among persons working in job settings characterized by a great deal of close interpersonal interaction under conditions of chronic stress and tension (Maslach & Jackson, 1979). The literature contains descriptions of it among the following mental-health-related disciplines: rehabilitation workers (Emener, 1979), counselors (Watkins, 1983), mental health workers (Pines & Maslach, 1978), social workers (Borland, 1981), special therapeutic community workers (Freudenberger, 1980, 1986), and physicians (Battle, 1981). Clearly, the conditions under which it occurs are endemic to community mental health settings and systems.

In our experience, this state involves various depression-like symptoms: low energy, disinterest, touchiness, unhappiness, and physical illnesses. Staff views of clients are affected by it as well; they will discuss clients in terms of hopelessness, chronicity, noncompliance, etc. (see Table 10.4). In fact, the symptoms of burnout generally parallel, in a less severe way, those of the clientele; low energy, lack of motivation, poor self-esteem, and a level of hopelessness that results in demoralization are generally sine qua non's of being a patient in the public mental health system.

The conventional view is that burnout stems, for the most part, from working with this difficult population, from the sense of powerlessness, helplessness, and frustration experienced by staff in their day-to-day work. While this is clearly an important factor, our experience has taught us that a more complete explanatory view is that burnout is an interactional product of setting, staff person, and client. Conventional wisdom attributes it almost exclusively to the client. In contrast, we ascribe great causal significance for burnout to the way in which the setting structures the staff's day-to-day working relationship with it and the clients it serves. The major issue is whether or not staff perceive themselves as being empowered to make, and feel responsible for, on-the-spot clinical decisions (see Table 10.5). The degree to which this empowered state can be truly experientially validated (thus preventing burnout) is closely tied to the size of the setting,

TABLE 10.4
Staff Burnout:
Description

1. No energy
2. No interest in clients
3. Clients frustrating, hopeless, chronic, unmotivated, untreatable, non compliant, acting out, etc.
4. High absenteeism
5. High turnover
The bottom line: Demoralization

TABLE 10.5
Staff Burnout:
Causes

---

1. Setting too hierarchical—staff not empowered
2. Too many externally introduced rules—no local authority and responsibility
3. Work group too large or noncohesive—no sense of "teamness"
4. Too many clients—not able to "understand," feels overwhelmed
5. Too little stimulation—routinization

The bottom line: Demoralization

---

number of layers in the organization's hierarchy, and the organization of the work group. We believe that these variables operate to reduce or produce burnout at all salary levels. Adequate pay, while it may reduce the incidence of burnout to some extent, will not, in and of itself, eliminate it.

An example: For intensive residential treatment settings the two ends of the hierarchy/size continuum are the large state hospital and small community alternatives. Twenty-to-thirty-bed wards in general hospitals fall midway on the continuum. In the large hospital hierarchy the lowest level of personnel ("aides," "technicians") have the most direct contact with patients and the least power. Clinical decisions must be cleared by a series of more powerful persons—the nursing staff, the head nurse, the ward administrator, the multi-unit administrator, and (occasionally) the hospital superintendent. Hierarchies like these tend to engender paralysis in the lowest level staff; they fear making important on-the-spot decisions as they may misstep; they fear taking responsibility as they may subsequently be blamed for a mistake. They want a rule from on high telling them what to do. These externally introduced constraints on their decision-making abilities in clinical situations are analogous to those often experienced by their clients in the mental health system. A similar psychological state results: learned helplessness, dependency, demoralization, and lack of motivation to participate actively in the planning and treatment processes.

For mental health center generalists, embedded in a context with a large number of actors, how the work is organized becomes crucial to whether or not burnout will be a frequent or unusual event. Mental health centers that pay reasonably, operate with small collegial teams, have reasonable workloads, and provide non-monetary educational "perks" will have a lower incidence of burnout than ones that don't organize the work this way. No matter how cleverly organized, community mental health programs must keep a watchful eye out for the sometimes subtle, but always pernicious, presence of burnout. Understanding why it occurs will allow its ongoing prevention and active treatment.

Regarding treatment and prevention of burnout (see Table 10.6), what must always be remembered is that, if the needs of clients are to be met, the staff must feel they have an accessible reservoir of energy from which to draw. Hence, meeting staff needs is no less important than meeting those of the clients. In fact, to avoid staff's exploiting clients, acting out against them, or being unresponsive to their needs requires constant attention to staff's own reasonable demands in the setting. Supervisor-staff relational processes should parallel those of staff-client relationships.

The principles involved in the "treatment" of burnout flow logically from the major causative factors outlined in Table 10.5. They are straightforward but may be difficult to apply in larger organizational units dealing with very disturbed and disturbing clients. The required elements: small working group size; minimal hierarchy; staff empowerment; and staff feeling they are valued members of a team whose needs will be responded to by

TABLE 10.6
Staff Burnout:
Prevention and Treatment

A. Principles
 1. Concrete accomplishments enhance morale.
 2. Staff must be empowered.
 3. Staff should feel membership in supportive team.
 4. Group experiences used to promote mutual trust and collectivity.
 5. Provide challenging new learning.

B. Specific techniques
 1. Group didactic teaching (e.g., incest, addiction, etc.).
 2. P.R.N. interpersonal problem resolution group.
 3. Regular problem case discussions with consultant.
 4. Staff teams learn and apply new techniques.
 5. Supervision (live, if possible).
 6. Parties.
 7. Coupling.

the bosses. These conditions are hard to attain in large hierarchical units. The importance of mutual support, consultative help, and a sense of trust and belonging that accrues from working in a small (six to ten person) collegial group should not be underestimated. Small is, once again, beautiful. The work group is the staff's social network in that context; as such, it is as deserving of care and attention as the clients' network.

A touching example of what can happen when staff are empowered and able to make decisions based on current circumstances is worth recounting:

> A 30-year-old woman came to Crossing Place after having been picked up wandering in a daze around the bus station. She arrived still dazed, very tired, uncommunicative and quasi-catatonic. She was able to tell us she was from a midwestern city and give a name and address. Her family (mother and uncle), had no phone so staff contacted the nearest police station and asked them to have family call Crossing Place. The relatives were overjoyed when they called because they had thought our client was dead since her purse had been found in New York City some days before. The uncle came by bus the next day to fetch his niece; our client came out of her daze when she saw her uncle. Staff offered them a ride to the bus station. In a simple, extraordinarily human gesture, the staff member asked the uncle if he'd ever been to Washington before. He said no. The staff member then took uncle and client on a whirlwind tour of the monuments, White House, and Capital Hill before dropping them at the bus station.

This is an example of immediately therapeutic interactions that occur frequently in settings where staff are empowered. The staff member's kindness, humaness, and generosity were subsequently acknowledged and complimented by staff-peers, director, and consultants.

A psychological principle underlying many helpful interventions is that restoration or maintenance of self-esteem, self-confidence, and morale is dependent on visible and acknowledged accomplishments or successes. Without being empowered, neither staff nor clients will be very willing to try things that might result in noticeable accomplishments. Hence, staff burnout is prevented by their feeling empowered so that their actions can facilitate success experiences with a notably unsuccessful clientele. In turn, they must both acknowledge clients' accomplishments, however small, and be acknowledged by peers and supervisors for having facilitated clients' successes.

For example, a client tells a staff person that he doesn't feel able to negotiate the process of getting into an apartment program (often based on a previous failure in trying to do so). Based on their judgment of that person's clinical state and knowledge of the nature of the application process to the apartment program, staff decide that the client will probably be successful if accompanied. If the process *is* then successfully negotiated, everybody wins; both staff and client have accomplished something that is real and visible. The staff person delivers lots of positive strokes to the client (who is also stroked by client-peers and other staff), and the staff person's role in the success is acknowledged by the client, supervisor, and staff-peer group. Remoralization is the outcome for client and maintenance of morale is the outcome for staff and setting.

There are a number of specific techniques for burnout prevention that flow from the five principles elucidated above:

1. *Didactic training exercises* focused around specific topics or techniques, such as dealing with incest victims or violence, use of trance, etc. They can be led by outside "experts" brought in specifically for the occasion or by in-house specialists. This provides the staff as a group with an opportunity to gain new knowledge and perhaps practice a new technique via role-playing. They grow together.

2. *Regular staff-only meetings focused on problems that have arisen between staff members.* These meetings can be led by the clinical supervisor. However, if similar issues keep resurfacing over time, we've found it's generally helpful to invite an outside "neutral" facilitator in to lead them. These therapy-like meetings not only solve problems, but also enhance group cohesion.

   These meetings (training and staff group with an outside facilitator) should be scheduled in response to problems as they arise. It is part of the clinical supervisor's job to be sure these needs are responded to in a timely and appropriate fashion.

3. *Client-oriented group consensus development meetings.* This activity is focused on perplexing and difficult clinical problems as related to individual and group relationship issues with clients and between staff. This meeting should be problem-focused, relationship-building, and supportive of both individual positions and differences among staff, while operating with the overall expectation that a consensus plan will eventually emerge. In our experience, this user-oriented meeting is best led by a consultant who knows the clients but doesn't run the program. It is focused on developing individualized approaches to each user's particular problems. These occasions would be called treatment planning meetings in most settings. Because of our emphasis on a collaborative planning and goal-setting process, we have tried, at times, to have clients attend these meetings. We've tried having one client at a time routinely present in these sessions, but this was experienced by many

clients as an inquisition or at least as overwhelming (there are usually 12–15 persons in the room because of students, split positions, etc.). We've also tried having several clients in attendance; this was difficult logistically and proved rather inefficient. It was also impossible to discuss certain background facts about clients (incest, abuse, etc.) in front of other clients because of issues of confidentiality. Our current practice is to ask individual clients to come to these meetings when there is a staff consensus and user agreement that it would be useful to hear their point of view firsthand.

4. and 5. *Team learning of new techniques* can occur didactically, by demonstration, by live supervision, or by case discussions. What is important is that staff continue to practice their new techniques within supportive peer groups. This will further mutual trust, collectivity, and validation of their acquisition of new techniques — a success, an accomplishment.

6. *Parties* are really just another way to ensure cohesion, trust, and mutual respect among staff. The basic paradigm is simple — parties away from the clinical setting. In the early phases of programs they are best organized by the power figures: the program director, supervisors, or specialist consultants. As a program becomes more settled and routinized, these events are best rotated among willing staff, whatever their programmatic role. We have found that two or three evening parties a year are important for maintenance of morale.

7. *Coupling*. Staff relationships outside the setting are another means by which staff treat or prevent burnout in themselves. These will generally evolve naturally out of the close working relationships established in family-like teams. They should be regarded by the program's leaders as interesting but basically none of their business. In our experience a number of such pairings have produced enduring relationships.

There are too many events over which individuals or groups have no control to ever guarantee minimal levels of burnout: Parents die, lovers leave, coworkers move on. However, careful attention to this burnout paradigm will at least allow the work setting to minimize its contribution to the demoralization that has come to be called "burnout."

CLINICAL SPECIALISTS

There are a number of persons with special technical knowledge and expertise who should be readily available as consultants to generic staff.

Concrete resources. At least one person should be specifically knowledgeable about what resources are available in the system, their criteria for eligibility, and how to facilitate client access to them. A non-inclusive list includes: jobs and job training; independent and supported housing; financial assistance (general relief, SSI, SSDI, housing subsidies, etc.); medical coverage and care.

Specialized therapeutic modalities. Consultation around these will require a psychiatrist and a Ph.D. clinical psychologist in most settings. A psychiatrist is unique in his psychopharmacologic and overall biopsychosocial integrative consultative expertise. Nurses can also provide this biopsychosocial integration, and hence are very valuable to programs, but they cannot prescribe and regulate medications.

A psychologist and in some instances a psychiatrist or other appropriately trained person can provide consultation/intervention around the use of trance and hypnosis, biofeedback, bioenergetics, acupuncture, meditation and relaxation, Gestalt practice, behavioral programming, social skills training, etc. Centers should attempt to have as many of these areas as possible covered by their own staff. It is also useful to have staff consultants in areas of family, individual, group, occupational, and art and other expressive therapies. It is our view that these areas are best dealt with when these consultants are individuals drawn from the generic staff pool who have special training, expertise, and interest in teaching.

Variety of therapeutic approach is as important to us as the heterogeneity of programs we espouse (our smorgasbord). Because of their focus on accomplishable tasks, occupational and art therapists are usually good staff for settings with acutely disorganized clients. As with other staff specialists, their roles should not be confined to the exercise of their unique skills.

In addition to providing consultation, teaching, and supervision around specific therapeutic techniques, Ph.D. psychologists give centers important research capabilities. This is particularly important because of our espousal of an outcome-based bonus system for clinicians. Its design requires considerable research expertise, sophistication, and experience. On-site psychologist(s) have the virtue of being part of the territory they will be researching—always an advantage for designing *relevant* research. They are more likely to be trusted to design evaluation research that taps variables clinicians define as appropriate to their approaches.

Good community mental health programs do not confine psychiatrists' or psychologists' roles to the areas of their *unique* competence. Doing so would artificially separate them from the team's overall functioning, provide them with decontextualized (hence limited) views of clients, and prevent their applying a variety of other skills they've acquired to a particular clinical situation. In sum, it would do the client and doctor a disservice. In the U.S. such selective use of highly degreed professionals is usually rationalized by the fact M.D.'s and Ph.D.'s are relatively expensive as compared with other disciplines. In Italy, with its doctor glut and flatter salary schedule, it is not a problem; in fact, M.D.'s usually outnumber social workers on the teams (see Chapter 11).

For us, to be able to recruit and retain highly trained professionals, who have a great deal to contribute if their training has been community oriented, it is important to have them apply the entire spectrum of what they know to clinical situations. In fact, these highly paid persons should be constantly challenged to expand and refine the breadth and depth of their skills. Although specialists in some respects, they are very useful generalists in others.

The American model program included in this volume (Chapter 12) uses its psychiatrists and Ph.D. psychologists in this way. Because their work is structured so that it provides them with the kinds of experiences described above, they are happy and stay despite pay that is lower than in private practice. Doctors, especially M.D.'s, have often been trained to believe that they are being poorly utilized if they are not "fully responsible for" or "in charge of" a patient's care. Experience in community mental health has shown that this is not only a false belief but one that gets in the way of being most effective in those contexts where authority and responsibility need to be widely shared. The consultative model we've described and recommended involves role reframing that should make the issue of professional territoriality moot for doctors. The staff teams in the Morrisania program are organized in this way; we detected little territorial concern and lots of job satisfaction.

In the system we propose there should be no financial reason not to hire as many doctoral-level persons as needed to maximize program effectiveness. Even without our proposed system of capitation-based national health insurance, the system's greatly reduced use of expensive hospital beds should free up adequate resources to hire "expensive" personnel. These savings are possible *now* within the public part of the American two-tier public/private mental health system. At the present time the average state spends 70% of its mental health budget on hospital care. As this percentage is reduced, a large number of dollars can be transferred to community programs. Proper planning on the state level will make *anticipated* savings from decreased bed utilization available to community programs on a 50 cents on the dollar basis a year or more *before* the savings actually occur. This will allow a transition period and provide money that community programs can use to start or expand the parts of their programs that will decrease hospital use (usually community residential alternatives). Reallocation of money from hospitals to community should be the highest priority. Experience has shown that it can be accomplished, despite institutional counter pressure, by a combination of strong leadership from the top and guaranteeing hospital workers continued employment, perhaps in a different setting.

ADMINISTRATORS

In our experience good clinicians find administration difficult and unrewarding. Hence, we believe that program administrators should be persons with relevant management training and experience. It is usually a mistake to use M.D.'s or Ph.D.'s in these roles. Their special expertise is more readily put to use if they do not have major administrative responsibilities. Their consultative roles are actually made more difficult if they are simultaneously "the boss."

There are, of course, clinicians who find administration challenging, interesting, and rewarding, and who have had sufficient experience with it to develop competence. These individuals (usually social workers in our experience) are extremely useful because they can manage programs in the context of their clinical knowledge.

Each program unit (e.g., adult services, alternatives to hospitalization, day programs; see Figure 8.2) should have one manager—an administrator—and one or more clinical supervisors. To ensure an ongoing mutual feedback and education process between clinicians and administrators, regular problem-focused meetings should be held involving all managers and program supervisors. In most cases one manager is sufficient for each service, whereas we estimate that one clinical supervisor will be needed for each extended family-size clinician group (six or eight or so). A relatively non-hierarchical organization of the mental health system preserves contact between individual program units and "the boss," while allowing each unit to operate relatively independently. Each unit has both responsibility for, and control over, its activities. Units that become larger than eight or ten clinical persons (as adult services would in this arrangement) should be subdivided. Again, small is not only beautiful, but functionally more effective as well.

CHAPTER 11

The Italian Experience

WHAT IS NOTABLE AND UNIQUE about the Italian psychiatric reform of 1978 is that a whole nation decided to do away with the state hospitals and has ever since demonstrated that it is possible to treat mental patients without resorting to these dinosaurs.

In the 1960s, when a movement for deinstitutionalization first started in Italy, the mental health care system was characterized by a massive institutionalization of mental patients, generally involuntarily committed, in large state hospitals. The legislation that supported the involuntary incarceration of mental patients in distant large institutions dated back to 1904.

Article 1 of the 1904 law opened: "People affected by mental illness *have* to be guarded and treated in mental hospitals when they are dangerous to themselves or others or of public scandal and are not, and cannot, be guarded and treated elsewhere." Initial admission, for up to one month of evaluation, was issued by the police magistrate, or in the case of an emergency by the police, after a medical certificate. Admission was entered on the person's criminal record. At the end of the evaluation, the patient was either discharged, or admitted permanently by court order. This implied the loss of his civil rights. In case of recovery, discharge was ordered by the court after the proposal of the superintendent of the hospital.

It was only in 1968, under the pressure of an already strong movement for psychiatric renewal, that amendments were issued as Law No. 431. This introduced several important innovations: Voluntary admissions were finally allowed, and the provision that admission to mental hospital be recorded on criminal record was revoked. The size of hospitals and of single wards and staff-to-patients ratios were also set and hospital words catchmented. Extramural facilities were established for aftercare.

Unfortunately, law 431 was implemented only partially, all the sections on commitment in the 1904 law remained unchanged.

DISSENT, 1961-78

In 1961 a group of radical psychiatrists led by the late Dr. Franco Basaglia took over the state hospital of Gorizia, a small city in northeastern Italy. They were imbued with the ideas of existential philosophy and shared a phenomenological approach.

Basaglia's approach was also clearly sociological in orientation, nonmedical, and to some extent antipsychiatric. However, it differed substantially from English antipsychiatry and the American radical movement in that it was less radical in principle and more pragmatic and action-oriented. Basaglia and associates were especially critical of the American radical movement, whose extreme libertarianism, in their eyes, could actually result in abandoning patients, especially in the case of the nonconsenting ones.

Basaglia did not question the existence of mental illness. He often used the term "bracketing," i.e., the suspension of judgments, applied to mental illness as disease (Scheper-Hughes & Lovell, 1987). The problem, he said, is not about the illness per se (its nature, causes, prognosis) but about the *consequences* of the illness. The consequences are very different according to the *kind of relationship* that exists between patient and treater, which in turn largely depends upon the social and economic status of the patient.

Thus the illness, as a clinical entity, plays just a secondary role; in fact, the same illness may result in very different outcomes depending on the degree to which the person's social role is preserved.

According to Basaglia, treatment is possible only if mental patients are free and have a relationship with clinicians characterized by reciprocity and empowerment. Within the institution, treatment is just another form of violence in that it aims at helping the patients adjust to the condition of being discriminated against.

What, then, can psychiatrists do? They can refuse to submit to, and carry out the institutional power mandate. Hence, they should "deny" or "negate" the institution. These ideas are synthesized in the Basaglian concept of "denial": The denied institutional mandate is replaced by attending to the real needs of individual patients.

The actual work within the hospital consisted in gradually removing all institutional barriers and restrictive practices. The wards were opened one after the other, allowing patients to move freely inside the hospital and even outside, in the city. Practices considered violent, like electroconvulsive treatment, isolation, and restraints were banned. In the case of an agitated person, members of the staff would remain with him as long as necessary; he would not be restrained.

Partial forms of patient government started within the first two years. A relatively small group of patients, the most active and motivated, formed a club and organized leisure activities. Meetings and assemblies were held in a great number. It is reported that in 1967 there were about 50 of them per week in the whole hospital. Everybody was invited to attend and express his own ideas. Especially "hot" institutional topics were welcomed and discussed animatedly.

Around 1970, the members of the original Gorizia group moved on to different cities (Arezzo, Ferrara, Parma and Reggio Emilia) where they showed that the model could be replicated in different geographic and sociocultural contexts. Basaglia moved to Trieste in 1971, where during the next six years he was able to phase out the state hospital and replace it with a comprehensive network of community services. Trieste became the prototype of the new Italian psychiatry, served as a model program for the reform, and was studied and publicized extensively (Bennett, 1985; Jones & Poletti, 1985; Mosher, 1982).

In 1973 Psichiatria Democratica (The Society for Democratic Psychiatry) was established, an organization constituted by the fathers and the followers of the movement.

THE REVOLUTION SUCCEEDS: LAW 180 OF 1978

Besides spreading ideas among mental health workers, administrators and the public domain, Democratic Psychiatry was also successful in getting political support. In the early '70s, left wing parties officially included the liberation of the mental patient and the reform of the psychiatric legislation in their political agenda.

However, in spite of the interest and the relatively universal agreement around the reform, nothing had been done legislatively by 1977. Then a small but very dynamic party, the Radical Party (holding about 5% of the seats in the parliament), launched a campaign to bring to referendum the 1904 psychiatric law. If the referendum passed, the existing psychiatric legislation would be completely repealed and the nation would be without a mental health system (no legal basis for the operation of mental hospitals and admissions, no budget, etc.).

Facing this possibility, the government quickly appointed a commission to compile a new law. Although Basaglia was not on the commission, he was consulted extensively and certainly set out its basic characteristics (although there were areas of compromise), so much so that the resulting law is popularly known as "the Basaglia law."

The law was ready and passed on May 13, 1978, just in time to avoid the referendum, as law N. 180: Voluntary and Compulsory Health Treatments. The main features of the law are the following:

1. Gradual phasing out of state mental hospitals by blocking all admissions. As an immediate provision of the law, no new patients could be admitted to state mental hospitals. Until December 31, 1980 (deadline postponed to December 31, 1981, in some regions), ex-hospital patients could be readmitted voluntarily; after the deadline no patient could be admitted.

   It is prohibited to construct new mental hospitals and to use the already existing ones as psychiatric facilities of general hospitals.

   New services to be developed have to be staffed by existing personnel, i.e., drawn from mental hospitals.

2. Treatment will ordinarily take place outside the hospital, with community-based facilities responsible for definite geographical areas, for which they have to provide the full range of psychiatric interventions.

3. Hospitalization (either voluntary or compulsory) is regarded as an exceptional intervention, to be used only if community treatment is not feasible or has already failed, and can take place only in small units located in general hospitals (no more than one 15-bed unit per hospital).

4. Compulsory evaluation and treatment in the hospital may take place only if (a) urgent intervention is required, (b) the necessary treatment is refused, (c) community treatment cannot be opportunely implemented. Certificates by two doctors (one must be from the National Health Service) making independent evaluations are required to initiate the compulsory action, which then has to be approved and actually ordered by the mayor, or his designate, acting as local health authority. Independent judicial review is required at two and seven days. The patient and any interested party may make a court appeal. Patient's civil rights must be safeguarded.

The closing of the "front door" of mental hospitals by blocking all admissions drastically interrupts the path of institutionalization and will eventually make the mental hospital disappear "by extinction." At the same time, existing mental hospital patients are not "dumped" in the community since the law does not force their discharge, instead recommending a gradual process of rehabilitation. Hence, it is better seen as a *non-institutionalization* rather than a deinstitutionalization law.

In contrast to other countries with community psychiatry, where alternative services have simply been added to those already existing, including the mental hospital, Italy has developed a psychiatric system *without* the mental hospital, knowing that the adding of new services eventually recruits new patients but leaves the mental hospital unaffected. Interestingly enough, the law dictates that the new services are to be staffed with the existing mental health personnel, thus stressing again the principle of reallocating the resources in order to change the system.

As to the provisions for involuntary commitment, notice that the criterion of dangerousness is not listed. In fact, Law 180 is conceived as a public health law and therefore deals with treatment, not with custody. In this it differs fundamentally from the 1904 law. The legislated characteristics of the inpatient facilities demonstrate concern with the risk of reproducing the mental hospital on a smaller scale.

On December 23, 1978, the law was incorporated in the act that launched the Italian National Health Service, Law N. 833. This fact, which deeply influenced the implementation process, is important in that it framed the psychiatric reform in a profound and comprehensive reform of the whole health system.

The Italian National Health service made health care available to all citizens and created a local administration (Unità Sanitaria Locale—U.S.L., i.e., Local Health Unit) that is responsible for planning and implementing the local health system and for distributing resources within each catchment area (50,000 to 200,000 inhabitants). Basaglia was appointed a special position, created for him in Rome, of superintendent of psychiatric services of the city and the surrounding region. Unfortunately, he died shortly afterwards, in August 1980; with his death the movement lost its charismatic leader and the law its promoter and principal supporter.

Moreover, law 180 was passed in times of economic recession and political instability following the assassination of Aldo Moro, the leader of the Christian Democrats, by the terrorists of the "Red Brigades." Rumors of both CIA and KGB involvement were rife. Fears of an Allende-type overthrow were also fairly widely engendered. Repressive antiterrorist measures running counter to traditional Italian anti-authoritarianism were allowed. Political activity became more muted and careful; the national reaction can be best described as widespread demoralization. In this context the energy, dedication, and zeal necessary to implement already legislated reforms was difficult to sustain. Security consciousness, control, and caution became the order of the day. Incidentally, Moro's body was found May 9; Law 180 was passed May 13, 1978.

Because the law was not being implemented at the same pace throughout the country, discontent grew and fed opposition to the law. A number of proposals were presented from different parties to modify Law 180, mitigating its revolutionary character. Although confirming the goal of phasing out existing mental hospitals, these proposals included a provision to allow the opening of departments for intermediate and long-term care of chronic patients. Family organizations were also instrumental in voicing discontent (but there is also a movement of families *in favor of* Law 180).

However, no proposal went very far. In addition, a proposal presented by the government in 1986, trying to integrate all previous ones, was abandoned *because there was no economic coverage.* Counterreformation is troubled, even before it starts, by the same problem as the reform!

For these reasons and because of other local economic and organizational difficulties, especially in southern regions, Law 180 has certainly not been fully, and especially *evenly*, implemented yet. No question, then, that it still elicits a fierce controversy. In the international literature, comments span from full and enthusiastic support (Lacey, 1984; Mosher, 1982, 1983a, 1983b) to a very critical and pessimistic stance (Jones & Poletti, 1985). Official appraisals of the services of specific areas have been very positive (Bennett, 1985; Jablensky & Henderson, 1983). In addition, there is already a bulk of data, regarding specific services, showing that where the reform has been appropriately implemented, it works well (Burti el al., 1986; Martini, Cecchini, Corhito, D'Arco, & Nasambeni, 1985; Tansella & De Salvia, 1986; Torre & Marinoni, 1985).

EFFECTS OF LAW 180 ON THE ITALIAN PSYCHIATRIC SYSTEM

For the purposes of this book, the effects of Law 180 on the Italian psychiatric system may be outlined as follows*:

1. The number of mental hospital inpatients has decreased from about 60,000 before the reform to less than 30,000. Figure 11.1 shows annual data regarding Italian state mental hospitals between 1962 and 1981. The maximum number of inpatients was in 1963, and has declined ever since.

---

*The interested reader will find an extensive appraisal of the implementation and effects of Law 180 in Mosher & Burti, 1989, Chapters 12 and 13.

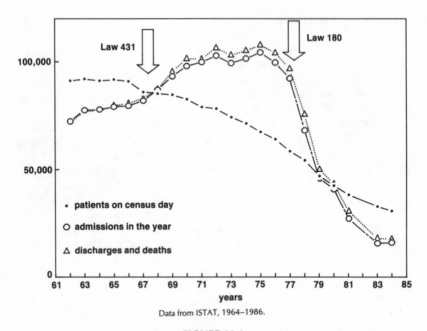

Data from ISTAT, 1964–1986.

FIGURE 11.1
Italy: State Mental Hospitals (1962–1984)
Indices of Hospital Activity

2. Closing of the front doors of the state mental hospitals *prevented*
   the institutionalization of new patients or the reinstitutionalization
   of those discharged. This has occurred without either an increase
   in the number of admissions to private hospitals or an increase of
   short-term admissions to general hospital units. Actually, the *over-*
   all inpatient care rate (including admissions) has remained stable
   since the reform. A visual inspection of Figure 11.2 shows that
   after the reform the overall rate of inpatient care did not increase,
   but remained stable, with the general hospital units progressively
   taking over the patient load at the expense of state hospitals, while
   private institutions maintain their positions. The most dramatic
   change occurred with regard to compulsory hospitalizations, which
   dropped from 32,521 in 1977 to 13,375 in 1979, with corresponding
   rates of 57 and 23 per 100,000 population, respectively (Misiti,
   Debernardi, Gerbaldo, & Guarnieri, 1981). In 1984 compulsory

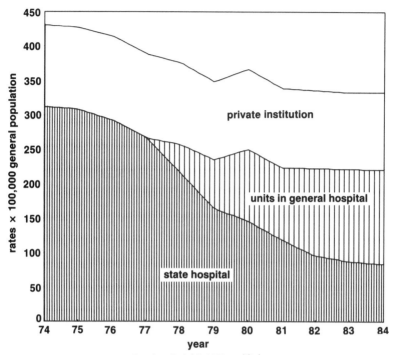

Data from De Salvia 1983, modified.

FIGURE 11.2
Global Inpatient Care in Italy (1974–84)

hospitalizations were about 15,800. In the areas with effective and comprehensive community services rates were even lower than 10 per 100,000 (De Salvia, 1984; Tansella, De Salvia, & Williams, 1987).

3. Both inpatient services (general hospital units) and outpatient services (community mental health centers) have been developed throughout the country and are available to more than 80% of the Italian population in their own catchment areas (U.S.L.s). According to most recent data provided by the Central Institute of Statistics (ISTAT, 1991) psychiatric units in general hospitals score 5441 beds (9.4 per 100,000 population), with 85,719 admissions a year and an average length of stay of 18 days.

A comprehensive national survey reports that one-fifth of admissions are involuntary commitments. The average national annual rate is about 36 per 100,000 adult (>14 years) population. As to readmissions, they are about one-third (34.1%) of all admissions (CENSIS, 1985). Staffing is mainly medical, having come from the mental hospitals and generally lacking formal training for the new job.

Regarding community services, the CENSIS survey reports 675 community services active as of December 31, 1984,* out of 694 U.L.S.s existing in Italy. Unfortunately, community services are not evenly distributed: considerable differences among regions exist. Yet, the overall picture is one of a comprehensive network of community services extended to the whole nation—a tangible sign that the implementation of the reform has actually progressed.

4. The flaws have mainly to do with limited resources. The reform has been made more difficult from the beginning by cuts in the health budget. In addition, the state hospital system still consumes about 80% of the national mental health budget, in spite of the fact that the number of patients has been reduced by 50% since the reform (Ongaro-Basaglia, 1987). There is also a delay in the transfer of the personnel from the mental hospitals to community services. All this results in delays in the development of community services. This is especially true of those regions in the south which were already lacking in social services. Other problems identified are poor integration of services, poorly trained personnel, and lack of routine participation by the medical schools.

However, the evidence is that where both hospital and community services have been developed, i.e., in a vast part of the country, the reform has been implemented successfully.

THE SOUTH VERONA COMMUNITY
PSYCHIATRIC SERVICE

The South Verona Community Psychiatric Service is presented here as a model program implementing the reform.

The psychiatric department of the University of Verona, established in 1970 as a typical Italian university psychiatric department, progressively developed a community program and was ready to assume responsibility of a catchment area when the reform was passed in 1978. In 1980, the Commu-

---

*Data on community services are not collected routinely by ISTAT.

nity Mental Health Center was founded, which has been operational ever since; it underwent successive changes over the years, as expected, because it is meant to be a flexible tool to meet the needs of the users at any given time (Faccincani, Burti, Garzotto, Mignolli, & Tansella, 1985).

The South Verona Area

Verona is a city of about 260,000 population, located in northeast Italy, halfway between Milan and Venice, in the region called Veneto (capital city: Venice). The South Verona area consists of three suburban districts and three small rural communities in the southern outskirts of the city. Resident population is 75,000.

Staff, Facilities and Service Organization

The permanent staff assigned to South Verona includes nine psychiatrists, three psychologists, three social workers, and 24 psychiatric nurses. There are also, at any given time, 13 psychiatric residents (they work full-time and on average stay two years and four to six medical students in training, who attend the service for four months on a rotation basis, and a variable number of volunteers. Professional staff are also engaged in teaching and research, so, for example, three of the eight psychiatrists do only limited clinical work. Staff members are divided into three multidisciplinary teams, each referring to a subsector of the catchment area (Figure 11.3).

With the exception of 10 nurses who cover the three round-the-clock shifts in the hospital unit, all staff work in both the intramural and the extramural programs. In other words, the *same* personnel staff *all* the programs ("single-staff" module) within and outside of the hospital.

The South Verona Community Mental Health Service offers the following programs (Zimmermann-Tansella, Burti, Faccincani, Garzotto, Siciliani, & Tansella, 1985):

- *Community Mental Health Center*, open six days a week, from 8 a.m. to 8 p.m. This facility is used in different ways: as a day hospital for chronic patients, as a walk-in center, as a place where staff meet and extramural interventions are planned and coordinated. It is considered the main facility of the service.
- *Psychiatric unit*, an open ward of 15 beds located in the university medical center (about 1,000 beds total).
- *Outpatient department*, which provides consultations, individual and family therapy. No group therapy is presently available, but there have been groups in the past.

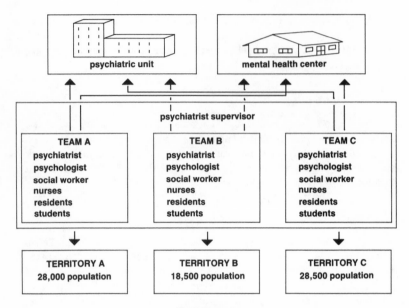

FIGURE 11.3
South Verona Community Psychiatric Service

- *Home visits and other extramural interventions*; these are made by all staff members in reply to emergency calls and for follow-up purposes and long-term care. The latter have proved very useful to *prevent* relapses of chronic patients and hence reduce the frequency of rehospitalization. Visits to known "high-risk" patients are planned in advance and offered on both a regular and an as-needed basis, so as to provide continuing support and care to our most difficult patients and their families.
- *Psychiatric emergency room*, part of the casualty department of the medical center. During working hours the psychiatrist on duty is usually assisted by a member of the team, who is (or will become) responsible of the patient requiring the emergency intervention; this is done in order to extend the practice of therapeutic continuity to persons to the emergency room.
- *Psychiatric consultation-liaison service*, providing consultations for patients and doctors of other departments of the hospital.
- *Residential facilities*. Two apartments are available for up to six

people who do not need supervision overnight. Two other apartments house a therapeutic community; it started on November 1, 1987 with three patients and can accommodate up to eight people. It is for disabled "veterans" who are unable to live independently and who either do not have a family or cannot, for whatever reason, live with their families. Although it is intended as a transitional accommodation, permanent stay is accepted if the patient does not have a more appealing alternative.

Transitional work opportunities are provided by two public sheltered workshops in town and a number of other initiatives run by charitable organizations and self-help groups. Some of these also offer residential accommodations.

A cooperative, paid for by the municipality, provides supporting persons at home to help the disabled and their families in tasks like cleaning, cooking, shopping, etc. Several South Verona mental patients receive this kind of service. The same cooperative provides job opportunities for those patients whose work incapacity is not too serious, yet serious enough to handicap them in these times of high unemployment rate. A gardening cooperative for more disabled mental patients is on the drawing boards.

Principles of Intervention

The service believes its principal responsibility is to the *more disturbed and disturbing* individuals, to whom it attempts to provide care in the *least restrictive environment*, i.e., with a minimum use of the hospital.

Since the use of crisis teams reduces hospitalization, as has been extensively documented by systematic research, crisis intervention techniques have been given high priority. Home visits are highly regarded and especially encouraged for this purpose. They are usually made by more than one worker, usually a *team* of two or three, *including a psychiatrist.*

In the experience of the South Verona group, home visits involving multidisciplinary teams serve also as an effective means to increase group spirit, to prevent burnout, and to train the staff in the development of effective, alternative intervention strategies. However, experience has shown that crisis intervention alone is not enough, especially in the case of chronic recidivists: The service has to focus on *preventing* crises by following up patients and providing counseling and support to families on a regular—usually weekly but at times daily—basis.

At the South Verona Community Service continuity of care is facilitated by the same staff members' working in both the intramural and extramural programs ("single staff" module). The same persons follow the same patient wherever he/she is treated at any given time. This greatly facilitates the build-up of personal, trusting, often affectionate relationships between staff and patients. Usually, and especially in the case of chronic patients and those at risk of becoming chronic, a core team of two or three workers is assigned to each patient so that at least one is available, in spite of turnover, shifts, vacations, etc. Patients are encouraged to come or call any time they feel they need help, without an appointment or a referral. If a patient shows up, he is likely to find one of his therapists, somebody he knows and trusts already—a real asset in case of excitement and behavior disorganization, when personal relationships are a key resource to solve the crisis.

Casework, case management and advocacy are everyday routines. The work with families deserves special mention. Since most patients (83%) live with their families, much work is done with them in terms of supportive counseling or family therapy. Some families are seen in formal family sessions, using the one-way screen and based on methods developed by the Milan school (Selvini-Palazzoli, Boscolo, Cecchin, & Prata, 1978), the so-called systemic family therapy. New cases seem to benefit greatly from this approach, both in terms of symptom reduction and prevention of dependency on hospitalization. In contrast, families with "veterans," i.e., patients with long careers as patients, resist, drop out easily, and look for more traditional approaches (hospitalization, medications; Burti, Faccincani, Mignolli, Siani, Siani, Siciliani, & Zimmerman-Tansella, 1984). However, the systemic approach has, overall, proved to be very useful in community work with families: It provides a relational model of interpretation for symptomatic behaviors and family reactions and also clarifies the role of the service and of other contextual components. Most professional members of the staff have training in family therapy and use the model extensively.

Teamwork and the Training of Residents

All important decisions regarding patients are taken within the team, after extensive discussion. A 15- to-30-minute case-centered meeting takes place every morning. In addition, there are two one-and-one-half-hour team meetings per week; one takes place in the center, while the other takes place in the unit, the latter in order to (1) have more direct information about those patients who are currently admitted, and (2) involve the nurses on duty in the unit, who otherwise have few opportunities to be involved in teamwork. In addition, there is a one-hour single case discussion once a week. Seminars are held on a quasi regular basis.

Minimal hierarchy and authority based on actual experience rather than academic credentials are stressed. Residents in training, who necessarily have only limited experience, work closely with the nurses, who have extended experience in community work, to their mutual advantage. Each resident has a caseload of 8–12 patients whom he follows continuously, across programs, during all his training period. This results in meaningful personal relationships between the residents and the patients and provides the trainee with a *longitudinal* perspective of the cases—a rare feature in residency programs. Residents and nurses are given a great deal of responsibility and initiative; if they have to make an important decision on the spot, such as admitting someone to the unit, they know it will be endorsed by the team. Staff professionals act more as coordinators and facilitators than as supervisors. In especially difficult cases they are ready to back up residents and nurses and to join them in the field. The fact that workers are never left alone, that they can count on reciprocal supervision in the team, as well as minimal hierarchy and empowerment, contributes to prevention of burnout, which is rarely seen in South Verona. Last but not least, although several professionals on the staff have had a formal training in systemic family therapy, teamwork encourages more interdisciplinarity than specialization—systems theory is by no means a credo.

Other Psychiatric Agencies in Town

In addition to the South Verona Community Psychiatric Service (CPS), in Verona there are the following mental health agencies:

- The state psychiatric hospital, with 366 long-stay patients, 18 of whom are from South Verona (as of December 31, 1986).
- Three outpatient services for children and adolescents (0–18 years).
- Two private psychiatric hospitals (with a total number of 220 beds). Their referrals come from the Verona province (including South Verona), but also from out of the region. According to our psychiatric register, 61 people from South Verona have been admitted to them in 1986.
- Two psychiatric units and two outpatient services in another general hospital in town, serving the two other territories of the U.S.L., which include part of downtown Verona and a mountainous district for an overall population of 111,000 (service No. 1), and the rest of downtown Verona and a rural district with an overall population of 123,000 (service No. 2). Unlike the South Verona service, these two do not have a community center yet; they use instead part of the ward for day care. There are consultation facili-

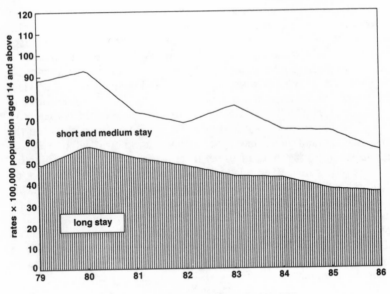

Data from Tansella, Balestrieri & Meneghill, 1979–1987.

FIGURE 11.4
Inpatient Care in South Verona (1979–86)
One-day Prevalence

ties outside, in the territory, with a psychiatrist and paraprofessionals one or two days a week, two sheltered workshops, and some
apartments.

PSYCHIATRIC CARE IN SOUTH VERONA: SOME DATA*

The great majority of the South Verona residents requiring some kind
of psychiatric intervention (long-stay inpatients of the mental hospital are
not included) are assisted by our Community Psychiatric Service. In the
years 1983–86, for example, an average 71.0% of the South Verona psychiatric patients were treated by the Community Psychiatric Service only,
4.2% by other institutions as well, and 24.8% only by other institutions.

---

*The data reported in this section have been extracted from the South Verona Psychiatric
Case Register's annual reports (Tansella, Balestrieri & Meneghelli, 1979–1987) as well as from
other relevant published papers.

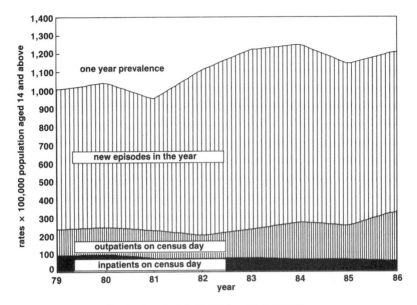

Data from Tansella, Balestrieri & Meneghill, 1979–1987.

FIGURE 11.5
Patient Care in South Verona (1979–86)
One Day and One Year Prevalence

Drug addicts, who by definition are followed by another service, are excluded. This low utilization of other services occurred despite ready availability of psychiatric beds in the private hospitals and outpatient facilities.

Distributions of various types of care in the years 1979 to 1986 are represented in Figures 11.4 and 11.5. Inpatients on one day (one-day prevalence represent the *rates* per 100,000 adult population, i.e., aged 14 and above) of patients already in the hospital on census day (December 31st of the previous year). Inpatients are divided by length of stay: long-stay patients were defined as those who have been in hospital for one year or longer on census day; short and medium-stay, those who have spent less than one year in hospital at the same date.

Outpatients on one day (one-day prevalence) are defined as those who had a contact on census day plus those with a "current episode" of outpatient care (i.e., those who had an outpatient contact both *before* and *after* the census day with less than three months between visits). One year preva-

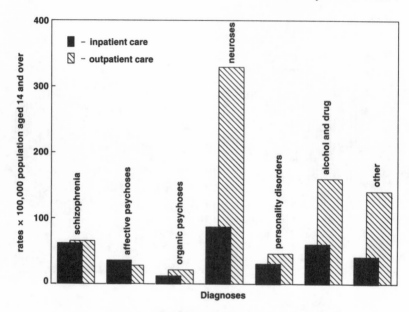

Data from Tansella, Balestrieri & Meneghill, 1979–1987.

FIGURE 11.6
Mean One-year Prevalence Rates by Diagnosis, South Verona (1979–86)

lence is also (one-day prevalence plus new episodes in the year) presented in Figure 11.5 (additive graph).

It may be observed in Figure 11.4 that the one-day prevalence of long-stay (one year or more in hospital on census day) inpatients remained unchanged from 1979 to 1982 and has been diminishing since, reflecting the trend of the mental hospital to disappear "by extinction." It is well-known that the mental hospital is the main place where long-stay used to accumulate. It is worthwhile to note that in South Verona, while the closure of the front door of the state mental hospital has stopped the main form of recruitment of potential new long-stay patients, these patients have not become long-stay elsewhere, i.e., either in the general hospital unit or in private hospitals (Balestrieri, Micciolo, & Tansella 1987). Short- and medium-stay patients show a noticeable decrease in the same period, thus giving an early indication of the shift from hospital to community care.

The total one-year prevalence remained fairly stable over the years (Figure 11.5). Rates (about 1%) are lower than those reported in other countries

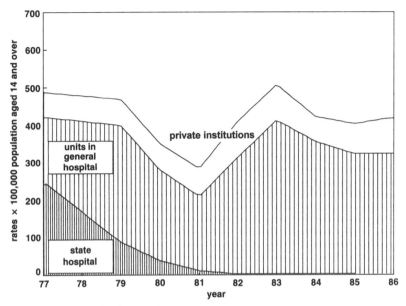

Data from Tansella, Balestrieri & Meneghill, 1979–1987.

FIGURE 11.7
Admissions of South Verona Residents
Before (1977) and After (1979–86) the Psychiatric Reform

(Babigian, 1977; Dupont, 1979; ten Horn, 1980; 1986; Wing & Fryers, 1976; Wing, Wing, Hailey, Bahn, Smith, & Baldwin, 1967), but similar to those found in other areas in Northern Italy (Tansella et al., 1987; Marinoni, Torre, Allegri, & Comelli, 1983).

Figure 11.6 reports the mean one-year reported prevalence (data cover the period 1979–1986; annual prevalences were averaged), by diagnosis and type of contact. All South Verona subjects who contacted psychiatric services during the calendar year were divided into two groups: those receiving outpatient care only (outpatient care) and those with at least one hospitalization during the year (inpatient care).

Schizophrenia and affective psychoses are the most represented diagnoses among patients admitted in the year. Neuroses and psychosomatic disorders are the most represented diagnoses among patients never admitted in the year, i.e., patients treated only in the community. However, it should be noted that a substantial proportion of subjects with a diagnosis of psychosis having psychiatric contacts during the year are treated without admission to the hospital. In the years 1979–1986 the ratio of patients receiving outpatient treatment only to patients admitted to the hospital during the year (outpatient care/inpatient care), is 2.41; i.e., people treated as outpatients *only* are more than twice as many as those admitted at least once in the year. These data confirm the community orientation of our approach.

Figure 11.7 shows data on inpatient care in South Verona one year before (1977) and eight years after (1979–1986) the psychiatric reform. The number of admissions to the state hospital dropped to zero in 1982, in compliance with the law. The total number of admissions to inpatient facilities decreased by 14%, (while the total number of hospital days and mean number of occupied beds decreased by 45%). These figures refer to *all* inpatient beds in Verona, including private ones. However, the most impressive feature regards compulsory admissions, which in the years after the reform (1979–1986) varied between ⅓ to ⅒ of those recorded before the reform (Figure 11.8).

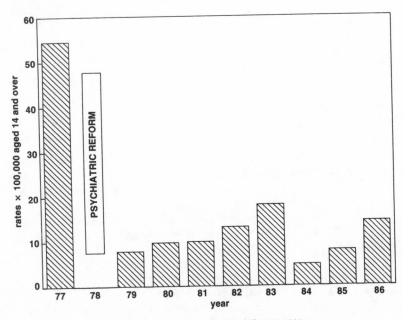

Data from Tansella, Balestrieri & Meneghill, 1979–1987.

FIGURE 11.8
Compulsory Admissions of South Verona Residents
Before (1977) and After (1979–86) the Psychiatric Reform

A study (Tansella, 1989) did not reveal any accumulation of *new long-stay* patients in the period 1980–1985. These results are in contrast with those reported in other countries (Häfner & Klug, 1982; Wykes & Wing, 1982). The study revealed instead a consistently increasing number of new long-term patients (Figure 11.9). However, in terms of outcome, there seem to be important differences between the long-stay and the long-term status. A follow-up study was performed on two cohorts of chronic patients: 25 long-stay and 29 long-term patients (Balestrieri et al., 1987). The two cohorts were comparable as to diagnostic category and sociodemographic characteristics. At two-year follow-up 22 (88%) of the long-stay patients were still long-stay and the remaining three had died. In contrast, only 13 (45%) of the long-term patients were still long-term (Figure 11.10); three had died, one had become long-stay, five were still followed, but not as intensively to qualify them as long-term, and seven were out of care.

The authors draw the conclusion that, unlike the mental hospital, community services do not foster a rigid pattern of "chronic" dependency on the institution. What happened to those patients was that after an acute

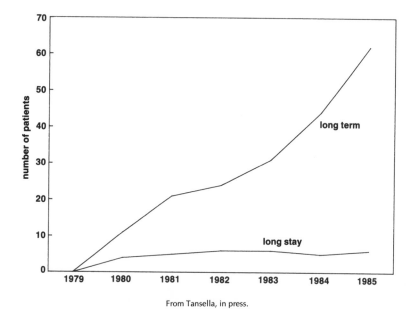

From Tansella, in press.

FIGURE 11.9
Number of New Chronic Patients
South Verona (1979–1985)

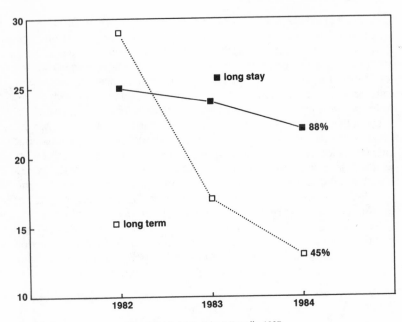

From Balestrieri, Micciolo, & Tansella, 1987.

FIGURE 11.10
Outcome of New Chronic Patients,
South Verona, 2 Year Follow-up

episode, during which they were closely followed by the services (and this qualified them for "long-term" users), they recovered or improved and had fewer contacts. In other words, community services would have more flexible patterns of care, with seemingly lower chronicity-inducing effects.

In addition, *none* of the *first-ever* patients contacting the South Verona community service since 1978 has become a long-stay inpatient, neither in the South Verona hospital unit nor in the private hospitals (which they can access easily if they wish), let alone in the state hospital, where admission is prohibited by law.

In conclusion, these data seem to show that in the past eight years the South Verona community psychiatric service has faced *all* the problems presented by psychiatric patients living in the territory, without the backup of the traditional state hospital. The stopping of all admissions (including readmissions) to the state hospital did not overload community services, nor did it bring about a shift to the private care system. Moreover, with the exception of a temporary increase in admissions to the South Verona inpatient unit in 1982–1983, probably a transient effect of the stopping of readmissions to the state hospital (effective January 1, 1982), total annual admissions have shown a decreasing trend: the revolving-door phenomenon has *not* been observed. This might be conservatively interpreted as an effect of the implementation and continuing improvement of alternative community services. In sum, data seem to confirm the expectation that a comprehensive, community-based psychiatric service providing both crisis intervention and continuity of care in the community can effectively reduce the need for hospitalization of psychiatric patients, including the most serious ones, who traditionally spent long periods of their lives in closed institutions.

CHAPTER 12

Working Against the Odds: Morrisania Mental Health Services, South Bronx, New York

INTRODUCTION AND BACKGROUND

THIS CASE STUDY IS ABOUT A VERY SPECIAL SOCIAL CONTEXT. It is about a program that struggles daily with America's most distressing social realities—unemployment, poverty, racism, homelessness, violence, substance abuse, teenage pregnancy, crime and family disruption—all resulting in multigenerational demoralization. It is the description of a mental health program located in one of America's worst urban disaster areas—the South Bronx.

The program's ten-year-old building faces the abandoned, decaying Morrisania Hospital, with its rock-broken windows. The four-block walk from the "L" on the Grand Concourse reminds one of a scene from an end-of-civilization science fiction movie. Former President Carter highlighted the plight of the South Bronx, but little construction or rehabilitation of buildings has taken place since then. The still extant small shops are triple locked and barred. Disillusionment, frustration, and hopelessness are almost palpable. At 9 o'clock in the morning, many of the men we passed were already intoxicated—why not, what else is there to do? An affluent society's garbage dump. Is it *possible* to be mentally healthy living in such a context? Can a mental health program be anything but a cruel sop tossed out amidst the rubble to give the *illusion* of addressing the problem? Would its budget be better spent as direct grants to families?

The Morrisania mental health program is a 9 a.m. to 5 p.m., five-day-a-week operation consisting of a day hospital and outpatient adult and children services. It is located in the Morrisania Family Care Center, the other half of which is occupied by an outpatient medical clinic.* Donald B. Brown, M.D., and Myrtle Parnell, M.S.W.,† both long-term veterans of the Morrisania program, describe the area as follows:

> In the ten years preceding the establishment of the Morrisania mental health program, the Southwest Bronx community had undergone drastic changes. It had been a well-established homogeneous middle-class Jewish family neighborhood centered on the broad and elegant boulevard known as the Grand Concourse. This community, however, was experiencing tensions on its fringes from the in-migration of poor, transient Puerto Ricans and Blacks. The more affluent families began to move to less stressed neighborhoods in nearby suburbs, thus beginning a process of "white flight."
>
> Greatly accelerating this flight was the opening of Coop City, a housing complex with its own schools and services. It was a new middle-class enclave for 60,000 people in a well-protected section of the Bronx which was well-insulated from the encroachment of urban blight by its remoteness and inaccessibility by public transportation. Having been subsidized by the state to be affordable to middle-class families, the complex allowed the remaining middle income families of the Morrisania area to move out en masse, leaving behind a neighborhood bereft of effective leadership, social cohesion and political clout.
>
> Unfortunately, the City did not take a "systems view" of the city-wide housing problem. It did not stop to wonder what the effect of the creation of an opportunity for many thousands of middle-class people to suddenly leave their old neighborhoods for "the better life" would be on threatened neighborhoods.
>
> Moving into the area were large numbers of poor Blacks and Puerto Ricans, attracted by good housing stock that was vastly superior to what they had left behind. Many of these new people were working poor and many were on Welfare. They could not afford the kind of rents the buildings had previously maintained. The housing stock rapidly deteriorated. An epidemic of arson was partially fueled by landlords who turned to insurance companies for their profits. Vacant lots containing piles of the unsightly rubble of burned out buildings became this area's most striking feature. The family-oriented shopping and services that the area had previously known left. Drugs, violence and crime became omnipresent. Community cohesion and political

---

*The center's 120,000-person catchment area lies in the southwest Bronx between the Grand Concourse and the Harlem River. Yankee Stadium is a famous and popular landmark.

†Dr. Brown, who collaborated on this chapter, is former Director of Mental Health Services, Morrisania Neighborhood Family Care Center. Subsequent to this description of the program, both Ms. Parnell and Dr. Brown left Morrisania. The economic difficulties of the late 1980s and early 1990s were seen there in decreased support and further social disorganization and impoverishment in the community it serves.

power had not developed, at least in part, due to the transient nature of the population.

A typical case in our clinic is a single parent, mother of several children, living in a deteriorated building that has no locks on the entrance door and where the mailboxes are regularly violated. The apartment door may have several locks attesting to the degree of concern about intruders. There may be one or more abandoned buildings on the block.

The presenting problem may be the mother's "nervousness," depression or disorganized behavior, or one of the children misbehaving in school. The mother regrets that she dropped out of school and wants her children to do better.

The family subsists on Welfare assistance, food stamps and Medicaid, has a two-party rent check (requiring the signatures of both the tenant and the landlord) because of previous non-payment.

The children are likely to be kept indoors after school because drugs and violence are so prevalent in the neighborhood. Many of our families have been the victims of burglaries, muggings, physical and sexual abuse, murder and/or have been touched by crime through family or social network connections.

There is usually a strong kinship network that includes friends and fathers of the children, which is essential to the family's survival. Resources, social and financial, are not the exclusive possessions of an individual or family. It is understood that in times of crisis "what's mine is yours." This system of reciprocal obligation is a major survival mechanism among the poor.

The religions may be different from those of the middle-class. The poor prefer the Pentecostal Church, Espiritismo or Santaria. Ministers, sisters of the church and faith healers are the natural helpers in time of emotional or spiritual crisis.

Our patients know that, at best, they are not valued and, at worst, they are seen by the larger society as burdens, lazy, dumb and worthless. Their existence is one of vulnerability to the violence in the streets. Life is a series of crises held together by their relationships with, and the resourcefulness of, their family, friends, and religion. (Brown & Parnell, 1990)

Some indicators of the urban disorganization in the Morrisania catchment area are:

1. In 1982, 45% of persons there received public assistance.
2. Out-of-wedlock births increased 107% (1970–78), versus 13% citywide (New York City Human Resources Administration, 1983). More than 20% of these infants are born to teenagers.
3. Fifty-five percent of the households earn less than $10,000 a year. A total of 71.8% of families are in the three lowest poverty categories.
4. The Morrisania area is educationally deprived as well. For persons over 18, only 29.5% are high school graduates and 2.2% graduated from college.
5. Violent death (homicide and suicide) and alcoholic cirrhosis of the liver are the third and fourth leading causes of death.

THE MORRISANIA PROGRAM

The clinic's annual budget is financed by a three million dollar contract for psychiatric services between the New York City Health and Hospitals Corporation (HHC) and the city's mental health department. The city then bills Medicaid to recover what it can. Roughly 75% of the clients seen in the clinic have either Medicaid or Medicare coverage. The clinic has 7.5 fulltime equivalent psychiatrists, 4 psychologists, and 3.5 R.N.'s on its staff. In addition, there are 27 other fulltime equivalent positions held by social workers, occupational therapists, and psychotherapists. This does not include staff from the child development section,* nor does it include administrative staff shared with the medical portion of the clinic occupying the same building. The outpatient department had a total of 1,450 active clients in 1987. There were, including sessions with children, 18,000 face-to-face contacts. The day hospital served 146 clients in 1986. Dr. Brown, program director since 1976, writes:

> In late 1976, the aging Morrisania City Hospital in the southwest Bronx was closed and moved to new facilities five miles north. The outpatient services for the hospital had been located across the street in the new Morrisania Neighborhood Family Care Center for two years. Primary care and specialty medical services continued to be situated there as a freestanding facility of the New York City Health and Hospitals Corporation.
>
> At the time the hospital closed, construction of a new wing to the N.F.C.C., the Mental Health Annex, was completed. It was funded by some of the very last federal monies appropriated for the construction of buildings as part of the original federal Community Mental Health Center's Act.
>
> As is common in the public hospital system in New York City, our program was set up with an affiliation contract with Montefiore Medical Center (part of the Albert Einstein College of Medicine). This allowed our program to be a training site for medical students and residents. Our staff psychiatrists and psychologists were eligible to become faculty in the medical school.

While the affiliation with the Albert Einstein College of Medicine provides an "academic" aura for the program, it also results in a fragmentation in staffing—the medical staff are Montefiore employees; the nonmedical staff and center administrator are employees of the City's Health and Hospital Corporation—thus creating two lines of authority.

Dr. Brown continues:

> Our Treatment Model:
> Making our clinical services relevant and useful to the poor community we were to serve was our primary goal in developing and running this new pro-

---

*Part of New York's mental retardation service system.

gram. Our patients would need validation of their strengths and coping abilities and not a clinical stance which focused on pathology and deficiency. The services needed to involve the natural support networks of our patients as well as be coordinated with other health and human service providers.

1. Systems Clinical Theory:

We believed that upon making a shift from the traditional individual clinical approach to one which encompassed the organization of the social world around the distressed individual or family, our therapeutic effectiveness would be enhanced in a number of ways:

First, we would become more attentive to cultural values and the norms of our patients and the communities in which they lived.

Second, many options for intervention would open beyond solely offering help to the individual. These would include working with natural support systems as well as other institutions important in the patient's life. Clinicians would work as systems brokers.

Third, our clinical approach would easily become problem oriented and pragmatic—emphasizing the present rather than the past. Systems clinical theory would provide an excellent basis for understanding and treating the crises of the poor and vulnerable mentally ill in terms of relevant changes in the immediate context of the life of individuals and families.

An additional benefit was that systems theory would remove, or shift to a larger social view, the stigmatizing effect of labeling the problem as belonging solely to the identified patient. Blame would be decreased. Our focus would be shifted toward the view of maximizing, strengths and coping abilities in a particular context.

2. Structure of the Services:

We designed our services to be brief (six to eight weeks) and crisis oriented and to be well integrated with longer term treatments. We wanted to be able to respond immediately, recognizing that much of the stress for which people seek help actually involves survival issues. We wanted to be sure we never had a waiting list.

Our charts were organized to include a time line and a genogram modified to show non-family members (important caretakers, Godparents and friends) as well as other agencies involved. The genogram structures information so that existing supports could be assessed for the patient and his/her family, along with the potential for therapeutic interventions.

We recognized at the outset of our program that our ideal of systematically making home visits as part of crisis treatment—and even offering ongoing family therapy in the home—would not be feasible. That idea involved too radical a departure from the established administrative structures and requirements in the N.F.C.C. and we did not pursue it.

3. Staffing:

Sixteen of the 34 staff originally hired were Black or Hispanic. Of the 13 highest trained professionals (the supervising nurses, doctors, psychologists and supervising social workers), ten were from the majority white, Anglo-American culture, while only two were Black and one was Hispanic. The importance of this early racial and cultural imbalance of the staff was to become clear in subsequent phases of the program's development.

4. Staff Supports and Training:

Systems theory teaches (and common sense tells us) that the characteristics of the interpersonal context in which psychiatric service delivery takes place will affect the nature of the service that is delivered. Thus, to the extent that we could succeed in providing staff with an effective support system, opportunities for their personal development, and for learning new skills, we expected that they could have a much better chance of achieving similar goals with their patients.

5. Supervision:

Clinical supervision of staff was set up according to a model derived from systems theory of the supervisor as consultant helping to increase competency and promote growth in the treatment social system, just as the therapist intervenes with similar goals in the social system of the identified patient and/ or family. Thus, wherever possible, supervision was live. It was conducted as a practical, live consultation built into the actual service delivery. Supervisors worked using the one-way mirror or sat in with the primary therapist to help untangle some complications in a case or to help in evaluating and developing a treatment plan.

6. Teams:

To maximize mutual support and sharing of skills, services were delivered by interdisciplinary teams consisting of approximately six to ten members (including trainees of various disciplines). Team leaders ran weekly team meetings that facilitated open interchange among staff regarding work-related problems as well as collaboration and mutual learning about cases by staff of different disciplines and cultural backgrounds.

Case conferences were held regularly. Everyone on a treatment team typically had a chance to observe and comment upon a live case as it was being supervised. In being observed, all clinicians (including the supervisors) were forced to confront issues of trust and fears of exposure in ways which are similar to what patients experience in any therapy situation. Once that trust is established, there develops a sense of support which increases the possibilities for both staff and patients to take risks and try new behaviors.

From the outset, our program had insufficient representation of Black and Hispanic professionals and supervisors. Our Hispanic paraprofessional staff struggled with an extra burden of having a large number of complex cases involving critical survival issues. This was due to their patients' inability to successfully negotiate in English such systems as Welfare, hospitals or the schools, or to handle a conflict with a landlord. These staff members were most intensely affected by the crisis of overwork.

Out of the strong feelings aroused by issues relating to race and ethnicity and feelings of exploitation, a Minority Coalition was formed during our second year. This group was interdisciplinary and included all levels of staff from paraprofessionals to psychiatrists. The Coalition directly met with me (the Program Director) to deal with the issues of hiring of more minority professional staff and improving the support of paraprofessionals by working towards giving each one a minority supervisor.

Coalition members became very involved in helping to successfully recruit new minority staff and worked to develop enriched staff training about cultural issues. In addition, the Coalition helped to bring the entire program to a new level of awareness and open discussion about issues of race and ethnicity in both our relationships with one another and with our patients. For example, I learned from my Black and Hispanic colleagues that as a White man trying to avoid what I believed to be further "oppression of minorities" some of my liberal permissive and egalitarian attitudes ran counter to the need for the effective executive authority, clear hierarchy and structure essential for the program's health and survival at this stage of its development.

ADMINISTRATION

This section is based on interviews with Donald Brown and Steven Goldstein (the Ph.D. chief psychologist who has been with the program since its inception) and Elsie Maldonado (now social work administrator of the facility, she started in the program as a psychiatric social worker in 1976).

The clinic suffers from a long history of fragmentation. The facility's life began split; the mental health side of the clinic was and still is affiliated with Montefiore Hospital, while the physical health side of the clinic was affiliated with a nearby Catholic hospital (it now has no affiliation). There is also a split in responsibility for dealing with the so-called chronically mentally ill. A majority of these patients, roughly 500 or so, many from Morrisania's catchment area, are followed in a continuing care clinic run by Bronx Psychiatric Center (the state hospital). Morrisania handles an additional 250 "veterans," some of whom live outside the catchment area. A few Morrisania patients attend the day center at the state hospital and are getting other services at Morrisania.

The center's particular administrative arrangement gives rise to further problems. For instance, facilities of the Health and Hospitals Corporation, designed to provide acute hospital care, lack the administrative support needed to develop community-based nonmedical programs, such as residences. In addition, when the community support concept was originally floated and given state and federal money, Morrisania was not able to apply. This has been changing in recent years, in that the HHC can now run Community Support Programs, of which Morrisania's homeless program is now one. However, this situation has meant that until recently they haven't been able to deal with the most common problem of their clientele – the lack of decent, affordable housing.

At the present time the staff is racially quite well balanced: Four of seven and a half psychiatrists are minority. All of the program's units are administered by minority professionals. In addition, the line staff is more than half minority, mostly Hispanic. The program finds it increasingly difficult to hire trained minority individuals because it pays less well than nearby voluntary hospitals. In addition, the pool of minority applicants is smaller since the decline in tuition aid under the Reagan administration. For example, at New York University there are only four Blacks and two Hispanics in a class of 144 social work students.

The housing problem threatens to overwhelm clients and staff alike. With upward revisions in early 1988 the New York City welfare housing allowance is $290 for a mother with two children. Apartments in the area, when available, rent for about $400 per month. Section eight housing subsidy and public housing waiting lists are years long. A seniors rental preference program also has a long waiting list. The SSI system is a bit more generous, providing $376 a month plus food stamps and Medicaid. In contrast to city and state welfare it does not require frequent face-to-face contacts for continuation. Eviction is a very common and devastating event. There are 4,000 per year in the Bronx alone. Entire families must frequently rely on shelters or double up in occupied apartments for periods of time.

The question may legitimately be asked: How has the program continued to exist and do its job and keep staff for as long as it has? Although occasionally ambitious professionals come to Morrisania for a year or two of training and then move on, many of the staff with whom we met had been there for seven or more years. The reasons are well captured by Ms. Maldonado (social work) and Mrs. Rosetta Jenkins, chief of nursing programs:

Ms. Maldonado: "I'm a Puerto Rican raised in the Bronx where I saw that the institutions were not serving the poor and minorities. My commitment to the work is an idealistic one. In the '60s and early '70s change and innovation were possible but now there are fewer resources and more bureaucratization. Despair is now much more common among the clients. Families have been depleted of economic and interpersonal resources. The stresses of crowding, poverty and lack of personal security contribute to family conflict and violence. They just can't take care of their sicker members because they are too stressed themselves. This helps explain why so many of our patients use the Franklin Avenue shelter as a second bedroom to the family home."

Mrs. Jenkins: "I believe and a lot of people agree with me that this is the very best place around. It's because of the family and systems philosophy of operation. It involves a lot of encouragement to do family work with a lot of collegial support and supervision available. The people who have been here for a long time are the old guard—we're sustaining a cause and carrying out a mission. The program's greatest virtue is the respect and dignity with which clients are treated. For them, this is a very unusual experience."

At one point, Mrs. Jenkins left Morrisania and went to work at another hospital's psychiatry program. She quite vividly contrasts the two programs' approaches:

"The other program is one of stagnation, sameness, homeostasis and chronicity. For example, the day hospital schedule at Morrisania is changed at least twice a year while the other one is never changed. Their only motivation is financial. At Morrisania minorities are all in key leadership positions with the exception of the directorship. At the other program only whites are in charge.

"Our own racial difficulties were addressed when the Minority Coalition became the watchdog of hiring. We were able to confront the myth of 'the happy family without differences.' In fact, forcing respect for cultural *differences* (as they did) actually muted racial issues in the program and led to an overall improved understanding of the patients."

Dr. Goldstein cited five factors as crucial to their survival:

1. They are really trying to serve.
2. There is substantial training available for everyone in family therapy and other forms of treatment.
3. They have an experimental attitude toward and encourage the application of new therapies.
4. There is less hierarchy than in most places because they use a family and systems model rather than a medical one. The egalitarianism that stems from the model is reinforced by the experience and skill of the operators themselves, which mutes professional/ nonprofessional differences.
5. The generally positive expectations at all levels create an ambiance that invites people to do well.

HOSPITALIZATION

The Morrisania program hospitalizes only clients (90 a year, 35 committed) who are already on their rolls. New clients who look like they will need hospitalization are sent directly to one of three public hospitals in the Bronx (all outside the catchment area). Psychiatric impatient beds in the Bronx are always scarce. Because of this, hospitalizing someone is a time-consuming and difficult process. There are a total of 315 acute adult and 530 long-stay psychiatric impatient beds in the Bronx (population 1.1 million). This is a ratio of 27 acute public beds per 100,000 population, as compared with 36 per 100,000 in New York City as a whole. This number of beds must be seen in the context of the Bronx: There are *no* mobile emergency services available, *no* residential alternatives to hospitalization, only 413 community residential beds, and a serious overall housing shortage. Hence, it is a situation in which hospital beds are in great demand.

Since the late '70s there has been an increasing number of admissions and a steady decline in the length of stay in the municipal hospitals' acute inpatient units in the Bronx. For example, Bronx Municipal Hospital Center's length of stay went from 27.7 days in 1979 to less than 14 days in

1987. The acute beds are serving as a rapidly revolving door. The center attempted to liaison with hospitals where their patients were admitted but soon found that it was a useless expenditure of staff time. Hospital staff were just too overwhelmed by admission and discharge pressures to deal with individual referral sources.

DAY HOSPITAL

The day hospital administrator is a Hispanic nurse who joined the program when she took it over in September 1986. In July 1987, she was joined by a white psychiatrist. The day hospital has 40 places and an average length of stay of about nine months. Eighty percent of the clients live with their families. The clients come from three sources:

1. Emergency rooms send patients who have decompensated but are not sick enough to require hospitalization.
2. The Morrisania outpatient clinic refers patients who are decompensating and need intensive care to avoid hospitalization.
3. State hospital inpatients are sent if they need further treatment and structure after discharge.

Most patients are schizophrenic; almost all are on neuroleptics. Basically, the criterion for admitting people to the day hospital is that they are sufficiently motivated about treatment to regularly get to the program or that their family or social network can assure their attendance. Staff have no problem with taking acutely psychotic clients. They will take active drug takers who can commit to a detoxification program and/or drug or alcohol ancillary programs like NA and AA. They try not to admit actively suicidal or homicidal people.

The treatment program is composed of three phases: Newly admitted clients are assigned to the lunch group (three to seven patients) that plans, shops, cooks, and serves lunch to the entire hospital. Upon graduation from the lunch group (usually three to six weeks), patients go to a goal-setting group and then to a predischarge group. Members of the predischarge group are focused primarily on what they need to have in place before they can leave the program. Woven in with these groups is a range of other activities: crafts, recreation, computer and other work-oriented skill groups. Once a week therapy groups are held in both English and Spanish. There are also weekly women's, nonverbal, movement, drama, and music groups in English and Spanish. The initial assessment is quite family and ecosystem oriented. In all cases, family members are urged to participate in multifamily psychoeducation sessions and/or once weekly family therapy. The program operates with 10 F.T.E.'s.

OUTPATIENT DEPARTMENT

Brown and Parnell write: (1990)

The outpatient service structure was designed to fit our systems theory concept that requests for help arise at a tune of failed adaptation and crisis. The first goal of clinical interventions was to help individuals and families attain a new level of adaptation. Some patients would not be expected to return for months or years until another crisis exceeded their problem-solving capacity. Others would continue for supportive and/or growth oriented psychotherapies, while still others benefited sufficiently from the brief intervention to go on with their lives without further help.

Continuity of patient care was achieved by organizing staff schedules for the outpatient department (O.P.D.) so as to allow each clinician time to see their crisis/walk-in patients for follow-up appointments. Interventions were made in the very first meeting. More thorough evaluations were made over subsequent visits. The possibilities of change were assessed by seeing how the patient (and family) responded to immediate efforts at change rather than through prolonged assessment interviews.

During the first interview, not only was the mental and medical (when indicated) state of the individual patient assessed and individual crisis treatment initiated, but information was gathered about family members and significant others in the patient's social field. The problems presented by our patients were varied, requiring at times medical/psychiatric assessment and intervention, social system, family/individual assessment and interventions by a therapist and/or advocacy and support by the paraprofessional.

In establishing our program with a systems clinical theory working culture, we were putting into operation new ideas about minorities and the poor. We were clear among ourselves that poverty itself is not a mental illness. We, therefore, assumed that our patients have strengths and organized our assessments to elicit the positives and coping abilities in individuals, families and social systems, rather than the pathology.

We assumed also that patients knew what they needed and our job was to help them with the problems presented. Our goal was to help resolve the crisis and return the person/family to regain their previous level of functioning as quickly as possible. It was often possible to achieve this goal by intervening in the social system and advocating for the patient.

Our purpose is to teach the patient about the particular system and how it works, so that s/he can eventually manage independently. Instead of escorting the patient ourselves, we may identify some person in the client's network who has the skills and availability to help the patient. For the clinician, resolving these issues is a very tedious and protracted task, requiring numerous calls and extreme frustration as the policies and procedures in other agencies, as well as the assigned worker, who changes so frequently.

Patients who first came alone were told that the possibilities for help would be increased if all relevant people involved came in for an assessment as part of a group meeting. Patients too frightened or ashamed to discuss their problems with anyone else were given the private help they requested, and the involvement of others was later encouraged.

Dr. Brown continues:

Group treatment for over 150 patients-a-year in 15 different groups is an important ongoing feature of our program. Our "menu" of groups includes activity, socialization, parenting skills, and insight oriented "personal growth" groups, to name a few. We have not yet achieved the hoped-for goals of seeding the development of self-help groups for our patients. Some groups are formed to meet a specific need in providing social supports. One such group consists of middle-aged Hispanic women who have recently migrated to New York City. This group, led by two middle-aged Spanish-speaking social workers, one a WASP (White Anglo-Saxon Protestant), the other a Puerto Rican who has lived in New York for over 30 years, addresses issues of acculturation and adaptation to life in New York, through direct example and open discussion.

New treatment modalities continue to be developed. One psychiatrist has become certified as an acupuncturist and offers this service four times a day to selected patients. A small group of clinicians have been learning stress reduction techniques and hypnosis. They have been applying this in their clinical work as well as training other staff in its use.

The outpatient department is run jointly by a black Ph.D. clinical psychologist and a Hispanic woman psychiatrist. It operates with 5.5. M.D. and 14 non-M.D. F.T.E.'s. In order to control patient flow more effectively, several changes have been instituted; there is no longer a separate crisis team and all new patients are seen in three or four brief treatment and evaluative sessions prior to a diagnosis and disposition meeting. Those who don't complete the series (about 50%) are dropped from the rolls. Psychotherapy, when offered, is usually individual (70%), focused on specific problems, time-limited, and whenever possible conducted by the evaluator. The staff work in three-person teams — one evaluator with a social worker and psychiatric supervisor. Currently outpatient staff carry 40–50 cases, except for the psychiatrists, who act as supervisors and consequently carry fewer individual patients (about 20). They are required to have 25 face-to-face contacts and 17½ hours of contact time each week. Outpatient clinicians are generalists; they do whatever is needed with every client, hence serving as designated case managers. This is not a term, or set of functions, about which one hears much talk in this setting. Recently a person has been hired to be exclusively responsible for keeping a roster of concrete available resources, that is, apartments, SSI, etc. There is also a renewed emphasis on use of groups. The 250 chronically mentally ill clients on their roster are seen usually on a monthly basis. Sixty are on injectable neuroleptics. Cecily Dell (a Ph.D. psychologist), a seven-year veteran out-patient therapist, describes her work as follows:

"We operate on 'dental model'—treat the cavity and ask people to come back when they have another. The solutions we have to offer are limited because we can't address the source of stress—the social and economic conditions. If we find someone with a developmental crisis we can be quite helpful. When my old clients call I'll see them again as frequently as needed to get them through the crisis. I have difficulty deciding exactly who should be logged into the clinic because if a person isn't registered you don't get credit for a visit against the required 25 contacts. However, registering all members of a family is time-consuming and duplicative. At the moment the city requires that those persons who don't have some form of insurance pay $7 per visit per family member. This is almost impossible for our families. For this fee to be waived I have to fill out a special form at specified intervals. So, it becomes a problem of my motivation and time. I spend about one-quarter of my time in the child program. I see about 20 to 25% of my clients on a strictly family basis. I see one-third of my clients weekly, one-third bimonthly, and one-third monthly. The weeklies are child clients and borderlines. Bimonthlies are bipolars who are generally functioning OK. Roughly one-quarter of my clients have had multiple hospitalizations. Our problem is that our family orientation clashes with the individual one of the rest of the system. The extra paperwork sorely tests my motivation to see families. Home visits are something that I'd like to do, but they are just too dangerous and too expensive. I have to take another person with me, it must be a male, and I have no car—so it becomes a real production. In spite of that, I do about one a month."

Everyone with whom we spoke had some concerns about his or her work. For example, one felt that groups are not used enough. Another felt the groups that are conducted are not properly organized. However, there was absolute agreement that they liked working at Morrisania. There was general agreement that is enjoyable because of the attitude toward innovation, the solidarity among the staff, and the amount of supervision and teaching available.

CHILD PROGRAM

This 4.5 F.T.E. program headed by a Chilean woman child psychiatrist started three years ago. The staff members now see 20 walk-in cases a month and have about 250 active cases at any given time. Referrals are equally split between schools and families. Eighty-five percent come from single-parent families, one-third are preschool age children, and another third are adolescents. They are treating 20 children with attention disorders with stimulants. Their principal clinical focus is problem-oriented immediate family intervention (60% receive only family therapy). About half the kids are also evaluated at school or at home. Learning-disabled children can be evaluated by either Morrisania's child development center or the schools.

The child clinic runs a variety of groups: parenting skills; parents with preschool age children; an evening group for working parents; and two regular therapy groups for kids, one latency age and the other adolescent. They use a consultant to make clinical decisions about the duration of groups and whether they will be open or closed. Drug-abusing adolescents are referred out to specialized programs. As elsewhere in the center, morale is good. To give therapists a sense of not leaving to face a difficult situation alone, problem cases are treated with live supervision behind a one-way mirror.

The service chief trained in a psychoanalytic child program in Manhattan but decided that for child work a family and community orientation would be more helpful than an analytic play therapy one. Her experience at Morrisania has confirmed her notion that at least with their clientele change is easier to produce from the outside in (behavior) than from inside out (insight).

HOMELESS PROGRAM – FRANKLIN AVE. MEN'S SHELTER IN SOUTH BRONX

1. *Background:* The homeless program grew out of Dr. Brown's involvement in the training of Albert Einstein psychiatric residents. In 1984–85 three residents began to visit shelters as part of their training in community psychiatry. In 1985 the three residents were granted approval of a proposal to form small groups of homeless men and move them together into apartments (à la Fairweather et al., 1969). The Community Support grant was awarded to Montefiore Hospital. No sooner had the grant been given than the hospital's insurers asked that an additional $250,000 premium be paid before they would assume liability for this program. A protracted series of negotiations between Montefiore and the City Department of Mental Health ensued. It was finally decided that the HHC would accept the program and it would be transferred to the Morrisania Neighborhood Family Care Center (MNFCC), with Dr. Brown as the director. However, during these negotiations (November '86 to October '87), the program's contract was frozen, making any changes in staff and purchasing impossible. This led to a loss of staff, demoralization – the usual consequences of such prolonged administrative haggling. As of November 1, 1987 the center will administer the grant.

2. *Description of the shelter:* New York City's current policy with regard to homelessness is to convert large underutilized buildings into shelters. Most are located in socially disorganized areas of the city where little com-

munity resistance is anticipated. The Franklin Avenue Armory barrack-type shelter is located in a particularly dilapidated section of the South Bronx. Four hundred and fifty of its 650 men are crowded into the Armory's large gym-like ground floor.

3. *The population:* The men are between 20 and 35 years old; 56% black and 41% Hispanic; 12% have reported previous psychiatric hospitalizations; 41% have been treated for substance abuse; 75–80% are currently abusing some substance; and 62% have been arrested and 22% convicted of a felony. Violence is common. Interestingly, 25% of the shelter users are *employed*, usually in entry-level jobs.

Because of the Bronx's housing shortage, the shelter functions as a second bedroom for 500 men from families in the surrounding community. Those with families within walking distance frequently go home during the day to eat, wash, and change their clothes and then return to the shelter to sleep.

The shelter has a staff of 150. Some staff are former homeless persons. Many have the same social problems and personal habits as the shelter inhabitants. The staff is focused on custodial and maintenance activities. Drug dealing is said to go on across staff and client lines.

4. *The mental health program:* The staff consists of one social worker, one case manager, one psychiatrist, and one program director in the day-time and two evening fulltime caseworkers. The original grant proposed forming groups of chronically mentally ill men within the facility to then be moved out as a group, as in the Fairweather model, into homes or apartments in the community. However, it soon became clear that there were two major problems with the plan: (1) There are only 413 community residence beds for mentally ill persons (estimated need: 1,500) in the entire Bronx. (2) Almost all the community placements *required* clients to be on medication. Shelters are known to attract persons adverse to taking psychopharmacologic agents. Although program staff discuss the role of medications with clients and encourage them to get them for specific indications, they do not prescribe them directly because they do not want to be seen as "controllers." They instead refer to a city clinic.

Their experience is that the nonpsychotic homeless man is often seen as a rather disturbed and disturbing individual because of his demoralization, depression, low frustration tolerance, frequent display of anger, and inability to follow through. Thus, even though these are *not* long-term psychiatric institution ex-inmates, they still have many of the qualities associated with institutionalism.

Because of the abovementioned problems, the program has been refocused on two groups of shelter residents: (1) newly admitted persons, and (2) persons in crisis. The crisis portion of the program is meant to serve the

12% of the population that is chronically mentally ill. Interventions involve intensive case management, attempting to link clients with various services, to help them form a network in the shelter with other men in similar situations, and whenever possible to negotiate a reunion with families. The staff encourage these men to play an active role in finding others in the shelter they believe could benefit from the program.

The first-timer portion of the program grew out of the workers' concern about the settling in they observed after two or three months at the shelter. In the six months prior to our visit the shelter had an average of two new first-timers a day.

The program served 172 shelter residents during its first year and helped 78 men move out into either temporary or permanent living arrangements, most (43 of the 78) into substance abuse rehabilitation programs. Located on the third floor of the armory, the program operates without appointments, has an open door, and gives free access to its phone as an incentive for involvement. The program is seen by its participants as a basically friendly place. Many of the men come up and spend time socializing. So, in addition to the more precisely defined functions, it operates an evening drop-in center.

Regarding the future of the program, Dr. Mullins (the program psychiatrist) believes that:

1. They need to find, renovate, and operate their own single room occupancy hotel (it should be noted here that there were 60% fewer SRO rooms available in New York City in 1980 than in 1973). They want to return to the single room occupancy model, with all of its problems, because they believe these men can best survive in a situation where they can control the amount of social contact they have.
2. Program staff need to do more home visiting and use a psychoeducational approach with the families to facilitate reintegration.
3. They need to expand their efforts for dealing with the systems that impinge on them. They are finding that their agency liaison is now easier and things happen much more quickly because they have developed personal relationships within the relevant agencies.

It is notable that the city has decided that its homeless problem is best addressed by renovated permanent shelters. In the South Bronx there is a plethora of abandoned apartment buildings that could be rehabilitated to become public housing. The city seems not to understand that it costs $20,000 a year per person in barracks arrangements and up to $300,000 a year per family in the hotels being used to house homeless families! City policy has also managed to break up couples by not allowing any unmarried persons who have lived together to be housed in their family program. The crowded first floor of the Armory, a sea of cots, seems a place devoted to dehumanized warehousing—a not very appealing long-term solution.

COMMENTARY

The Morrisania program is a lesson in the power of ideology to sustain effort in the face of seemingly insurmountable odds. Staff struggle daily to transform the machinations of an unfriendly system into a positive influence on the lives of a multiproblem clientele. They continue to struggle both because of the consistency of the philosophy and because of the attention devoted to staff morale. It seems to have been very effective in preventing staff burnout. They have evolved a coherent systemic model within a fragmented, disjointed system. Elements we consider vital to effective program functioning—mobile crisis intervention, intensive residential care, and transitional and permanent supported housing—are totally absent. They have limited control over the entry and exit gates and their efforts vis-à-vis the larger system are mostly ineffective.

While most public mental health clients are poor and have multiple problems, the Morrisania catchment area contains a much larger number of such persons because of the pervasiveness of the poverty (55% of families earn less than $10,000 a year) and lack of community resources. Despite all the programmatic and bureaucratic deficiencies, this program most nearly approximates what we would consider to be an effective clinical approach to a community mental health clientele. The following summary and conclusion from an article by Brown and Parnell (1990) state very well how closely their principles are to those we've described elsewhere in this volume:

> Emphasize Mutual Support and Networking: In dealing with the special stressors of working with the poor and mentally ill, it has been important to have a working environment in which our staff can share information and emotional support. Likewise, we have worked hard to develop an administrative style which provides a model for respecting difference, while cooperating and resolving conflicts. Frequent parties, mutual sharing of ethnic foods and maintaining team cohesiveness have made work in this domestic war zone not only bearable, but exciting. Administrators who don't understand the special issues of dealing with our patient population have become uncomfortable with this different approach and pressure continues to be exerted, which threatens the spirit of sharing and teamwork. This requires constant sharing of information and "advocacy work" on our own behalf.
>
> Recognize Strengths, Normalize the Problems: The stresses we experience are a "normal" aspect of delivering human services to the poor in public

institutions. What we do achieve, often against great odds, needs special recognition and praise. Our sense of helplessness and demoralization is mitigated when we learn that others are in the same situation and have found ways to cope.

Encourage Growth and Change: Patients, families, staff, programs, communities and the entire service system each have their own cycles of development, crisis and adaptation. A spirit of encouraging learning, growth, innovation and change, keeps us moving forward in trying new clinical interventions redesigning aspects of the program, or teaching/advocating for our needs with other service providers, administrators, or politicians.

Morrisania is serving substantial numbers of homeless persons. Unfortunately, a basically sound approach to the problem may be foundering because of bureaucratic problems and poor city planning. Given what we saw in the South Bronx, we wonder whether government wants to do anything serious about the homelessness problem. In an area with literally hundreds of empty buildings available for renovation, and where housing is the most obvious and pressing need, it boggles the mind that shelters are the principal solution. No one seems to be focused on developing and providing permanent, affordable, decent housing to all of the citizens of the South Bronx — some of whom are currently homeless, some of whom are mentally ill, some of whom are just plain poor folks trying to survive.

The problems within the center's setting are ones that are extraordinarily difficult to address, mostly because they are often ones generated in the bureaucracy that controls the setting but is unresponsive to the center's change efforts. Worse yet, it's not just one outside bureaucracy but *several*. Within the center itself, there are some racial problems, principally the result of a *bureaucratic* inability to let experience and competence count as much as degrees in the promotion ladder. This greatly affects the paraprofessionals who have been with Morrisania for quite some time, are now well trained family and system clinicians, but who cannot get management positions because they don't have proper credentials in the city's personnel system. As a result they feel, justifiably, exploited. Again, it's a *system* problem. Fortunately, some paraprofessionals have been able to take advantage of the program's special support for them to get credentials (i.e., special schedules have been arranged so that they can attend school while working). Maintaining balance in the Center's multiracial staff is an ongoing concern. However, because Morrisania is a ship full of persons trying to hang on and get through a storm together this issue is really secondary.

This program is being documented in the literature (Brown & Parnell, 1990; Goldstein, 1986; Goldstein & Dyche, 1983; Simon, 1986). We hope this publicity will help it become more widely known so that its clinical model can be applied in other, perhaps more salubrious, settings.

Ingredients of Success

CHAPTER 13

What We Have Learned from All This

BASED ON OUR EXPERIENCE WITH A LARGE NUMBER of community programs, we have identified a number of common elements that contribute in varying degrees to programmatic success.

STRONG LEADERSHIP

Successful programs usually have strong, dedicated, committed, consistent leadership. This is true of the programs we have presented. To be a major force behind a transformation in an entire nation's mental health program may, however, require the charisma of a Basaglia. Nevertheless, fine local programs can be led by trusted, highly involved persons with sufficient power to make things happen. For programs to continue to grow and evolve, consistency of leadership over time seems necessary. Common sense tells us that it is easier to pass the baton of noncharismatic leaders; Italy's experience with Basaglia's loss is certainly a testimony to this phenomenon. The vacuum he left when he died in 1980 has never really been completely filled. Without its strong leader the Democratic Psychiatry movement found it difficult to press for more rapid implementation of Law 180.

Stable leadership in a setting that allows experiential validation of new clinical practices also serves an important training and dissemination function. Basaglia's original group in Gorizia drew students from all over Italy.

A cadre of community mental health workers was trained in a paradigm that represented a dramatic change from previous practice. They subsequently went out to work in other parts of the country. By the time the law was actually changed in 1978, Gorizia and Trieste-like community programs were already in place in a number of Italian cities. The positive clinical role models provided by the leadership in the programs we've described are very important to both recruiting and training students. In turn, students provide them with new energy and enthusiasm and take what they learn to implement in new settings.

PROFESSIONAL SUPPORT GROUPS

Transforming a system from a hospital to a community orientation is personally risky. Leaders who propose this change are out of step with existing realities and hence viewed as deviant. Basaglia, for example, was still defending himself in court when he died. The suit was one that had been filed six years earlier. One important lesson we can learn from Basaglia relates to his foresight in forming the alternative psychiatric society, Democratic Psychiatry, in Italy. This society provided a sense of belonging, a place where professionals who held similar views could share them and where a new consensus could be evolved. This view was dramatically different from the existing one but difficult to define as deviant, since the group evolved an alternative consensus representing many mental health professionals. Although dominated by psychiatrists, the Society for Democratic Psychiatry was ecumenical in its membership. This professional proletarianization provided a living model for the way Basaglia believed mental health structures should be reorganized. That is, they should be nonhierarchical insofar as possible, be democratic in terms of the power residing in developing consensus, and be competence-based rather than degree-based in terms of task assignments. The programs we describe generally operate in this way as well — small, collegial teams with decision-making power.

Democratic Psychiatry served as a magnet drawing mental health professionals from all disciplines. Most especially it provided a format for expression to students committed to human rights reform. These high energy recruits provided the fuel that powered Democratic Psychiatry's engine. This is still true of South Verona. Morrisania's recruiting ability is due to its application of a consistent theoretical model and an unusual context. Although they're not volunteers, its trainees are surely high energy recruits.

A CONSENSUS THAT CHANGE IS NEEDED

It is notable that if there was ever a popular consensus in the U.S. that the mental health system needed reform it was in the Kennedy era. A wide array of professional and lay groups (36 in all) came together to produce the 1961 Report of the Joint Commission on Mental Health. There is some disagreement about whether President Kennedy proposed his 1963 bill to please his sister Eunice Shriver or whether he had in fact read the Joint Commission's report and taken on its cause. Dr. Jack Ewalt (Chairman of the Joint Commission) maintains it was the latter, but the former explanation is most prevalent in the present-day mythology. It is likely that both versions are true to some extent. There was, it seems, a modest consensus in the early '60s that dramatic changes in the U.S. mental health system were needed. The consensus did not evolve until nearly a decade later in Italy.

In Italy the strategy used to gain popular support for the plight of the mental patient in the *manicomio* was to pair it with that of the exploited factory worker. Hence, the labor unions (mostly leftwing) became major sources of popular blue-collar support for the work of Democratic Psychiatry.

In the U.S. "popular" support came mostly from professionals and mental health laymen's advocacy groups like the Mental Health Association. The rhetoric in this country really seemed to have been humanistic: We should not treat members of a free, open, democratic society in a way that may imprison them against their wills for long periods of time and deprives them of their civil liberties.

In the U.S., attention to the "cause" of the mental patient seems to have been diverted to the war in Viet Nam. When the country found it could not support both guns and butter and as guns consumed more and more of the federal budget, the initial dream of 2,000 CMHC's covering the entire U.S. was scaled back.

In Italy it would appear that, although a consensus for change still exists, it has been tempered economically by the end of Italy's "miraculous" economic development post World War II and socially by the paralysis that followed by Aldo Moro's assassination.

After perhaps a decade of relative quiescence a new popular consensus for change seems to be evolving in the U.S. The major new player in this game is the National Alliance for the Mentally Ill (NAMI) (also see Chapter 3). Formed only in 1979, this group's influence has grown by leaps and bounds. Its members lobby effectively in Congress, browbeat television programs that misrepresent images of mental patients, and have been actively involved in a major restructuring of the NIMH that resulted in their achieving a number of their goals. They are an ever vigilant group looking for ways to get better care for, improve the image of, and destigmatize their offspring.

A second new player in the newly redeveloping consensus for change is former mental patient mutual-help movement. Although not as well organized, moneyed and powerful as NAMI, these groups have begun to develop their own alternative mental health programs. They have been effective in initiating change through class action suits against various state mental health systems about hospital conditions, patient rights, involuntary administration of psychotropic medications, and lack of treatment in least restrictive environments. By the mere fact of their having been filed, these suits have caused changes in behavior within state mental health systems.

If these two new teams (clients and parents) don't get stalemated in a serious adversarial posture, they may well be able to press for the contextual conditions necessary to implement widely the types of effective community-based programs described in this book. The individual programs described have developed supportive local networks to varying extents. Morrisania is operating in political and economic context that is not always supportive. It seems to survive through internal networking and consensus-building.

A STABLE, PREDICTABLE SOURCE
OF FINANCIAL SUPPORT

Law 180 was passed in Italy in May 1978. A comprehensive national health insurance scheme combining features of the British and Scandinavian schemes was passed by the Italian parliament in December 1978. The plan provided for countrywide catchment-area-based health services utilizing general practitioners as the first line of service. The plan is paid for by a payroll tax and the money is distributed more or less on a capita basis to each region (equivalent to states in the U.S.). Hence, support for community-based psychiatry was made available. Within regions and catchment areas competition among the medical specialties for funds has been keen and has sometimes led to inequities. Also, Italian economic problems result in the National Health Service constantly being buffeted by spending and personnel freezes. What is important, however, is that the National Health Service is here to stay and mental health will receive a reasonably predictable share of the financial pie. Programs will expand and contract but their survival should not be threatened.

The situation is more complex and difficult in the United States. Support for CMHC's went through several permutations. Basically, CMHC's received eight-year staffing grants that required increasing levels of local matching funds. It rapidly became important for CMHC's to develop their local resources to meet the match. While the ways in which this was done varied widely, the result was almost always a patchwork of local monies from a variety of sources. State funds, the traditional support for public mental health care, were often withheld or given only grudgingly because of the early federal decision to bypass the states in funding the CMHC'S.

Interestingly, this need to develop local resources contributed to the legitimate criticism of the CMHC's as not serving the most seriously disturbed and disturbing persons. That is, *financial needs* encouraged CMHC's to treat middle-class neurotic patients who had health insurance.

In 1981, when federal CMHC money was converted into block grants to states, each center became beholden to the state for its share of federal support. In fact, as was the case in Washington, DC, when federal staffing grants ran out, a number of jurisdictions closed CMHC's or merged them into existing programs at reduced funding levels. In a sense, the declining eight-year federal staffing grant support contained the seeds of destruction of the program designers intentions. They had banked on state and local support to take over when the federal support ran out. Predictably, this did not always occur. Hence, uncertainty over its eventual survival was built into every federally funded CMHC.

Exemplary U.S. programs survive by serving the perceived needs of their communities, by the successful lobbying at local and state levels for money, and by having enough political power from boards, legislators, etc., to be a force with which to be reckoned. In addition, enlightened state leadership (whence support comes) is very helpful.

Today, the two biggest obstacles to the widespread development of adequate community-based care in the U.S. are: (1) the absence of a reliable, predictable source of support, such as national health insurance; and (2) the presence of far too many hospital beds that eat up a disproportionate share of resources. Italy is still spending a lot on its state hospitals. However, since new patients can't be admitted, they will eventually disappear. Unfortunately, this policy of non-institutionalization does not look like it's going to make the transatlantic voyage. For the most part, America seems to have tacitly agreed to continued production of new "veterans." So far as we know, no state has yet proposed closing all of its mental hospitals to admissions. This is so despite the availability of cost-effective alternatives (e.g., mobile crisis intervention and intensive residential alternatives).

Other obstacles to community program development in the U.S. are: (1) It's out of fashion; (2) appropriate training programs are lacking; and (3) divisive professional territoriality with CMHC programs persists. The training issue is also a problem in Italy, but the other two basically don't exist. Community mental health is mandated by law, so it can't be out of fashion. In Italy there are such high rates of unemployment, even among doctors, that most people are just happy to have a job; unlike doctoral-level professionals in the U.S., they don't need to control the program to feel useful.

Based on this analysis, what kinds of changes are needed in the American system to make the type of community mental health system we espouse widely available?

First, and most critically, a system of national health insurance is needed.

Such a system would pay for *what* is delivered, not where. It would provide a reliable source of funding for a true community smorgasbord of programs and facilities. We hope current U.S. efforts in this regard succeed.

Second, a guaranteed annual income or some other form of nondependency-inducing and -perpetuating welfare is needed. It should provide enough money so recipients can live, not merely struggle to exist. Poverty, because of the endless stress it engenders, is a major contributing cause of *prolonged* mental illness (Warner, 1985).

Third, the relevant professional disciplines must provide in-vivo experiential training in community mental health. As part of this, stable community and academic program leadership should be rewarded. Sufficient numbers of role models are needed to assure a continual supply of appropriately trained new professionals.

Fourth, a policy of non-institutionalization should be implemented by blocking admissions to *all* large psychiatric institutions. As buildings are emptied they should be demolished or *immediately* converted to some other use, such as nursing homes for the elderly long-stay patients already in them. They should not be targeted as terminal care centers for AIDS patients. They have never been good places in which to be crazy and are certainly not good places in which to die in a dignified manner. *Anticipated* savings should be transferred to community programs on a $0.50 on the dollar basis.

Leadership, money, and non-institutional contexts are critical to the development of effective community mental health programs.

CHAPTER 14

Summary: Contextual Confusions and Some Recommended Remedies

WHAT IS COMMUNITY MENTAL HEALTH ANYWAY? For us it is the delivery of prompt, adequate, and consistent answers to the real social, psychological, and medical needs of a defined population. It is the provision of a wide enough array of services, programs and facilities so that everyone sent for or seeking help can find options relevant to his or her needs in the smorgasbord offered. It is a system organized for and by the customers.

Community mental health in the United States has had a checkered, on again, off again, career. It was in vogue from the mid-18th century until the civil war era. It flickered a bit in the early 20th century but was basically dormant until the appearance of the Joint Commission's report in 1961 and the CMHC legislation of 1963 that flowed from it. In the '60s it grew like topsy as a consequence of federal support, only to flatten out and then decline in the '80s. In the late '70s it spawned a child (C.S.P.) that seems to have provided a conceptualization to rejuvenate community programs. Meanwhile, the "old" CMHC program got its politics straightened out by the Reagan administration—no more were the "feds" going to dictate where, and for what, their support for mental health would be spent within individual states.

Community mental health is *public* mental health. The American two-tier health care system has not yet invented private community mental health for seriously disturbed and disturbing persons. If there were health insurance money available, it is likely that it would soon be available. Many

Italians believe that everything in life is politics; public mental health is politics with poverty, racism, sexism, marginalization, stigmatization, and social control thrown in for good measure. Community workers are faced constantly with the effects of society's ills. Their clients are usually powerless, unorganized, demoralized and dependent. The somewhat paradoxical definition of "mental health" as a quasi "medical" undertaking frequently confuses staff. Is "mental illness" for real or is it a metaphor of convenience — one that legitimizes attention to what are really social problems with psychological sequelae? Have we just reframed social ills as medical problems so someone might pay to have them addressed? Following the mental illness model with its defect in the individual assumptions, staff are constantly confronted with the fact that the political system impinges negatively on their clients. Confusion mounts — if so and so has this genetically determined chemical imbalance that's produced his disease, why is it his disease seems always to get worse when he can't find housing or loses his woman friend? Even the *presumed magical* drugs can't prevent his getting worse under these conditions.

Physicians imbued with too much power are asked (in some instances required) to be agents of social control. They hospitalize and "treat" patients against their wills. Yet physicians are ill trained to be controllers; they've been led to believe they're healers who will be voluntarily sought out for their ministrations. In community work real choices for clients and staff are limited by what the community (however defined) wants done. Just trying to get a clear picture of who wants to do what to whom can be very confusing. Throw in the contradictions of systems versus individual defect theories and the social problem versus medical disease issue and you've got potential for a real mess. So it goes daily in community mental health work; it's messy. The private practice voluntary model does not usually apply. Unfortunately, that's how almost everyone's been trained, so it's applied anyway and doesn't work. Who is to blame? Why the clients, of course, because they're "unmotivated" or "chronic"! Unfortunately, they are not often powerful enough to resist these blame attributions. Program directors and staff are relieved while clients acquire yet another unneeded failure experience to go with all their others.

Given the confusing, demoralizing, and often degrading state of many public mental health programs, it's not surprising that staff may forget their manners in interactions with the users. To do so is to contribute personally to an already unpleasant state of affairs. In talking to users, especially public mental health ones, it's vital to be respectful, truly attentive, and nonjudgmentally understanding — in short, to treat them with dignity. The golden rule must apply to these interactions, in order to establish a reciprocal relationship that may provide an opportunity for staff to be helpful in an ongoing way. Without such a relationship, especially one that's focused non addressing real client problems and needs, helping becomes coercive manipulation of objects. Proper relationships provide support, sustain effort, and facilitate change.

The helping process, even if begun under auspicious circumstances, has a number of potential pitfalls. Basically, overenthusiastic intrusion into all aspects of clients' lives will leave them expectant, dependent, and ultimately disillusioned when this month's savior proves to be no more reliable than last's. Hence, we strongly recommend that staff be encouraged to "be with" and "do with" clients, while expecting them to learn better how to help themselves. Staff may also suffer disappointment at their clients' perceived failures. Their burnouts will likely be attributed to their clients' lack of motivation or "chronicity." These problems can be minimized by having staff working in small teams and being sure clients are actively involved in, and exercise control over, the helping process. Staff must always remember that clients' lives are theirs to live, not the staff's. With this in mind, power and status issues must be acknowledged and discussed. Staff should do only as much as needed, and asked for, in the helping process. The process should pay constant attention to the principles of contextualization, normalization and preservation of power described in this volume.

Working in community mental health programs is often regarded as second-class citizenship because the pay is low, the clientele notoriously difficult, the setting's reputation tarnished, and the working conditions usually unpleasant. This is true because the resources needed to make community mental health into a first-class operation are being spent on inpatient care. Most workers know that in order to be more effective their programs need more resources. They are not likely to be the benefactors of some wonderful governmental largesse. So, what to do? Follow the Willie Sutton model: "Willie, why do you keep robbing banks?" "'Cuz, that's where the money is." Ergo, mental health money must be gotten out of hospitals, particularly large ones. Until this happens community programs will get only leftovers. This does not mean that clients should be forced out of institutions. Rather, large institutions (state hospitals) should not be allowed to admit anyone. In a few years they'll disappear by attrition. We know how to operate effective community programs that use only a few beds in places called hospitals.

Magical relief of pain and suffering is an almost universal human wish. As the source of fulfilling this wish, pills have replaced religion in many parts of our society. The pain and suffering experienced by community mental health clients are all too real and must be addressed. Are pills the best way to deal with their problems? In some situations yes, they may be, at least temporarily. In other situations they may do more harm than good, especially if used for a long time. We seem to have become accustomed to using pills too frequently, often without attending to their long-range costs — especially tardive dyskinesia. These need to be subtracted from the benefits accrued in the short run. Because psychotropic drugs are the sole purview of powerful, unquestioned physicians, nonphysicians tend to overlook or disregard what's going on with medications in clients they otherwise know very well. Good information about the use, abuse, and toxic potential of the various classes of psychotropic drugs must be made available and used by clients and staff. Lack of such information is irresponsible and dangerous.

In order to design a well functioning community system there needs to be a coherence and coordination of administrative and clinical principles, staff attitudes and values, and types of programs and facilities offered. Actually the distinction drawn between administrative and clinical issues, on the one hand, and staff values and attitudes, on the other, is arbitrary; they should be all of a piece. Perhaps the differences between them are better understood as different organizational levels within an overall open system. For example, without a defined catchment area within which the program controls the gates, it will not be possible to plan how much crisis intervention or how many residential alternative, day program, and housing spaces will be needed. Without this information it is not possible to know how many staff members with the correct attitudes, values, practices, and relevant training should be hired. Elements of a system are by definition interdependent; changing one part is inevitably reflected throughout it. We believe that it is possible to plan and implement effective community mental health programs only if all the elements are attended to; piecemeal planning is fruitless.

Services and facilities provided by programs should comprise a widely varied array; we use the word "smorgasbord" frequently to help visualize this notion. The array will have three major subdivisions: outpatient, residential, and day and evening programs.

The outpatient service, especially through its provision of in-residence crisis intervention and resolution, should be the linchpin in the system. Multiperson groupings (e.g., families, networks, problem-focused groups) should be the preferred modus operandi. A variety of brief, focused, psychosocial interventions should be readily available for particular problems. However, the thoughtful application of newly developed or researched approaches should also be encouraged. Case management functions should be provided by the *team* responsible for each client so that someone is available who knows, and has a relationship with the client, at all times.

Residential programs, especially the intensively staffed ones (e.g., hospital wards and alternatives), are the system's most expensive single element.

Hence, their use should be carefully monitored and controlled. However, barring compelling reasons against doing so, every newly identified functional psychotic deserves one or more trials of drug-free psychosocial treatment, usually in a residential alternative to hospitalization. Drug-free treatment trials may require many days of residential care. We recommend use of this expensive resource for this purpose because of the long-term savings that will accrue to the system if disability can be prevented or minimized. Halfway houses should be available to facilitate transition to supported permanent housing. The housing staff is to be flexibly available to families, group homes, apartments, single room occupancy hotels, etc., on an as-needed basis.

Homelessness is mostly an economic problem. Its long-term solution *awaits* serious governmental attention and intervention. Meanwhile, the current bandaid solution — shelters — is creating another problem — shelter institutionalism. Interestingly, it appears that these nocturnal pseudo-voluntary almshouses are no less "total" in their deleterious effects on persons than large involuntary mental hospitals.

Day and evening programs are necessary in part because many public mental health clients can't, or won't work. Those who can't work should be repeatedly offered opportunities to try again. Unfortunately, until a workable incentive system is developed, it will be impossible to motivate those who won't work. Even though it might break the poverty-dependence cycle, giving up the security of a welfare dole for an entry-level job that consigns them to membership in the working poor is not a worthwhile trade-off for most mental health clients.

Good community mental health staff are raised, not trained. It's very hard to train adults to do no harm, follow the golden rule, and treat people with respect and dignity if they don't already embody these key values and attitudes. There are guidelines for selecting staff from among groups of candidates; however, it's not a very scientific process. If new staff do the job as it's described and convey the necessary values and attitudes, the program will reinforce and expand whatever they bring to it. Of course, staff who have special technical training in a variety of areas, e.g., research, psychopharmacology, family therapy, are needed. Their work should be organized so that they remain firmly embedded as team members while using their special expertise. If staff work is organized in nonhierarchical, supportive family-like teams that accomplish goals, risk of "burnout" is reduced. If it does occur it can be dealt with in a variety of ways, principally focused on the remoralizing effects of being successful.

The Italian mental health reform of 1978 addressed the issue of *preventing* institutionalization in a radical way. It decreed the phasing down of state mental hospitals by prohibiting admissions to them. However, it did not prescribe the rapid discharge of existing patients, thus avoiding the risks related to mass deinstitutionalization. Admissions, if necessary, have to take place in small units (no more than 15 beds) located in general hospitals. Catchmented, community-based mental health services have to provide all interventions for the psychiatric needs of a given population (50,000 to 200,000 population) *without the backup of the state hospital.*

A number of studies have shown the successful implementation of the reform in different settings. Negative reports have also been published, and pessimistic opinions on the applicability of such an innovative reform on a national basis have been expressed.

However, a nationwide survey (CENSIS, 1985) has shown that a fairly comprehensive network of services has been developed in all of Italy since the reform. Community mental health centers have opened in 675 of 698 catchment areas (versus 750 out of 2,000 in the U.S.). Inpatient units in general hospitals have been developed in all regions. Although the bed rate (5.4 per 100,000 population) is still lower than the one planned, and is unevenly distributed among regions, these units do not seem to be overburdened by their caseloads. As a consequence of stopping admissions, the number of inpatients of state mental hospitals decreased from 60,000 in 1977 to less than 30,000 in 1984. Most importantly, the lack of state hospital backup has precipitated neither an increase in short-term admissions to the general hospital units nor a shift to private hospitals.

We have had a great deal to say about the central importance of *context* to effective community work — client context, staff working context, organizational context, administrative context, community context, political context, etc. In Italy a context developed at each level that allowed for a dramatic change in the way mental health services would be delivered. A seemingly radical notion was legislated into standard practice for an entire country. For a variety of reasons America's 1963 attempt at reforming its mental health system has had only limited success. Yet, a great deal of useful experience was acquired in the process. What we've presented is a selected amalgamation of the Italian and American experiences with community mental health. We believe that the open system psychosocial intervention model we propose can be implemented in most locales if it is properly adapted to fit local conditions and if attention is directed to contextual constraints. Even without a *system* of national health coverage (as is true in the U.S.), what we propose will cost no more than is presently being spent on public mental health — *if* a policy of non-institutionalization is put in place. It need not be a national policy to work; states, counties, and cities could develop quality community programs with savings derived from reduction in use of hospital-based care.

It had been our intention to provide practical, commonsense, flexible, good enough administrative and clinical guidelines to allow the development and implementation of effective psychosocially oriented community mental health systems in a wide variety of locales. Only their thoughtful application over time, in many contexts, will tell us whether or not we have been successful.

Medications for Mental Illness and Other Mental Disorders

ANYONE CAN DEVELOP a mental disorder — you, a family member, a friend, or the fellow down the block. Some disorders are mild, while others are serious and long-lasting. These conditions can be helped. One way — an important way — is with psychotherapeutic drugs. Compared to other types of treatment, these medications are relative newcomers in the fight against mental illness. It was only about 30 years ago that the first one, chlorpromazine, was introduced. But considering the short time they've been around, psychotherapeutic drugs have made dramatic changes in the treatment of mental disorders. People who, years ago, might have spent their entire lives in mental hospitals because of crippling mental illness may now only go in for brief treatment, or might receive all their treatment at an outpatient clinic.

Psychotherapeutic drugs also may make other kinds of treatment more effective. Someone who is too depressed to talk, for instance, can't get much benefit from psychotherapy or counseling, but often, taking medication will improve symptoms so that the person can respond better.

SYMPTOM RELIEF, NOT CURE

Just as aspirin can reduce a fever without clearing up the infection that causes it, psychotherapeutic drugs act by controlling symptoms. Like most

Information from DHHS Publication No. (ADM)87-1509 Alcohol, Drug Abuse, and Mental Health Administration. Printed 1987.

drugs used in medicine, they correct or compensate for some malfunction in the body. Psychotherapeutic drugs do not *cure* mental illness, but they do lessen its burden. These medications can help a person get on with life despite some continuing mental pain and difficulty coping with problems. For example, drugs like chlorpromazine can turn off the "voices" heard by some people with schizophrenia and help them to perceive reality as others do. And antidepressant drugs can lift the dark, heavy moods of depression.

How long someone must take a psychotherapeutic drug depends on the disorder. Many depressed and anxious people may need medication for a single period—perhaps for several months—and then never have to take it again. For some conditions, such as schizophrenia or manic-depressive illness, medication may have to be taken indefinitely or, perhaps, intermittently.

Like any medication, psychotherapeutic drugs do not produce the same effect in everyone. Some people may respond better to one drug than another. Some may need larger doses than others do. Some experience annoying side effects, while others do not. Age, sex, body size, body chemistry, habits, and diet are some of the factors that can influence a drug's effect.

QUESTIONS FOR YOUR DOCTOR

To increase the likelihood that a medication will work well, patients and their families must actively participate with the doctor prescribing the drug. They must tell the doctor about the patient's past medical history, other drugs being taken, anticipated life changes—such as planning to have a baby—and, after some experience with a drug, whether it is causing side effects. When a drug is prescribed, the patient or family member should ask the following questions recommended by the U.S. Food and Drug Administration and other groups:

- What is the name of the drug, and what is it supposed to do?
- How and when do I take it, and when do I stop taking it?
- What foods, drinks, drugs, or activities should I avoid while taking the drug?
- What are the side effects, and what should I do if they occur?
- Is there any written information available about the drug?

In this booklet, medications are described by their generic (general) names and in italics by their trade names (brand names used by drug companies). They are divided into four large categories based on the symptoms for which they are primarily used—antipsychotic, antimanic, antidepressant, and antianxiety drugs. Some are used for more than one purpose;

antidepressants, for example, have been found helpful for treating some anxiety disorders.

An index at the end of the booklet gives the trade name of the most common prescribed drugs and notes the section that contains information about each type of drug. Another index lists the generic name of the drug and tells which section to refer to for information.

ANTIPSYCHOTIC DRUGS

A person who is psychotic is out of touch with reality. He may "hear voices" or have strange and untrue ideas (for example, thinking he is the President of the United States, a religious leader, or a movie star).* He may get excited or angry for no apparent reason, or spend a lot of time off by himself, or in bed, sleeping during the day and staying awake at night. He may neglect his appearance, not bathing or changing his clothes, and may become difficult to communicate with—saying things that make no sense, or barely talking at all.

These kinds of behaviors are symptoms of psychotic illness, the principal form of which is schizophrenia. All of them may not be present when someone is psychotic, but some of them always are. Antipsychotic drugs, as their name suggests, act against these symptoms. These drugs cannot "cure" the illness, but they can take away many of the symptoms or make them milder. In some cases, they can shorten the course of the illness as well.

There are a number of antipsychotic drugs available. They all work; the main differences are in the potency—that is, the dose (amount) prescribed to produce therapeutic effects—and the side effects. Some people might think that the higher the dose of medication, the more serious the illness, but this is not always true.

A doctor will consider several factors when prescribing an antipsychotic drug, besides how "ill" someone is. These include the patient's age, body weight, and type of drug. John A., a 6-foot, 180-pound, 25-year-old, might be taking three times as much medication as Mary B., a 5-foot, 105-pound, 65-year-old, but they may both be equally ill. Past history is important, too. If a person took a particular medication before and it worked, the doctor is likely to prescribe the same drug again. Some less potent drugs, like chlorpromazine (*Thorazine*), are always prescribed in higher numbers of milligrams than others of high potency, like haloperidol (*Haldol*).

A person has to take a large amount, of a "high-dose" antipsychotic drug (such as chlorpromazine) to get the same effect as a small amount of

---

*"He" is used here to refer to both men and women.

a "low-dose" drug (such as haloperidol). Why don't doctors just prescribe "low-dose" drugs? The main reason is the difference in side effects (actions of the drug other than the one intended for the illness). These drugs vary in their side effects, and some people have more trouble with certain side effects than others. A side effect may sometimes be desirable. For instance, the sedative effect of some antipsychotic drugs is useful for patients who have trouble sleeping or who become agitated during the day.

Unlike some prescription drugs, which must be taken several times during the day, antipsychotic medications can usually be taken just once a day. Thus, patients can reduce daytime side effects by taking the medications once, before bed. Another feature of some of these drugs is their availability in forms that can be injected once or twice a month, thus assuring that the patient complies with the doctor's orders.

Most side effects of antipsychotic drugs are mild. Many common ones disappear after the first few weeks of treatment. These include drowsiness, rapid heartbeat, and dizziness or faintness when changing position.

Some people gain weight while taking antipsychotic drugs and may have to change their diet to control their weight. Other side effects which may be caused by some antipsychotic drugs include decrease in sexual ability or interest, problems with menstrual periods, sunburn, or skin rashes. If a side effect is especially troublesome, it should be discussed with the doctor, who may prescribe a different drug, change dosage level or pattern, or prescribe an additional medication to control the side effects.

Movement difficulties may occur with some antipsychotic drugs. These include muscle spasms (of the neck, eye, back, or other muscles), agitation, restlessness, pacing, difficulty concentrating, or a general slowing-down of movement and speech and a shuffling walk. Some of these side effects look a lot like symptoms of psychotic illness, but aren't. If they appear or continue when someone is taking an antipsychotic drug, notify the doctor, who can prescribe a specific medication to control the side effects.

Just as people vary in their responses to antipsychotic drugs, they also vary in their speed of improvement. Some symptoms diminish in days, while others take weeks or months. In many cases, improvement is seen over a period of several weeks. For many patients, substantial improvement is seen by the sixth week of treatment (although this is not true in every case). If someone does not seem to be improving, a different type of medication may be tried. Drug treatment for a psychotic illness can continue for up to several months, sometimes even longer. When the patient is totally or largely symptom-free for a period of time, the dose of the drug may gradually be lowered. If the symptoms do not return, the drug may be tapered off and discontinued.

Even if a person is feeling well, or at least better, he should not just stop taking the medication. Suddenly stopping an antipsychotic drug may cause a withdrawal reaction which could include nightmares, sleep disturbances, stomach cramps, and diarrhea. Tapering off medication while continuing to see the doctor is important.

Some people may need to take medication for an extended period of time, or even indefinitely, to remain symptom-free. These people usually have chronic (long-term, continuous) schizophrenic disorders, or have a history of many schizophrenic episodes, where the likelihood of becoming ill again is high. In these cases, medication may be continued in as low a dose as possible to still control symptoms. This type of treatment, called maintenance treatment, prevents relapse in many people and removes or reduces symptoms for others.

While maintenance treatment is helpful for many people, a drawback for some is the possibility of long-term side effects, particularly a condition called tardive dyskinesia. This condition is characterized by involuntary movements of the lips, tongue, and jaw—and, sometimes, of the hands and feet. The disorder may range from mild to severe. For some people, it cannot be reversed, while others recover partially or completely. Tardive dyskinesia is seen most often after long-term treatment with antipsychotic drugs and is more common in elderly women. There is no way to determine whether someone will develop the disorder, and if it develops, whether the patient will recover. At present, there is no effective treatment. The possible risks of long-term treatment with antipsychotic drugs must be weighed against the benefits in each individual case by patient, family, and doctor.

Clinical researchers are investigating two new types of long-term treatment designed to provide the advantages of medication while reducing the risks of tardive dyskinesia and other possible side effects. A "low-dosage" approach uses far lower maintenance doses of antipsychotic drugs than have generally been employed, while an "intermittent dose" treatment involves stopping the drug when the patient is symptom-free and beginning it again only when symptoms reappear. Both approaches are promising and will continue to be explored.

A new, so-called "atypical" antipsychotic drug (clozapine) is now available. It has two especially important salutary features: it does not cause tardive dyskinesia; and about a third of patients who have not responded to other antipsychotic drugs will be helped. It also has two serious problems: it may cause agranulocytosis, a potentially fatal disease of white blood cells; and it has a relatively high incidence of seizures. It is also very expensive, in part because weekly blood tests are required to monitor the white blood cell count.

Antipsychotic drugs can have unwanted effects when taken with other medications. Therefore, the doctor should be told about all drugs being taken, including over-the-counter preparations, and the extent of the use of alcohol. Some antipsychotic drugs interfere with the action of antihypertensive drugs (taken for high blood pressure), anticonvulsants (taken for epilepsy), and drugs used for Parkinson's disease. Some antipsychotic drugs add to the effects of alcohol and other central nervous system depressants, such as antihistamines, antidepressants, barbiturates, some sleeping and pain medications, and narcotics.

ANTIMANIC DRUGS

Manic-depressive illness (bipolar disorder) is characterized by mood swings: severe highs (mania) and lows (depression). Patients may have several episodes of mania and only one of depression—or just the opposite. Sometimes, these mood swings follow each other very closely (within hours or days), but they may also be separated by months or years.

When someone is in a manic "high," he is overactive, overtalkative, and has a great deal of energy. He will switch quickly from one topic to another, as if he cannot get his thoughts out fast enough; his attention span is often short, and he can easily be distracted. Sometimes, the "high" person is irritable or angry and has false or inflated ideas about his position or importance in the world. He may be very elated, full of grand schemes which might range from business deals to romantic involvements. He may engage in wild spending sprees. Often, he shows poor judgment in these ventures.

Depression will show in a "low" mood, lack of energy, changes in eating and sleeping patterns, feelings of hopelessness, helplessness, and guilt, and sometimes thoughts of suicide.

These "highs" and "lows" may vary in intensity and severity. The drug used most often to combat a manic "high" is lithium. It is unusual to find mania without a subsequent or preceding period of depression. Lithium evens out mood swings in both directions, so that it is used not just for acute manic attacks, or flare-ups of the illness, but also as an ongoing treatment for bipolar disorder.

Lithium will diminish severe manic symptoms in about 5 to 14 days, but it may be anywhere from days to several months until the condition is fully controlled. Antipsychotic drugs are sometimes used in the first several days of treatment to control manic symptoms until the lithium begins to take effect.

Someone may have one episode of bipolar disorder and never have another, or be free of illness for several years. However, for those who have more than one episode, continuing (maintenance) treatment on lithium is usually given serious consideration.

Some people respond well to maintenance treatment and have no further episodes. Others have moderate mood swings that lessen as treatment continues and may disappear entirely. Some people may continue to have episodes that are diminished in frequency and severity. Some manic-depressive patients may not be helped at all. Who will respond in what way cannot be determined beforehand. Providing there are no physical conditions which present problems, and there are no serious adverse reactions, lithium can continue to be taken indefinitely.

Regular blood tests are an important part of treatment with lithium. These tests measure the amount of the drug in the body. If too little is taken, the drug will not be effective. If too much is taken, it may be toxic (poisonous). The range between an effective dose and a toxic one is small. Blood tests are given often at the beginning of treatment, to determine the best lithium level for the patient, and less often as treatment goes on. How much lithium needs to be taken may vary over time, depending on how ill a person is, his body chemistry, and his physical condition.

Anything that lowers the level of sodium (table salt is sodium chloride) in the body may cause a lithium buildup and lead to toxicity. Reduced salt intake, heavy sweating, fever, vomiting, or diarrhea may do this. An unusual amount of exercise or a switch to a low-salt diet are examples. It's important to be aware of conditions that lower sodium and to share this information with the doctor. The lithium dose may have to be adjusted.

Signs of lithium toxicity may include nausea, vomiting, drowsiness, and mental dullness, slurred speech, confusion, dizziness, muscle twitching, abnormal muscle movement, and blurred vision. A serious lithium overdose can be life-threatening.

When a person first takes lithium, he may experience side effects, such as drowsiness, weakness, nausea, vomiting, tiredness, hand tremor, or increased thirst and urination. These usually disappear or subside quickly, but hand tremor may persist. Weight gain may also occur. Diet will help, but crash diets should be avoided because they may affect the lithium level. Drinking low-calorie or no-calorie beverages will help keep weight down. Kidney changes, accompanied by increased thirst and urination may develop during treatment. These conditions and the thyroid problems that may occur are generally reversible and treatable.

Because of possible complications, lithium may either not be recommended or may be given with caution when a person has existing thyroid, kidney, or heart disorders, epilepsy, or brain damage. Women of childbearing age should be aware that lithium can cause deformities in babies born to women taking lithium. Special caution should be taken during the first 3 months of pregnancy.

Lithium, when combined with certain other drugs, can have unwanted effects. Some diuretics (drugs that remove water from the body) increase the level of lithium and can cause toxicity. Other diuretics, like coffee and tea, can lower the level of lithium. Problems may occur when lithium is combined with hydroxyzine (*Atarax, Vistaril*), antipsychotic drugs, or methyldopa (*Aldomet* and others). *Someone who is taking lithium should tell all the doctors he sees about all other medications he is taking.*

With regular monitoring, lithium is a safe and effective drug that enables many people, who otherwise would suffer from incapacitating mood swings, to lead normal lives.

Not all patients with symptoms of mania benefit from lithium. Some have been found to respond to another type of medication, the anticonvulsant drugs (which are usually used to treat epilepsy). Carbamazepine is the anticonvulsant that has been most widely used. Manic-depressive patients who cycle rapidly — that is, they change from mania to depression and back again over the course of hours or days, rather than months — seem to respond particularly well to carbamazepine.

Early side effects, although generally mild, include drowsiness, dizziness, ataxia, confusion, disturbed vision, perceptual distortions, memory impairment, and nausea. They are usually transient and often respond to temporary dosage reduction. More serious are the skin rashes that can occur in 15 to 20 percent of patients. These rashes are sometimes severe enough to require discontinuation of the drug. Two other anticonvulsants, valproic acid and divalproex, are now also being used in the treatment of mania. Their side effects are rather similar to those of carbamazepine, plus liver toxicity, increased appetite, weight gain, and tremor. They cause skin rashes less frequently. However, neither carbamazepine nor any other anticonvulsants have been approved by the Food and Drug Administration for manic-depressive illness. These drugs must undergo further study and testing before they merit FDA approval and general use.

ANTIDEPRESSANT DRUGS

The kind of depression that can benefit from drug treatment is more than just "the blues" or the "downs" of everyday life. It's a condition that's prolonged, lasting 2 weeks or more, and it interferes in a marked way with a person's ability to carry on daily tasks and to enjoy activities that previously brought pleasure.

The depressed person will seem sad or "down." He may have trouble eating and lose weight (although some people eat more and gain weight when depressed). He may sleep too much or too little, have difficulty going to sleep, sleep restlessly, or awaken very early in the morning. He may speak of feeling guilty, worthless, or hopeless. He may complain that his thinking is slowed down. He may lack energy, feeling "everything's too much," or he might be agitated and jumpy. A person who is depressed may cry. He may think and talk about killing himself and may even make a suicide attempt. Some people who are depressed have psychotic symptoms, such as delusions (false ideas) that are related to their depression. For instance, a psychotically depressed person might imagine that he is already dead, or "in hell," being punished.

Not everyone who is depressed has all these symptoms, but everyone who is depressed has at least some of them. A depression can vary in intensity from severe to moderate to mild.

Antidepressant drugs are used most widely for serious depressions, but they can also be helpful for some milder depressions. These drugs take away or reduce the symptoms of depression, and help the depressed person return to normal life and functioning. They are not "uppers" or stimulants—they can't make someone feel any better than he usually does, but they can help a person to feel as good as he did before he became depressed.

Antidepressant drugs are also used for disorders characterized principally by anxiety. They can block the symptoms of panic, including rapid heartbeat, terror, dizziness, chest pains, nausea, and breathing problems. They can also be used to treat some phobias.

When someone is taking antidepressant drugs, improvement will not generally begin to show immediately. With most of these drugs, it will take from 1 to 3 weeks before changes begin to occur. Some symptoms diminish early in treatment; others, later. For instance, a person's energy level or sleeping or eating patterns may improve before his depressed mood lifts. If there is little or no change in symptoms after 3 to 6 weeks, a different drug may be tried. Some people will respond better to one drug than another. Since there is no way of determining which drug will be effective beforehand, the doctor may have to prescribe first one drug, then another, until an effective one is found. Treatment is continued for a minimum of several months and may last up to a year or more.

While some people have one episode of depression and then never have another or remain symptom-free for years, others have more frequent episodes or very long-lasting depressions that may go on for years. Some people find that their depressions become more frequent and severe as they get older. For these people, continuing (maintenance) treatment with antidepressant drugs can be an effective way of reducing the frequency and severity of depressions. Those that are commonly used have no known long-term side effects and may be continued indefinitely. The dose of the drug may be lowered if side effects become troublesome.

Lithium can also be used in maintenance treatment of repeated depressions where there is evidence of a manic or manic-like episode in the past.

There are a number of antidepressant drugs available. They differ in their side effects and, to some extent, in their level of effectiveness. Tricyclic antidepressants (named for their chemical structure) are considered more effective for treatment of depression than monoamine oxidase inhibitors (MAOIs), but MAOIs are often helpful in so-called "atypical" depressions, where there are symptoms like overeating, oversleeping, anxiety, panic attacks, and phobias. Newer antidepressants, principally, serotonin reuptake inhibitors like fluoxetine, may prove to have advantages in terms of more rapid onset of action, fewer adverse side effects, and greater safety because of low toxicity from overdosage. In addition, one of them, clomipramine, is effective with obsessive-compulsive disorder.

Dosage of antidepressant drugs is variable, depending on the type of drug, the person's body chemistry, age, and, sometimes, body weight.

Doses are generally started low — and raised gradually over time until the desired effect is reached without the appearance of troublesome side effects.

There are a number of possible side effects with tricyclic antidepressants that vary, depending on the drug. For example, amitriptyline (*Amitril, Elavil, Amitid,* and *Endep*) tends to make people very drowsy and sleepy, while protriptyline (*Vivactil*) hardly does this at all. Because of this kind of variation in side effects, one antidepressant might be highly desirable for one person and not recommended for another. Most tricyclics complicate some specific heart problems. Other side effects with tricyclics may include blurred vision, dry mouth, constipation, dizziness when changing position, increased sweating, difficulty urinating, changes in sexual desire, decrease in sexual ability, weight gain, muscle twitches, fatigue, and weakness. Not all these drugs produce all side effects, and not everybody gets them. Some will disappear quickly, while others may remain for the length of treatment. Some side effects are similar to symptoms of depression (for instance, fatigue and constipation). For this reason, the patient or family should discuss all symptoms with the doctor, who may change the medication or dosage.

MAOIs may cause some side effects similar to tricyclics. Dizziness when changing position and rapid heartbeat are common. MAOIs also react with certain foods, alcoholic beverages, and other drugs (such as aged cheeses, Chianti and other red wines, and over-the-counter cold preparations) to cause severe high blood pressure, headaches, seizures, and stroke. For this reason, people taking MAOIs *must* stay away from restricted foods, drinks, and medications.

The serotonin reuptake inhibitors clomipramine, fluoxetine, sertraline and paroxetine must not be used in conjunction with monoamine oxidase inhibitors. Their most common side effects are nausea, sleepiness, weakness, dizziness, difficulty sleeping, tremor, nervousness, decreased appetite, ejaculatory disturbance, and rarely, increased suicidality.

An overdose of antidepressants is serious and potentially lethal. It requires immediate medical attention. These drugs should be taken only in the amount prescribed and should be kept in a secure place away from children.

Symptoms of a tricyclic overdose develop within an hour and may start with rapid heartbeat, dilated pupils, flushed face, and agitation, and progress to confusion, loss of consciousness, seizures, heart irregularities, cardiorespiratory collapse, and death. Reactions caused by mixing MAOIs with aged cheeses and other restricted foods often do not appear for several hours. Signs may include raised blood pressure, headache, nausea, vomiting, rapid heartbeat, possible confusion, psychotic symptoms, and coma.

When taking antidepressant drugs, it is important to tell all doctors being seen (not just the one who is treating the depression) about all medications being used, including over-the-counter preparations, and alcohol, if it is used regularly. Antidepressants interact with a large number of drugs and other substances; these interactions may change the effect of the antidepressant or cause unwanted reactions. Tricyclics may interact with thyroid hormone, antihypertensive drugs, oral contraceptives, some blood coagulants, some sleeping medications, antipsychotic drugs, diuretics, antihistamines, aspirin, bicarbonate of soda, vitamin C, alcohol, and tobacco.

MAOIs also have negative interactions with a large number of drugs and other substances. The more common include local anesthetics, over-the-counter cold and allergy preparations, amphetamines, antihistamines, insulin, narcotics, antiparkinsonian drugs, alcohol, and monosodium glutamate (MSG).

When used with proper care, following doctors' instructions, antidepressants are extremely useful drugs that can reverse the misery of a depression and help a person feel like himself again.

ANTIANXIETY DRUGS

Everyone experiences anxiety at one time or another — "butterflies in the stomach" before giving a speech or sweaty palms during a job interview are common symptoms. Other symptoms of anxiety include irritability, uneasiness, jumpiness, feelings of apprehension, rapid or irregular heartbeat, stomach ache, nausea, faintness, and breathing problems.

Anxiety is often manageable and mild. But sometimes it can present serious problems. A high level or prolonged state of anxiety can be very incapacitating, making the activities of daily life difficult or impossible.

Phobias, which are persistent, irrational fears and are characterized by avoidance of certain objects, places, and things, sometimes accompany anxiety. A panic attack is a severe form of anxiety that occurs suddenly and is marked by intense fear, breathlessness, pounding heart, and feelings that one may die.

Antianxiety drugs calm and relax the anxious person and remove the troubling symptoms. There are a number of antianxiety drugs currently available. The preferred drugs for most anxiety disorders are the benzodiazepines. Antidepressant drugs are also very effective for panic attacks and some phobias and are often prescribed for these conditions. Recently, antidepressants have also been used for more generalized forms of anxiety, especially when accompanied by depression.

The most commonly used benzodiazepines are chlordiazepoxide (*Librium*, Librax, Libritabs, and others) and diazepam (*Valium*). Benzodiazepines are relatively fast-acting drugs. Most will begin to take effect within hours, some in even less time. These effects are long lasting, so that often the benzodiazepines can be taken only two or three times a day. Dosage of the drug is generally started at a low level and gradually raised until symptoms are diminished or removed. The dosage will vary a great deal depending on the symptoms and the individual's body chemistry. Benzodiazepines have few side effects. Drowsiness and loss of coordination are most common. Fatigue and mental slowing or confusion can also occur. These effects make it dangerous to drive or operate some machinery when taking benzodiazepines — especially when the patient is just beginning treatment. Other side effects are rare.

Benzodiazepines combined with other drugs can present a problem, notably when taken together with commonly used substances such as alcohol. Following the doctor's instructions is important. The doctor should be informed of all other drugs the patient is taking, including over-the-counter medications (those available without a prescription). Benzodiazepines increase central nervous system depression when combined with alcohol, anesthetics, antihistamines, sedatives, muscle relaxants, and some prescription pain medications. Particular benzodiazepines may influence the action of some anticonvulsant and cardiac drugs. Benzodiazepines have also been associated with abnormalities in babies born to mothers who were taking these drugs.

With benzodiazepines, there is a potential for the development of tolerance and dependence as well as the possibility of abuse and withdrawal reactions. For this reason, the drugs are generally prescribed for brief periods of time (days or weeks), and sometimes intermittently, for stressful situations or anxiety attacks. For the same reason, ongoing or continuous treatment with benzodiazepines is not recommended for most people. A very small number of patients may, however, need long-term treatment.

Consult with the doctor before discontinuing a benzodiazepine. A withdrawal reaction may occur if the drug is abruptly stopped. Thus, after benzodiazepines are taken for an extended period, the dosage is gradually tapered off before being completely stopped. Symptoms may include anxiety, shakiness, headache, dizziness, sleeplessness, loss of appetite, and, in more severe cases, fever, seizures, and psychosis. A withdrawal reaction may be mistaken for a return of the anxiety, since many of the symptoms are similar.

Except for alprazolam (*Xanax*), an overdose of benzodiazepines is almost never life-threatening, but taken together with alcohol or other drugs, it may lead to serious and possibly life-threatening complications.

Although benzodiazepines or tricyclic antidepressants are the preferred drugs for most anxiety disorders, occasionally, for specific reasons, one of the following drugs may be prescribed: antipsychotic drugs; antihistamines (such as *Atarax, Vistaril*, and others); barbiturates such as phenobarbital; propanediols such as meprobamate (*Equanil*); and propanolol (*Inderal, Inderide*).

INDEX OF DRUGS

To find the section of the text that describes the drug you or a friend or family member is taking, find either the generic (chemical) name and look it up on the first list, or the trade name and look it up on the second list. If you do not find the name of the drug on the label, ask your doctor or pharmacist for it. (Note: some drugs, such as amitriptyline and chlordiazepoxide, are marketed under numerous trade names, not all of which can be mentioned in a brief list such as this. If your drug's trade name does not appear in this list, look it up by its generic name or ask your doctor or pharmacist for more information.)

Alphabetical Listing of Medications by Generic Name

GENERIC NAME	TRADE NAME	TYPE OF DRUG
acetophenazine	Tindil	antipsychotic
alprazolam	Xanax	antianxiety
amitriptyline	Amitid	antidepressant
	Amitril	
	Elavil	
	Endep	
amoxapine	Asendin	antidepressant
butaperazine	Repoise	antipsychotic
carbamazepine	Tegretol	antimanic
carphenazine	Proketazine	antipsychotic
chlordiazepoxide	Librax	antianxiety
	Libritabs	
	Librium	

chlorpromazine	Thorazine	antipsychotic
chlorprothixene	Taractan	antipsychotic
clomimpramine	Anafranil	antiobsessive-compulsive
clorazepate	Azene	antianxiety
	Tranxene	
clozapine	Clozaril	antipsychotic
desipramine	Norpramin	antidepressant
	Pertofrane	
dextroamphetamine	Dexedrine	stimulant
diazepam	Valium	antianxiety
divalproex	Depakote	antimanic
doxepin	Adapin	antianxiety
	Sinequan	
fluoxetine	Prozac	antidepressant
fluphenazine	Permitil	antipsychotic
	Prolixin	
haloperidol	Haldol	antipsychotic
halazepam	Paxipam	antianxiety
imiprmine	Imavate	antidepressant
	Janimine	
	Presamine	
	Tofranil	
isocarboxazid	Marplan	antidepressant
lithium carbonate	Eskalith	antimanic
	Lithane	
	Lithobid	
lithium citrate	Cibalith-S	antimanic
lorazepam	Ativan	antianxiety
loxapine	Daxolin	antipsychotic
	Loxitane	
maprotiline	Ludiomil	antidepressant
mesoridazine	Serentil	antipsychotic
methylphenidate	Ritalin	stimulant
molindone	Lidone	antipsychotic
	Moban	
nortriptyline	Aventyl	antipsychotic
	Pamelor	
oxazepam	Serax	antianxiety
paroxetine	Paxil	antidepressant
perphenazine	Trilafon	antipsychotic
phenelzine	Nardil	antidepressant
piperacetazine	Quide	antipsychotic
prazepam	Centrax	antianxiety
	Vestran	
prochlorperazine	Compazine	antipsychotic
protriptyline	Vivactil	antidepressant
sertraline	Zoloft	antidepressant
thioridazine	Mellaril	antipsychotic
thiothixene	Navane	antipsychotic
tranylcypromine	Parnate	antidepressant
trazodone	Desyrel	antidepressant
trifluoperazine	Stelazine	antipsychotic
triflupromazine	Vesprin	antipsychotic
valproic acid	Depakene	antimanic

Alphabetical Listing of Medications by Trade Name

TRADE NAME	GENERIC NAME	TYPE OF DRUG
Adapin	doxepin	antidepressant
Amitid	amitriptyline	antidepressant
Amitril	amitriptyline	antidepressant
Anafranil	clomimpramine	anti-obsessive compulsive
Asendin	amoxapine	antidepressant
Ativan	lorazepam	antianxiety
Aventyl	nortriptyline	antidepressant
Azene	clorazepate	antianxiety
Centrax	prazepam	antianxiety
Cibalith-S	lithium citrate	antimanic
Clozaril	clozapine	antipsychotic
Compazine	prochlorperazine	antipsychotic
Daxolin	loxapine	antipsychotic
Depa-kene	valproic acid	antimanic
Depa-kote	dival-proex	antimanic
Dexedrine	dextroamphetamine	stimulant
Elavil	amitriptyline	antidepressant
Endep	amitriptyline	antidepressant
Eskalith	lithium carbonate	antimanic
Haldol	haloperidol	antipsychotic
Imavate	imipramine	antidepressant
Janimine	imipramine	antidepressant
Librax	chlordiazepoxide	antianxiety
Libritabs	chlordiazepoxide	antianxiety
Librium	chlordiazepoxide	antianxiety
Lidone	molindone	antipsychotic
Lithane	lithium carbonate	antimanic
Lithobid	lithium carbonate	antimanic
Loxitane	loxapine	antipsychotic
Ludiomil	maprotiline	antidepressant
Marplan	isocarboxazid	antidepressant
Mellaril	thioridazine	antipsychotic
Moban	molindone	antipsychotic
Nardil	phenelzine	antidepressant
Navane	thiothixene	antipsychotic
Norpramin	desipramine	antidepressant
Pamelor	nortriptyline	antidepressant
Parnate	tranylcypromine	antidepressant
Paxil	paroxetine	antidepressant
Paxipam	halazepam	antianxiety
Permitil	fluphenazine	antipsychotic
Pertofrane	desipramine	antidepressant
Presamine	imipramine	antidepressant
Proketazine	carphenazine	antipsychotic
Prolixin	fluphenazine	antipsychotic
Prozac	fluoxetine	antidepressant
Quide	piperacetazine	antipsychotic
Repoise	butaperazine	antipsychotic
Ritalin	methylphenidate	stimulant
Serax	oxazepam	antianxiety
Serentil	mesoridazine	antipsychotic
Sinequan	doxepin	antidepressant

Stelazine	trifluoperazine	antipsychotic
Taractan	chlorprothixene	antipsychotic
Tegretol	carbamazepine	antimanic
Thorazine	chlorpromazine	antipsychotic
Tindal	acetophenazine	antipsychotic
Tofranil	imipramine	antidepressant
Tranxene	clorazepate	antianxiety
Trilafon	perphenazine	antipsychotic
Valium	diazepam	antianxiety
Vesprin	trifluopromazine	antipsychotic
Vestran	prazepam	antianxiety
Vivactil	protriptyline	antidepressant
Xanax	alprazolam	antianxiety
Zoloft	sertraline	antidepressant

References

A network for caring: The community support program of the National Institute of Mental Health (1982). U.S. Department of Health and Human Services, National Institute of Mental Health, DHHS Pub. No. (ADM) 81-1063.

Anthony, W. A., & Blanch, A. (1987). Supported employment for persons who are psychiatrically disabled: A historical and conceptual perspective. *Psychosocial Rehabilitation Journal, 11*, 5-23.

Anthony, W. A., Buell, G. J., Sharrett, S., & Althoff, M. E. (1972). Efficacy of psychiatric rehabilitation. *Psychological Bulletin, 78*, 447-456.

Anthony, W. A., & Dion, G. (1986). *Psychiatric rehabilitation: A rehabilitation research review.* Washington, DC: National Rehabilitation Information Center.

Arce, A. A., & Vergare, M. J. (1985a). Psychiatrists and interprofessional role conflicts in community mental health centers. In *Community mental health centers and psychiatrists.* Edited by the Joint Steering Committee of the American Psychiatric Association and the National Council of Community Mental Health Centers. Washington, DC and Rockville, MD.

Arce, A., & Vergare, M. (1985b). An overview of community residences as alternatives to hospitalization. *Psychiatric Clinics of North America, 8*, 423-436.

Babigian, H. M. (1977). The impact of community mental health centers on the utilization of services. *Archives of General Psychiatry, 34*, 385-394.

Bachrach, L. L. (1976). *Deinstitutionalization: An analytical review and sociological perspective.* Washington, DC: U.S. Government Printing Office.

Backes, R., Cohen, J., Gundlach, E., Myers, T., Propst, R., Rawls, A., & Hennings, B. (1987). *Medical services in the Fountain House model.* Presented at the Fourth Annual Fountain House Seminar, Seattle, WA.

Balestrieri, M., Micciolo, R., & Tansella, M. (1987). Long-stay and long-term psychiatric patients in an area with a community-based system of care. A register follow-up study. *International Journal of Social Psychiatry, 33*, 251-262.

Barton, R. (1959). *Institutional neurosis.* Bristol: Wright.

Barton, W., & Sanborn, C. J. (Eds.) (1977). *An assessment of the community mental health movement*. Lexington, MA: D. C. Heath.

Basaglia, F. (1985). What is psychiatry? In R. F. Mollica (Ed.), The unfinished revolution in Italian psychiatry: An international perspective. *International Journal of Mental Health, 14*, 42–51.

Battle, C. J. (1981). The iatrogenic disease called burnout. *Journal of American Medical Women's Association, 36*, 357–359.

Beard, J. H., Malamud, T. J., & Rossman, E. (1978). Psychiatric rehabilitation and long-term rehospitalization rates: The findings of two research studies. *Schizophrenia Bulletin, 4*, 622–636.

Beard, J. H., Propst, R., & Malamud, T. J. (1982). The Fountain House model of psychiatric rehabilitation. *Psychosocial Rehabilitation Journal, 5*, 47–53.

Beck, A. T., Rush, A. J., Shaw, B., & Emery, G. (1979). *Cognitive therapy of depression*. New York: Guilford.

Beers, C. W. (1939). *A mind that found itself*. New York: Doubleday.

Beigel, A., & Levenson, A. I. (Eds.) (1972). The *community mental health center*. New York: Basic Books.

Beiser, M., Shore, J. H., Peters, R., & Tatum, E. (1985). Does community care for the mentally ill make a difference? A tale of two cities. *American Journal of Psychiatry, 142*, 1047–1052.

Bellack, A. S., Turner, S. M., Hersen, M., & Luber, R. F. (1984). An examination of social skills training for chronic schizophrenic patients. *Hospital and Community Psychiatry, 35*, 1023–1028.

Bellak, L. (Ed.) (1974). *A concise handbook of community psychiatry and community mental health*. New York: Grune & Stratton.

Bennett, D. H. (1985). The changing pattern of mental health care in Trieste. In R. F. Mollica (Ed.). The unfinished revolution in Italian psychiatry: An international perspective. *International Journal of Mental Health, 14*, 70–92.

Bennett, D. H., & Wing, K. K. (1963). Sheltered workshops for the psychiatrically handicapped. In H. Freeman, & J. Farndale (Eds.). *Trends in the mental health services*. London: Pergamon.

Bertelsen, K., & Harris, M. R. (1973). Citizen participation in the development of a community mental health center. *Hospital and Community Psychiatry, 24*, 553–556.

Black, B. J. (1970). *Principles of industrial therapy for the mentally ill*. New York: Grune & Stratton.

Bleuler, M. (1975). Personal communication.

Bleuler, M. (1968). A 23-year longitudinal study of 208 schizophrenics and impressions in regard to the nature of schizophrenia. In D. Rosenthal, & S. S. Kety (Eds.), *The transmission of schizophrenia*. Oxford: Pergamon Press.

Bockoven, J. S. (1963). *Moral treatment in American psychiatry*. New York: Springer.

Bolman, W. (1972). Community control of the community mental health center: II. Case Examples. *American Journal of Psychiatry, 129*, 181–186.

Bond, G. R., Witheridge, T. F., Setze, P. J., & Dincin, J. (1985). Preventing rehospitalization of clients in a psychosocial rehabilitation program. *Hospital and Community Psychiatry, 36*, 993–995.

Bordin, E. S. (1979). The generalizability of the psychoanalytic concept of the working alliance. *Psychotherapy, 16*, 252–260.

Borland, J. J. (1981). Burnout among workers and administrators. *Health and Social Work, 6*, 73–78.

Braun, P. B., Kochansky, G., Shapiro, R., Greenberg, S., Gudeman, J. E., Johnson, S., & Shore, M. F. (1981). Overview: Deinstitutionalization of psychiatric patients: A critical review of outcome studies. *American Journal of Psychiatry, 138*, 736–749.

Brown, D., & Parnell, M. (1990). Mental health services for the urban poor: A systems approach. In M. P. Mirkin (Ed.), *The social & political contexts of family therapy*. Boston: Allyn and Bacon.

Brown, G. W. (1981). Life events, psychiatric disorder and physical illness. *Journal of Psychosomatic Research, 25*, 461–473.

Brown, G. W., & Birley, J. (1968). Crises and life changes and the onset of schizophrenia. *Journal of Health and Social Behavior, 9,* 203-214.

Budson, R. D. (1978). *The psychiatric halfway house.* Pittsburgh, PA: University of Pittsburgh Press.

Budson, R. D., Meehan, J., & Barclay, E. (Eds.). (1974). *Developing a community residence for the mentally ill.* Boston: Commonwealth of Massachusetts.

Burti, L., & Mosher, L. R. (1986). Training psychiatrists in the community: A report of the Italian experience. *American Journal of Psychiatry, 143,* 1580-1584.

Burti, L., Faccincani, C., Mignolli, G., Siani, R., Siciliani, O., & Zimmermann-Tansella, Ch. (1984). Terapia sistemica e servizio territoriale: un addio allo specchio? In L. Boscolo, & G. Cecchin (Eds.), *Atti del IV Convegno Annuale del Centro Milanese di Terapia della Famiglia.* Milano: Centro Milanese di Terapia Familiare.

Burti, L., Garzotto, N., Siciliani, O., Zimmerman-Tansella, Ch., & Tansella, M. (1986). South Verona's psychiatric service: An integrated system of community care. *Hospital and Community Psychiatry, 37,* 809-813.

Canton, G., & Santonastaso, P. (1984). Psychological distress and life events in neurotic patients. *Psychopathology, 17,* 144-148.

Caplan, G., & Caplan, R. B. (1967). Development of community psychiatry concepts. In A. M. Freedman, & H. I. Kaplan (Eds.), *Comprehensive textbook of psychiatry (1st ed.).* Baltimore: Williams & Wilkins.

Carling, P. (1984). *Developing family foster care programs in mental health: A resource guide.* Washington, DC: U.S. Department of Health and Human Services.

Carpenter, M. D. (1978). Residential placement for the chronic psychiatric patient: A review and evaluation of the literature. *Schizophrenia Bulletin, 4,* 384-398.

Carpenter, W. T., Jr., Hanlon, T. E., Heinrichs, D. W., Summerfelt, A. T., Kirkpatrick, B., Levine, J., & Buchanan, R. W. (1990). Continuous versus targeted medication in schizophrenic outpatients: outcome results. *American Journal of Psychiatry, 147,* 1138-1148.

Carpenter, W. T., Heinrichs, D. W., & Hanlon, T. E. (1987). A comparative trial of pharmacologic strategies in schizophrenia. *American Journal of Psychiatry, 144,* 1466-1470.

Cauce, A. M. (1986). Special networks and social competence: Exploring the effects of early adolescent friendships. *American Journal of Community Psychology, 14,* 607-628.

Centro Studi Investimenti Sociali (CENSIS) (1985). *L'attuazione della riforma psichiatrica nel quadro delle politiche regionali e dell'offerta quantitativa e qualitativa dei servizi.* Mimeo. Roma: CENSIS.

Centro Studi Ministero della Sanità (1977). *L'assistenza Psichiatrica Ospedaliera ed Extraospedaliera. Rapporto no. 14.* Roma.

Chamberlin, J. (1978). *On our own: Patient-controlled alternatives to the mental health system.* New York: McGraw-Hill.

Chien, C., & Cole, J. O. (1973). Landlord-supervised cooperative apartments: A new modality for community-based treatment. *American Journal of Psychiatry, 130,* 156-159.

Chouinard, G., Bradwejn, J., Jones, B. D., & Ross-Chouinard, A. (1984). Withdrawal symptoms after long-term treatment with low-potency neuroleptics. *Journal of Clinical Psychiatry, 45,* 500-502.

Ciompi, L. (1980). Catamnestic long-term study of the course of life and aging of schizophrenics. *Schizophrenia Bulletin, 6,* 606-618.

Clark, G. H., & Vaccaro, J. V. (1987). Burnout among CMHC psychiatrists and the struggle to survive. *Hospital and Community Psychiatry, 38,* 843-847.

Cohen, S., & Syme, S. L. (Eds.). (1985). *Social support and health.* Orlando: Academic Press.

Day, R., Nielsen, J. A., Korten, A., Ernberg, G., Dube, K. C., Gebhart, J., Jablensky, A., Leon, C., Marsella, A., Olatawura, M., Sartorius, N., Stromgren, E., Takahashi, R., Wig, N., & Wynne, L. C. (1987). Stressful life events preceding the acute onset of schizophrenia: A cross-national study from the World Health Organization. *Culture, Medicine and Psychiatry, 11,* 123-205.

Davis, J. M. (1980). Antipsychotic drugs. In H. Kaplan, A. M. Freedman, & B. J. Sadock (Eds.), *Comprehensive Textbook of Psychiatry, Volume 3.* Baltimore: Williams & Wilkins.

Davis, T., & Specht, P. (1978). Citizen participation in community mental-health programs:

A study in intergroup conflict and cooperation. *Group and Organization Studies, 3*, 456–466.

Dean, A., & Lin, D. (1977). The stress buffering role of social support. *Journal of Nervous and Mental Disease, 166*, 7–15.

De Salvia, D. (1983). Lo sviluppo dell'assistenza psichiatrica in Italia. Uno studio valutativo. *Prospettive Sociali e Sanitarie, 14–15*, 22–28.

De Salvia, D. (1984). Elementi di statistica ed epidemiologia sull'applicazione della 180. *Fogli di Informazione, 106*, 1–22.

De Salvia, D., & Crepet, P. (Eds.). (1982). *Psichiatria Senza Manicomio. Epidemiologia Critica della Riforma*. Milano: Feltrinelli.

Deutsch, A. (1948). *Shame of the states*. New York: Arno Press.

Dohrenwend, B. P. (1975). Sociocultural and sociopsychological factors in the genesis of mental disorders. *Journal of Health and Social Behavior, 16*, 365–392.

Dohrenwend, B. P., & Egri, G. (1981). Recent stressful life events and episodes of schizophrenia. *Schizophrenia Bulletin, 7*, 12–23.

Dupont, A. (1979). Psychiatric case registers. In H. Haefner (Ed.), *Estimating needs for mental health care*. Berlin: Springer Verlag.

Emener, W. G. (1979). Professional burnout: Rehabilitation's hidden handicap. *Journal of Rehabilitation, 45*, 55–58.

Ewalt, J. R. (1987). Personal communication.

Faccincani, C., Burti, L., Garzotto, N., Mignolli, G., & Tansella, M. (1985). Organizational aspects of community care. The South-Verona mental health center. *New Trends in Experimental and Clinical Psychiatry, 1*, 201–216.

Fairweather, G. W., Sanders, D., Cressler, D., & Maynard, H. (1969). *Community life for the mentally ill: An alternative to institutional care*. Chicago: Aldine.

Falloon, I. R. H., Boyd, J. L., McGill, C. W., Razani, J., Moss, H. B., & Gilderman, A. M. (1982). Family management in the prevention of exacerbations of schizophrenia. *New England Journal of Medicine, 306*, 1437–1440.

Fenton, W. S., Leaf, P. J., Moran, N. L., & Tischler, G. L. (1984). Trends in psychiatric practice, 1965–1980. *American Journal of Psychiatry, 141*, 346–351.

Foley, H. A., & Sharfstein, S. S. (1983). *Madness and government: Who cares for the mentally ill?* Washington, DC: American Psychiatric Press.

Fountain House. (1985). Summary of Transitional Employment Results, Memorandum 279, 10 December.

Frank, J. D. (1971). Therapeutic factors in psychotherapy. *American Journal of Psychotherapy, 25*, 350–361.

Frank, J. D. (1973). *Persuasion and healing: A comparative study of psychotherapy*. Baltimore: Johns Hopkins University Press.

Frank, L. R. (1986). The policies and practices of American psychiatry are oppressive. *Hospital and Community Psychiatry, 137*, 497–501.

Freudenberger, H. J. (1980). *Burnout*. New York: Anchor Press.

Freudenberger, H. J. (1986). The issues of staff burnout in therapeutic communities. *Journal of Psychoactive Drugs, 18*, 247–251.

Fromm-Reichmann, F. (1948). Notes on the development of treatment of schizophrenics by psychoanalytic psychotherapy. *Psychiatry, 11*, 263–273.

Galzina, M., & Terzian, H. (1980). *L'Archivio della Follia*. Padova: Marsilio Editori.

Gardos, G., Cole, J. O., & Torey, D. (1978). Withdrawal syndromes associated with antipsychotic drugs. *American Journal of Psychiatry, 135*, 1321–1324.

Glasscote, R. M., Cumming, E., Rutman, I., Sussex, J. N., & Glassman, S. M. (1971). *Rehabilitating the mentally ill in the community*. Washington, DC: Joint Information Service of the American Psychiatric Association and the National Association for Mental Health.

Goldberg, D. P., & Huxley, P. (1980). *Mental illness in the community: The pathway to psychiatric care*. London: Tavistock.

Goldman, H. H., & Morrissey, J. P. (1985). The alchemy of mental health policy: Homelessness and the fourth cycle of reform. *American Journal of Public Health, 75*, 727–731.

Goldman, H. H., Adams, N. H., & Taube, C. A. (1983). Deinstitutionalization: The data demythologized. *Hospital and Community Psychiatry, 34*, 129–134.

Goldman, H., Morrissey, J., Ridgely, M., Frank, R., Newman, S., & Kennedy, C. (1992). The Robert Wood Johnson Program on Chronic Mental Illness: Implementation analysis and policy findings. *Health Affairs, 11*, 51–68.

Goldmeier, J. (1977). Community residential facilities for former mental patients: A review. *Psychosocial Rehabilitation Journal, 1*, 1–45.

Goldmeier, J., Shore, M. F., & Mannino, F. V. (1977). Cooperative apartments: New programs in community mental health. *Health and Social Work, 2*, 119–140.

Goldstein, S. (1986). Bye bye Brady bunch. *The Family Therapy Networker.* January–February, 31–32/76–78.

Goldstein, S. J., & Dyche, L. (1983). Family therapy of the schizophrenic poor. In W. R. McFarlane (Ed.), *Forces from outside the family.* New York: Guilford.

Golomb, S. L., & Kocsis, A. (1988). *The halfway house: On the road to independence.* New York: Brunner/Mazel.

Gottlieb, B. H. (1985). Social networks and social support: An overview of research, practice and policy implications. *Health Education Quarterly, 12*, 5–22.

Greenberg, R. P., Bernstein, R. F., Greenberg, M. D., & Fisher, S. (1992). A meta-analysis of antidepressant outcome under "blinder" conditions. *Journal of Counseling and Clinical Psychology, 60*, 664–669.

Greenblatt, M., Becerra, R. M., & Serafetinides, E. A. (1982). Social networks and mental health: An overview. *American Journal of Psychiatry, 139*, 977–984.

Grob, G. (1973). *Mental institutions in America, social policy to 1875.* New York: Free Press of Clencoe.

Grob, G. (1983). *Mental illness and American society, 1875–1940.* Princeton: Princeton University Press.

Gruenberg, E. M., Snow, H. B., & Bennett, C. L. (1969). Preventing the social breakdown syndrome. In F. C. Redlich, *Social Psychiatry.* Baltimore: Williams & Wilkins.

Grunebaum, H. (1986). On harmful therapy. *American Journal of Psychotherapy, 60*, 165–176.

Gunderson, J. G. (1978). Defining the therapeutic processes in psychiatric milieus. *Psychiatry, 41*, 327–335.

Gunderson, J., Will, O. A., & Mosher, L. R. (Eds.). (1983). *Principles and practice of milieu therapy.* New York: Jason Aronson.

Gunderson, J. G., Frank, A. F., Katz, H. M., Vannicelli, M. L., Frosch, J. P., & Knapp, P. H. (1984). Effects of psychotherapy on schizophrenia: II. Comparative outcome of two forms of treatment. *Schizophrenia Bulletin, 10*, 564–598.

Häfner, H., & Klug, J. (1982). The impact of an expanding community mental health service on patterns of bed usage: Evaluation of a four-year period of implementation. *Psychological Medicine, 12*, 177–190.

Hammer, M. (1981). Social supports, social networks and schizophrenia. *Schizophrenia Bulletin, 7*, 45–57.

Hammer, M. (1983). 'Core' and 'extended' social networks in relation to health and illness. *Social Science and Medicine, 17*, 405–411.

Harding, C. M., Brooks, G. W., Ashikaga, T., Strauss, J. S., & Breier, A. (1987a). The Vermont longitudinal study of persons with severe mental illness, I: Methodology, study sample and overall status 32 years later. *American Journal of Psychiatry, 144*, 718–726.

Harding, C. M., Brooks, G. W., Ashikaga, T., Strauss, J. S., & Breier, A. (1987b). The Vermont longitudinal study of persons with severe mental illness, II: Long-term outcome of subjects who retrospectively met DSM-III criteria for schizophrenia. *American Journal of Psychiatry, 144*, 727–735.

Hatfield, A. (1984). *Coping with mental illness in the family.* NAMI.

Hatfield, A. (1985). *Consumer guide to mental health services.* NAMI.

Heptinstall, D. (1984). Psichiatria democratica: Italy's revolution in caring for the mentally ill. *Community Care, 1*, 17–19.

Herz, M. I., Endicott, J., Spitzer, R., & Mesnikoff, A. (1971). Day versus inpatient hospitalization: A controlled study. *American Journal of Psychiatry, 127*, 1371-1382.

Hirschfeld, R. M., Matthews, S. M., Mosher, L. R., & Menn, A. Z. (1977). Being with madness: Personality characteristics of three treatment staffs. *Hospital and Community Psychiatry, 28*, 267-273.

Hogarty, G. E., Anderson, C. M., Reiss, D. J., Kornblith, S. J., Greenwald, D. P., Javna, C. D., & Madonia, M. J. (1986). Family psychoeducation, social skills training and maintenance chemotherapy in the aftercare treatment of schizophrenia. *Archives of General Psychiatry, 43*, 633-642.

Hogarty, G. E., Schooler, N. R., Ulrich, R., Mussare, F., Ferro, P., & Herron, E. (1979). Fluphenazine and social therapy in aftercare of schizophrenic patients. Relapse analyses of a two-year controlled study of fluphenazine decanoate and fluphenazine hydrochloride. *Archives of General Psychiatry, 36*, 1283-1294.

Horowitz, M., & Marmar, C. (1985). The therapeutic alliance with difficult patients. *Psychiatry Update, 4*, APA Press.

Horvath, A. O., & Greenberg, L. (1986). The development of the working alliance inventory. In L. Greenberg, & W. Pinsof (Eds.), *The psychotherapeutic process: A research handbook*. New York: Guilford.

Hoult, J. (1986). The community care of the acutely mentally ill. *British Journal of Psychiatry, 149*, 137-144.

Huber, G., Gross, G., Schuttler, T., & Linz, M. (1980). Longitudinal studies of schizophrenic patients. *Schizophrenia Bulletin, 6*, 592-605.

Imber-Black, E., Roberts, J., & Whiting, R. J. (Eds.). (1988). *Rituals in families and family therapy*. New York: W. W. Norton.

Istituto Centrale di Statistica (ISTAT). *Annuario statistico Italiano, 1964-1991 edns*. Roma: ISTAT.

Jablensky, A., & Henderson, J. (1983). Report on a visit to the South-Verona community psychiatric service. *WHO Assignment Report*. Copenhagen and Geneva: WHO.

Jansen, E. (1970). The role of the halfway house in community mental health programs in the United Kingdom and America. *American Journal of Psychiatry, 126*, 1498-1504.

Jerrell, J. M., & Larsen, J. K. (1983). Trends in outcome indicators in sample community mental health centers: 1976-1982. National Institute of Mental Health, Technical Report 83-9.

Jervis, G. (1975). *Manuale critico di psichiatria*. Milano: Feltrinelli.

Joint Commission on Mental Illness and Health (1961). *Action for mental health: Final report of the Joint Commission on Mental Illness and Health 1961*. New York: Basic Books.

Jones, K., & Poletti, A. (1985). Understanding the Italian experience. *British Journal of Psychiatry, 146*, 341-347.

Jones, K., & Poletti, A. (1986). The 'Italian experience' reconsidered. *British Journal of Psychiatry, 148*, 144-150.

Kane, J. M. (1983). Low dose medication strategies in the maintenance treatment of schizophrenia. *Schizophrenia Bulletin, 9*, 528-532.

Kane, J. M. (1984). *Drug maintenance strategies in schizophrenia*. American Psychiatric Press: Washington, DC.

Kane, J. M. (1987). Treatment of schizophrenia. *Schizophrenia Bulletin, 13*, 133-156.

Kane, J. M., Rifkin, A., Woerner, M., Reardon, G., Sarantakos, S., Schiebel, D., & Ramos-Lorenzi, J. (1983). Low dose neuroleptic treatment. *Archives of General Psychiatry, 40*, 893-896.

Kane, J. M., Woerner, M., Weinhold, P., Wagner, J., Kinon, B., & Borenstein, M. (1984). Incidence of tardive dyskinesia: Five year data from a prospective study. *Psychopharmacology Bulletin, 20*, 382-386.

Kanter, J. (1984). *Coping strategies for relatives of the mentally ill*. NAMI.

Kaplan, B., Cassel, J., & Gore, S. (1977). Social support and health. *Medical Care, 15*, 47-58.

Kiesler, C. A. (1982a). Mental hospitals and alternative care: Noninstitutionalization as potential public policy for mental patients. *American Psychologist, 37*, 349-360.

Kiesler, C. A. (1982b). Public and professional myths about mental hospitalization: An empirical reassessment of policy-related beliefs. *American Psychologist, 37*, 1323-1339.

Klerman, G., Weissman, M., Rounsaville, B., & Chevron, E. (1984). *Interpersonal psychotherapy of depression*. New York: Basic Books.

Klorman, R., Strauss, J., & Kokes, R. (1977). Premorbid adjustment in schizophrenia: Concepts, measures, and implications. Part III. The relationship of demographic and diagnostic factors to measures of premorbid adjustment in schizophrenia. *Schizophrenia Bulletin, 3*, 214-225.

Knesper, D. J., & Carlson, B. W. (1981). An analysis of the movement to private psychiatric practice. *Archives of General Psychiatry, 38*, 943-949.

Kresky-Wolff, M., Matthews, S., Kalibat, F., & Mosher, L. (1984). Crossing Place: A residential model for crisis intervention. *Hospital and Community Psychiatry, 35*, 72-74.

Kresky, M., Maeda, E. M., & Rothwell, N. D. (1976). The apartment program: A community living option for halfway house residents. *Hospital and Community Psychiatry, 27*, 153-154.

Kupfer, D. J., Frank, E., Perel, J. M., Cornes, C., Mallinger, A. G., Thase, M. E., McEachran, A. B., & Grochocinski, V. J. (1992). Five-year outcome for maintenance therapies in recurrent depression. *Archives of General Psychiatry, 49*, 769-73.

Lacey, R. (1984). Where have all the patients gone? *Guardian*, July 4.

Laing, R. D. (1967). *The politics of experience*. New York: Ballantine.

Lamb, H. R. (1979). Roots of neglect of the long-term mentally ill. *Psychiatry, 42*, 201-207.

Lamb, H. R. (Ed.) (1984). *The homeless mentally ill*. Washington, DC: American Psychiatric Association.

Lamb, H. R., & Lamb, D. M. (1984). A nonhospital alternative to acute hospitalization. *Hospital and Community Psychiatry, 35*, 728-730.

Landy, D., & Greenblatt, M. (1965). *Halfway houses*. Washington, DC: U.S. Department of Health, Education and Welfare, Vocational Rehabilitation Administration.

Langsley, D. G., & Kaplan, D. M. (1968). *The treatment of families in crisis*. New York: Grune & Stratton.

Langsley, D. G., Pittman III, F. S., & Swank, G. F. (1969). Family crisis in schizophrenics and other mental patients. *Journal of Nervous and Mental Disease, 149*, 270-276.

Langsley, D. G., Berlin, I. N., & Yarvis, R. M. (1981). *Handbook of community mental health*. Garden City, New York: Medical Examination Publishing Co.

Lazare, A., & Eisenthal, S. (1979). A negotiated approach to the clinical encounter, chapter 1. In A. Lazare (Ed.), *Outpatient psychiatry, diagnosis and treatment*. Baltimore: Williams & Wilkins.

Lazare, A., Eisenthal, S., & Frank, A. (1979). A negotiated approach to the clinical encounter, chapter 2. In A. Lazare (Ed.), *Outpatient psychiatry, diagnosis, and treatment*. Baltimore: Williams & Wilkins.

Leff, J., & Vaughn, C. (1980). The interaction of life events and relatives expressed emotion in schizophrenia and depressive neurosis. *British Journal of Psychiatry, 136*, 146-153.

Leff, J., & Vaughn, C. (1987). Expressed emotion. *Hospital and Community Psychiatry, 38*, 1117-1118.

Leff, J., Kuipers, L., Berkowitz, E., Vries, R., & Sturgeon, D. (1982). A controlled trial of social intervention in the families of schizophrenic patients. *British Journal of Psychiatry, 141*, 121-134.

Levine, I. S. (1984). Homelessness: Its implications for mental health policy and practice. *Psychosocial Rehabilitation Journal, 8*, 6-16.

Levine, I. S., Lezak, A. D., & Goldman, H. H. (1986). Community support systems for the homeless mentally ill. In E. Bassuk (Ed.), *The mental health needs of homeless persons*. San Francisco: Jossey-Bass.

Luborsky, L., McLellan, A. T., Woody, G. E., O'Brien, C. P., & Auerbach, A. (1985). Therapist success and its determinants. *Archives of General Psychiatry, 42*, 602-614.

Luchons, D. J., Freed, W. J., & Wyatt, R. J. (1980). The role of cholinergic supersensitivity in the medical symptoms associated with withdrawal and anti psychotic drugs. *American Journal of Psychiatry, 137*, 1395-1398.

262

Community Mental Health

Madness Network News, Journal of the Psychiatric Inmate Liberation Movement (no longer published). Back issues available from MNN, 2054 University Avenue, Room 405. Berkeley, CA, 94704.

Mandiberg, J., & Telles, L. (1990). The Santa Clara County clustered apartment project. *Psychosocial Rehabilitation Journal, 14*, 21–28.

Mannino, F. V., Ott, S., & Shore, M. F. (1977). Community residential facilities for former mental patients: An annotated bibliography. *Psychosocial Rehabilitation Journal, 1*, 1–43.

Marder, S. R., Van Putten, T., Mintz, J., Lebell, M., McKenzie, J., & May, P. R. A. (1987). Low and conventional dose maintenance therapy with fluphenazine decanoate. *Archives of General Psychiatry, 44*, 518–522.

Marinoni, A., Torre, E., Allegri, G., & Comelli, M. (1983). Lomest psychiatric case register: The statistical context required for planning. *Acta Psychiatrica Scandinavica, 67*, 109–117.

Martini, P., Cecchini, M., Corlito, G., D'Arco, A., & Nascimbeni, P. (1985). A model of a single comprehensive mental health service for a catchment area: A community alternative to hospitalization. *Acta Psychiatrica Scandinavica, 316*, 95–120.

Maslach, C., & Jackson, S. E. (1979). Burned-out cops and their families. *Psychology Today, 12*, 59–62.

Matthews, S. M., Roper, M. T., Mosher, L. R., & Menn, A. Z. (1979). A non-neuroleptic treatment for schizophrenia: Analysis of the two-year postdischarge risk of relapse. *Schizophrenia Bulletin, 5*, 322–333.

Mayer-Gross, W. (1920). Uber die Stellungnahme zur Abgelaufenen akuten Psychose. *Zectung Gesselahaft Neurologie Psychiatrie, 60*, 160–212.

McGlashan, T. H., Levy, S. T., & Carpenter, W. T. (1975). Integration and sealing over: Clinically distinct recovery styles from schizophrenia. *Archives of General Psychiatry, 32*, 1269–1272.

Miller, J. (1983). Psychiatry as a tool of repression. *Science for the People*, March–April.

Minkoff, K., & Stern, R. (1985). Paradoxes faced by residents being trained in the psychosocial treatment of people with chronic schizophrenia. *Hospital and Community Psychiatry, 36*, 859–864.

Misiti, R., Debernardi, A., Gerbaldo, C., & Guarnieri, M. (1981). *La riforma psichiatrica: Prima fase di attuazione*. Roma: Il Pensiero Scientifico.

Mollica, R. F. (1985). From Antonio Gramsci to Franco Basaglia: The theory and practice of the Italian psychiatric reform. In R. F. Mollica (Ed.), The unfinished revolution in Italian psychiatry: An International perspective. *International Journal of Mental Health, 14*, 22–41.

Moos, R. H. (1974). *Evaluating treatment environments: A social ecological approach*. New York: John Wiley.

Moos, R. (1975). *Evaluating correctional and community settings*. New York: John Wiley.

Mosher, L. R. (1977). Societal barriers to learning: The community psychiatry example. In G. Serban (Ed.), *A critical appraisal of community psychiatry*. New York: John Wiley.

Mosher, L. R. (1978). Can diagnosis be non-pejorative? In L. C. Wynne, R. L. Cromwell, & S. Mattysse (Eds.), *The Nature of Schizophrenia*. New York: John Wiley.

Mosher, L. R. (1982). Italy's revolutionary mental health law: An assessment. *American Journal of Psychiatry, 139*, 199–203.

Mosher, L. R. (1983a). Radical deinstitutionalization: The Italian experience. *International Journal of Mental Health, 11*, 129–136.

Mosher, L. R. (1983b). Recent developments in the care, treatment, and rehabilitation of the chronic mentally ill in Italy. *Hospital and Community Psychiatry, 34*, 945–950.

Mosher, L. R. (1983c). Alternatives to psychiatric hospitalization: Why has research failed to be translated into practice? *New England Journal of Medicine, 309*, 1479–1480.

Mosher, L. R. (1986). The current status of the community support program: A personal assessment. *Psychosocial Rehabilitation Journal, 9*, 3–14.

Mosher, L. R. (1989). Community residential treatment: Alternatives to hospitalization. In A. Bellack (Ed.), *A clinical guide for the treatment of schizophrenia* (pp. 136–161). New York: Plenum Press.

Mosher, L. R., & Gunderson, J. G. (1979). Group, family, milieu and community support system treatment for schizophrenia. In L. Bellack (Ed.), *Disorders of the Schizophrenic Syndrome*. New York: Grune & Stratton.

Mosher, L. R., Kresky-Wolff, M., Matthews, S., & Menn, A. (1986). Milieu therapy in the 1980's: A comparison of two residential alternatives to hospitalization. *Bulletin of the Menninger Clinic, 50*, 257–268.

Mosher, L. R., & Menn, A. Z. (1977). Lowered barriers in the community: The Soteria model. In L. A. Stein, & M. A. Test (Eds.), *Alternatives to mental hospital treatment*. New York: Plenum Press.

Mosher, L. R., & Menn, A. Z. (1978). Community residential treatment for schizophrenia: Two-year follow-up. *Hospital and Community Psychiatry, 29*, 715–723.

Mosher, L., & Menn, A. (1979). Soteria: An alternative to hospitalization for schizophrenia. In H. R. Lamb (Ed.), *New directions for mental health services—Alternatives to acute hospitalization, 1*. San Francisco: Jossey-Bass.

Mosher, L. R., & Menn, A. (1983). Scientific evidence and system change: The Soteria experience. In H. Stierlin, L. Wynne, & M. Wirsching (Eds.), *Psychosocial interventions in schizophrenia*. Heidelberg: Springer-Verlag.

Mosher, L. R., Menn, A. Z., & Matthews, S. M. (1975). Evaluation of a home-based treatment for schizophrenia. *American Journal of Orthopsychiatry, 45*, 455–467.

Mosher, L. R., Reifman, A., & Menn, A. (1973). Characteristics of nonprofessionals serving as primary therapists for acute schizophrenics. *Hospital and Community Psychiatry, 24*, 391–396.

Mosher, L. R., Vallone, R., & Menn, A. Z. (March 1992). The Soteria project: Final progress report; R01MH35928, R12MH20123 and R12MH25570. Submitted to the NIMH. (Available from the author)

Murphy, G. E., Simons, A. D., Wetzel, R. D., & Lustman, P. J. (1984). Cognitive therapy and pharmacotherapy: Singly and together in the treatment of depression. *Archives of General Psychiatry, 41*, 33–41.

Murphy, H. B. M., Engelsmann, F., & Tcheng-Laroche, F. (1976). The influence of foster home care on psychiatric patients. *Archives of General Psychiatry, 33*, 179–183.

National Institute of Mental Health, ADAMHA, DHHS (1987). Toward a model plan for a comprehensive community-based mental health system.

Niskanen, P., & Achte, K. A. (1972). *Course and prognosis of schizophrenic psychoses in Helsinki: A comparative study of first admissions in 1950, 1960, and 1965*. Monographs from the Psychiatric Clinic of the Helsinki University Central Hospital, No. 4.

New York City Human Resources Administration (1983). Report on the Borough of the Bronx. Mimeo.

Newton, P. (1973). Social structure and process in psychotherapy. A sociopsychological analysis of transference, resistance and change. *International Journal of Psychiatry, 11*, 480–526.

Ongaro-Basaglia, F., and 10 co-sponsors (1987). Disegno di Legge: Provvedimenti per la programmazione, l'attuazione e il finanziamento dei servizi di salute mentale ad integrazione ed attuazione di quanto disposto dagli articoli f33, 34, 35 e 64 della legge 23 dicembre 1978, n. 833. *Atti Parlamentari, Senato della Repubblica, 2312*, 1–14.

Pancheri, A. (1986). *L'urgenza psichiatrica nel dopo-riforma. Analisi degli interventi di crisi nel dipartimento di psichiatria di Portogruaro*. Unpublished doctoral dissertation, University of Verona, Italy.

Paul, G. L. (1969). The chronic mental patient: Current status-future directions. *Psychological Bulletin, 71*, 81–94.

Paul, G. L. (1978). The implementation of effective treatment programs for chronic mental patients: Obstacles and recommendations. In J. A. Talbott (Ed.), *The chronic mental patient*. Washington, DC: American Psychiatric Association.

Paul, G. L., & Lentz, R. J. (1977). *Psychosocial treatment of chronic mental patients: Milieu vs. social-learning programs*. Cambridge: Harvard University Press.

Paykel, E. S. (1978). Contribution of life events to the causation of psychiatric illness. *Psychological Medicine, 8*, 245–253.

Perry, J. W. (1962). Reconstitutive process in the psychopathology of the self. *Annals of the New York Academy of Sciences, 96*, 853–876.

Phillips, L. (1966). Social competence, the process-reactive distinction and the nature of mental disorder. *Proceedings of American Psychopathology Association, 54*, 471–481.

Phoenix rising, ex-mental patient Newsletter, Box 7251, Sta. A, Toronto, Canada, Ontario, M5W 1X9.

Pines, A., & Maslach, C. (1978). Characteristics of staff burnout in mental health settings. *Hospital and Community Psychiatry, 29*, 233–237.

Polak, P. R., & Kirby, M. W. (1976). A model to replace psychiatric hospitals. *Journal of Nervous and Mental Disease, 162*, 13–22.

Polak, P., Kirby, M., & Dietchman, W. (1979). Treating acutely psychiatric patients in private homes. In H. R. Lamb (Ed.), *New directions for mental health services—Alternatives to acute hospitalization, 1*. San Francisco: Jossey-Bass.

Potasnik, H., & Nelson, G. (1984). Stress and social support: The burden experienced by the family of a mentally ill person. *American Journal of Community Psychology, 12*, 589–607.

Prien, R., Kupfer, D., Mansky, P., Small, J., Tuason, V., Voss, C., & Johnson, W. (1984). Drug therapy in the prevention of recurrences in unipolar and bipolar affective disorders. *Archives of General Psychiatry, 41*, 1096–1104.

Purnell, T. L., Sachson, S. M., & Wallace, E. C. (1982). A quarterway house program for hospitalized chronic patients. *Hospital and Community Psychiatry, 33*, 941–942.

Rabkin, J. G., & Struening, E. L. (1976). Life events, stress and disease. *Science, 194*, 1413–1420.

Ramon, S. (1982). The Italian job. *Social Work Today, 14*, 5.

Randolph, F., Lanx, R., & Carling, P. G. (1988). *In search of housing: Creative approaches to financing integrated housing*. Burlington, VT: The Center for Change.

Rappaport, M., Goldman, H., Thorton, P., Moltzen, S., Steener, B., Hall, K., Gurevitz, H., & Attkisson, C. C. (1987). A method for comparing two systems of acute 24-hour psychiatric care. *Hospital and Community Psychiatry, 38*, 1091–1095.

Rausch, H. L., & Rausch, C. L. (1968). *The halfway house movement: A search for sanity*. New York: Appleton-Century-Crofts.

Report on Bronx Community District #4, New York City Human Resources Administration, 1983.

Rifkin, A., Quitkin, F., Rabiner, C., & Klein, D. F. (1977). Fluphenazine decoanoate, fluphenazine hydrocholoride given orally, and placebo in remitted schizophrenics. I. Relapse rates after one year. *Archives of General Psychiatry, 34*, 43–47.

Rogers, C. R. (1957). The necessary and sufficient conditions of therapeutic personality change. *Journal of Consultative Clinical Psychology, 51*, 557–564.

Rose, S. M. (1985). *Advocacy and empowerment: Mental health care in the community*. Boston: Routledge and Kegan Paul.

Rosen, B., Klein, D., & Gittelman-Klein, R. (1971). The prediction of rehospitalization: The relationship between age of first psychiatric treatment contact, marital status and premorbid asocial adjustment. *Journal of Nervous and Mental Disease, 152*, 17–22.

Rothman, D. (1971). *The discovery of the asylum: Social order and disorder in the new republic*. Boston: Little, Brown.

Rothman, D. (1980). *Conscience and convenience: The asylum and its alternatives in progressive America*. Boston: Little, Brown.

Rothman, D. J., & Rothman, S. M. (1984). *The Willowbrook wars: Decade of struggle for social justice*. New York: Harper & Row.

Rothwell, N. D., & Doniger, J. M. (1966). *The psychiatric halfway house: A case study*. Springfield: Charles C. Thomas.

Schaffer, N. D. (1982). Multidimensional measures of therapist behavior as predictors of outcome. *Psychological Bulletin, 92*, 670–681.

Scheper-Hughes, N., & Lovell, A. M. (Eds.). (1987). *Psychiatry inside out. Selected writings of Franco Basaglia*. New York: Columbia University Press.

Schumacher, E. F. (1973). *Small is Beautiful*. New York: Harper & Row.

Schwartz, C., & Myers, J. K. (1977). Life events and schizophrenia: parts I and II. *Archives of General Psychiatry, 34*, 1238–1248.

Segal, S. P., Baumohl, J., & Moyles, E. W. (1980). Neighborhood types and community reaction to the mentally ill: A paradox of intensity. *Journal of Health and Social Behavior, 21*, 345–359.

Selvini-Palazzoli, M., Boscolo, L., Cecchin, G., & Prata, G. (1977). Family rituals: A powerful tool in family therapy. *Family Process, 16*, 445–453.

Selvini-Palazzoli, M., Boscolo, L., Cecchin, G., & Prata, G. (1978). *Paradox and Counterparadox.* New York: Aronson.

Selvini-Palazzoli, M., Boscolo, L., Cecchin, G., & Prata, G. (1980). Hypothesizing-circularity-neutrality: Three guidelines for the conductor of the session. *Family Process, 19*, 3–12.

Semrad, E. V. (1966). Long-term therapy of schizophrenia: Formulation of the clinical approach. In G. L. Wilson (Ed.), *Psychoneurosis and schizophrenia.* Philadelphia: Lippincott.

Semrad, E. V., & Zaslow, S. L. (1964). Assisting psychotic patients to recompensate. *Mental Hospital, July*, 361–366.

Simon, R. (1986). Across the Great Divide. *The Family Therapy Networker*, January–February, 21–30/74.

Slavich, A. (1987). Personal communication.

Solomon, P., & Davis, J. M. (1984). Community attitudes toward residential facilities for psychiatric patients. *Psychosocial Rehabilitation Journal, 8*, 38–41.

Sonkin, D. S., & Durphy, M. (1985). *Learning to live without violence: A handbook for men.* San Francisco: Volcano Press.

Soskis, D. A., & Bowers, M. B. (1969). The schizophrenic experience: A follow-up study of attitude and post hospital adjustment. *Journal of Nervous and Mental Disease, 149*, 443–449.

Spivak, M. (1974). A conceptual framework for the structuring of the living of psychiatric patients in the community. *Community Mental Health Journal, 10*, 345–350.

Srole, L., Langner, T. S., Michael, S. T., Opler, M. K., & Rennie, T. A. C. (1962). *Mental health in the metropolis: The midtown Manhattan study.* New York: McGraw-Hill.

Stein, L. I., & Test, M. A. (Eds.). (1985). *Training in the community living model—a decade of experience. New Directions for Mental Health Services, no. 26.* San Francisco: Jossey-Bass.

Steinberg, H. R., & Durrell, J. (1968). A stressful social situation as a precipitant of schizophrenic symptoms: An epidemiological study. *British Journal of Psychiatry, 114*, 1097–1105.

Stern, R., & Minkoff, K. (1979). Paradoxes in programming for chronic patients in a community clinic. *Hospital and Community Psychiatry, 30*, 613–617.

Straw, R. B. (1982). *Meta-analysis of deinstitutionalization.* (Doctoral dissertation). Ann Arbor, MI: Northwestern University.

Stroul, B. A. (1986). *Models of community support services: Approaches to helping persons with long-term mental illness.* National Institute of Mental Health, Community Support Program.

Stroul, B. A. (1987). *Crisis residential services in a community support system.* Report prepared for National Institute of Mental Health Community Support Program.

Struening, E. L. (1986). *A study of residents of the New York City shelter system: Report to the New York City Department of Mental Health, Mental Retardation, and Alcoholism Services.* New York, New York State Psychiatric Institute, Epidemiology of Mental Disorders Research Department.

Strupp, H. H., Hadley, S. W., & Gomes-Schwartz, B. (1977). *Psychotherapy for better or worse: The problem of negative effects.* New York: Jason Aronson.

Sullivan, H. S. (1931). The modified psychoanalytic treatment of schizophrenia. *American Journal of Psychiatry, 11*, 519–540.

Sullivan, H. S. (1970). *The psychiatric interview.* New York: W. W. Norton.

Susser, E., & Struening, E. L. (1987). *First time users of the New York City shelter system: Report to the New York City Department of Mental Health, Mental Retardation, and*

Alcoholism Services. New York, New York Psychiatric Institute, Epidemiology of Mental Disorders Research Department.

Tansella, M. (1989). Evaluating community psychiatric services. In P. Williams, G. Wilkinson, & K. Rawnsley (Eds.), *The scope of epidemiological psychiatry.* London: Routledge.

Tansella, M., Balestrieri, M., & Meneghelli, G. (1979–1987). *Statistics from the South-Verona psychiatric case register.* Cattedra e Servizio di Psicologia Medica Istituto di Psichiatria. Unpublished annual reports, Universit di Verona, Italy.

Tansella, M., & De Salvia, D. (1986). Case registers in comprehensive community psychiatric service areas in Italy. In G. H. M. M. ten Horn, R. Giel, W. H. Gulbinat, & J. H. Henderson (Eds.), *Psychiatric case registers in public health. A worldwide inventory. 1960–1985.* Amsterdam: Elsevier.

Tansella, M., De Salvia, D., & Williams, P. (1987). The Italian psychiatric reform: Some quantitative evidence. *Social Psychiatry, 22,* 37–48.

ten Horn, G. H. M. M. (1980). Register study: A small cohort of multiple service users from a geographically delimited area. *Acta Psychiatrica Scandinavica, Suppl.* 285, 305–314.

ten Horn, G. H. M. M., Giel, R., Gulbinat, W., & Henderson, J. (Eds.). (1986). *Psychiatric case registers 1960–1985.* Amsterdam: Elsevier.

Test, M. A., & Stein, L. I. (1978a). Training in community living: Research design and results. In L. I. Stein & M. A. Test (Eds.), *Alternatives to mental hospital treatment.* New York: Plenum Press.

Test, M., & Stein, L. I. (1978b). The clinical rationale for community treatment: A review of the literature. In L. I. Stein, & M. A. Test (Eds.), *Alternatives to mental hospital treatment.* New York: Plenum Press.

Torre, E., & Marinoni, A. (1985). Register studies: Data from four areas in Northern Italy. *Acta Psychiatrica Scandinavica, Suppl., 316,* 87–94.

Torrey, E. F. (1983). *Surviving schizophrenia: A family manual.* New York: Harper & Row.

Torrey, E. F., & Wolfe, S. (1986). *Care of the seriously mentally ill: A rating of state programs.* Washington, DC: Public Citizen Health Research Group.

Turner, J. C., & Ten Hoor, W. J. (1978). The NIMH community support program: Pilot approach to a needed social reform. *Schizophrenia Bulletin, 4,* 319–348.

Vandenbos, G. R., & Karon, B. P. (1971). Pathogenesis: A new therapist personality dimension related to therapeutic effectiveness. *Journal Personality Assessment, 35,* 252–260.

Vaughn, C., Snyder, K., Jones, S., Freeman, M., & Falloon, I. (1984). Family factors in schizophrenic relapse. *Archives of General Psychiatry, 41,* 1169–1177.

Wadsworth, W. V., Wells, B. W. P., & Scott, R. F. (1962). The organization of a sheltered workshop. *Journal of Mental Science, 108,* 780–785.

Walsh, M. (1985). *Schizophrenia: Straight talk for families and friends.* San Francisco: Warner Books.

Wansbrough, N., & Miles, A. (1968). *Industrial therapy in psychiatric hospitals.* London: Kings Fund.

Warner, R. (1985). *Recovery from schizophrenia: Psychiatry and the Political Economy.* Boston: Routledge and Kegan Paul.

Washburn, S., Vannicelli, M., Longabaugh, R., & Scheff, B. J. (1976). A controlled comparison of psychiatric day treatment and inpatient hospitalization. *Journal of Consulting and Clinical Psychology, 44,* 665–678.

Watkins, C. E. (1983). Burnout in counselling practice. Some potential professional and personal hazards of becoming a counselor. *Personnel and Guidance Journal, 61,* 304–308.

Weisman, G. (1985a). Crisis houses and lodges: Residential treatment of acutely disturbed chronic patients. *Psychiatric Annals, 15,* 642–644, 647.

Weisman, G. (1985b). Crisis-oriented residential treatment as an alternative to hospitalization. *Hospital and Community Psychiatry, 36,* 1302–1305.

Wendt, R. J., Mosher, L. R., Matthews, S. M., & Menn, A. Z. (1983). Comparison of two treatment environments for schizophrenia. In J. G. Gunderson, O. A. Will, & L. R. Mosher (Eds.), *Principles and practices of milieu therapy.* New York: Jason Aronson.

Wilder, J., Levin, G., & Zwerling, I. (1966). A two-year follow-up evaluation of acute psychiatric patients treated in a day hospital. *American Journal of Psychiatry, 122*, 1095-1101.

Wilson, H. S. (1983). Usual Hospital Treatment in the USA's Community Mental Health System. *International Journal of Nursing Studies, 20*, 75-82.

Wing, J. K., & Brown, G. W. (1970). *Institutionalism and schizophrenia: A comparative study of three mental hospitals 1960-1968.* Cambridge: Cambridge University Press.

Wing, J. K., & Fryers, T. (1976). *Psychiatric services in Camberwell and Salford: Statistics from the Camberwell and Salford psychiatric registers 1964-74.* MRC Social Psychiatry Unit, Institute of Psychiatry, London, and Department of Community Medicine, University of Manchester.

Wing, L., Wing, J. K., Hailey, A., Bahn, A. K., Smith, H. E., & Baldwin, J. A. (1967). The use of psychiatric services in three urban areas: An international case register study. *Social Psychiatry, 2*, 158-167.

Wolfensberger, W. (1970). The principle of normalization and its implications to psychiatric services. *American Journal of Psychiatry, 127*, 291-297.

Wykes, T., & Wing, J. K. (1982). A ward in a house: Accommodation for "new" long-stay patients. *Acta Psychiatrica Scandinavica, 65*, 315-330.

Wynne, L. C., McDaniel, S. H., & Weber, T. T. (Eds.). (1986). *Systems consultation: A new perspective for family therapy.* New York: Guilford Press.

Zimmermann-Tansella, Ch., Burti, L., Faccincani, C., Garzotto, N., Siciliani, O., & Tansella, M. (1985). Bringing into action the psychiatric reform in South-Verona. A five-year experience. *Acta Psychiatrica Scandinavica, Suppl. 316*, 71-86.

Zinman, S. (1986). Self-help: The wave of the future. *Hospital and Community Psychiatry, 37*, 213.

Zinman, S., Harp, H., & Budd, T. (Eds.). (1987). *Reaching across: Mental health clients helping each other*, California Network of Mental Health Clients.

Zusman, J., & Lamb, H. R. (1977). In defense of community mental health. *American Journal of Psychiatry, 134*, 887-890.

Zwelling, S. (1985). *Quest for a cure.* Williamsburg, VA: The Colonial Williamsburg Foundation.

Index